Growing Food the Natural Way

Growing Food the Natural Way

By Ken and Pat Kraft

Illustrated by Ed Nuckolls

DOUBLEDAY & COMPANY, INC.
GARDEN CITY, NEW YORK

ISBN: 0-385-02039-2
Library of Congress Catalog Card Number 72–92226

This book is for Jean Arthur,
who loves a garden.

Acknowledgments

OUR GRATEFUL THANKS are due to many—gardeners, horticulturists, friends, and others—who have helped us with this book. Among them we want especially to mention Gerald Burke, Floris Hartog, Jerome Kantor, Miss Margaret Lial, Gordon Baker Lloyd, Miss Ellen Mastroianni, Mrs. William McCampbell, Mrs. Kay Newell, Miss Maud Oakes, Mrs. Dorothy Retallack, and Paul Stark, Jr.

And we owe a great deal, as always, to the help and patience of the staff of the Harrison Memorial Library of Carmel, California, particularly to the kindness of Mrs. Vicki Jones and Mrs. Sheila Baldridge.

KEN AND PAT KRAFT

Carmel, California

Contents

1

Why Organic...?

It was in the chilly wartime District of Columbia spring of 1944 that we decided there was room enough in the little back yard of our rented cottage to start a garden and do something about food shortages. We had been busily planning a postwar farm and had just run across the new, to us, Bio-Dynamic concept of farming, so we thought we'd try it out on a small scale with our war garden.

Almost at once we discovered we had always been pretty much Bio-Dynamic, or organic or natural gardeners without knowing it. This was no great credit to us; we each had learned gardening from a grandparent who knew no gardening except this natural kind because that is all there was in their days, if you discount a few asides such as an occasional whiff of Paris green for leaf-chewing insects.

In the nearly three decades since that war garden we have had more than twenty gardens in various climates of this country. In them we experimented with many an organic idea of our own and others, and with non-organic ones. In the course of this trial-and-error gardening we learned both sides of the coin. We also had the chance to test natural and chemical methods on many soil types and in gardens of many sizes, from some no larger than the top of a card table to others that could have fed a neighborhood. So when we tell you later in this book what compost can do for a garden and for the environment, and the merits of natural fertilizers, and some safe ways to come to terms with pests, we aren't passing along the one and only thing we know on the subject. We are giving you, so far as our experience now permits, a balanced judgment.

Although writing has been a lifetime pursuit with us, for years it never occurred to us to write about our gardening, so that when we did start to do so, we were able to draw on a considerable experience with it. In the course of this we had gradually learned that soil has a great power of healing itself. It didn't matter very much what kind of gardening had been practiced on a piece of land as long as the topsoil had not been stripped away by erosion, excavation, or sheer ignorance. The chemicals in chemical fertilizers are arrangements of atoms and molecules, as in rocks and organic matter. Rains carry them away; the topsoil's micro-organisms impartially break them down. Give such soil an abundance of organic matter, we noticed, and it quickly restored itself from whatever depressing effects remained of chemical fertilizers' sand or other fillers, by-products and overloads.

Besides the healing effect on the soil, this return to nature also has an effect on the gardener, we have noticed—and, in fact, we think that one of the strongest urges for going organic is something nature has built into people. Feeding the earth with the earth's own products, with manures, plant parts, animal matter, feels *right* and for the long run. By contrast, dusting the soil with a sacked chemical that looks uneasily like cement and even smells something like it is artificial and short-term. By the same reasoning, dooming pests with broadcasts of poison turns out to be no permanent doom, but rebounds instead in the form of new scourges enhanced by the falling off of their enemies. You don't have to think hard to see there is something wrong with that.

And there is a solid nutritional basis for organic gardening. Growing good food by giving back to the earth what it has given to previous crops is the natural way to restore essential elements that form part of the next crop. These are the things that people need in order to be healthy. If they don't get them, the deficiency diseases follow—rickets, pellagra, scurvy . . . even excessive tooth decay, bone troubles, nervous disorders. And according to one of the country's best-known nutritionists, Adelle Davis, use of chemical fertilizers destroys the infection fighter, vitamin A.

There is a game we play in our house every now and then. It starts when one of us asks: "Be honest, now. Of all the places we've lived, which one would you go back to, if you could only choose one?"

"The farm. Wouldn't you?"

"What about that climate?"

"Well, sure—we had too-hot and too-cold. But I'd still choose the farm. And so would you!"

"What about the work?"

"Oh, we worked too hard. Sometimes, anyway. But we were doing it because we wanted to. And anyway I give us credit for having sense enough now to know what to do and what not to do."

"No cows, no chickens?"

"I don't mean that. I'd like everything again, but we'd run it differently—more dwarf fruit trees instead of standards; that algae control for the pond with hay bales; the fast compost method . . ."

"And just as big a garden as before?"

"That's part of the fun. And on the farm we had so much to nourish the garden with, from the fields and the barn and all."

"I certainly remember the hauling and spading. And composting and mulching. And weeding and—"

"Listen, you were worse than I was. You wanted the garden still bigger!"

It was certainly big enough. But it *was* part of the fun, a pretty big part. And whether we always admit it or not, the fun or whatever you want to call it—satisfaction, achievement, freedom—is what keeps tugging us gently back toward that big, glorious, organic farm garden, or one like it that we'll be setting up when we find the likely place—with the huge compost piles, the pond alive with bass and bluegills, the orchard on a gentle slope, a clear spring flowing from bedrock, sundappled clearings in the woods and a cushion of leaf mold underfoot, the winter's cordwood under cover in autumn, and a stone cellar crammed with harvest goodness grown well and naturally.

And so if we had to settle on a single reason to urge organic gardening to you, we'd choose the fun and satisfaction you're going to get from it. All the solid bonuses of good nutrition and environment-saving will come along with it—but the fun, the pure joy of a partnership with nature is what makes organic gardening so right and good.

2

How to Start an Organic Garden

BEFORE WE GO into some of what you need to start a natural or organic garden let us tell you how to make a midget instant organic garden. You can even do it in a window box.

First dig a little trench with a trowel, about as wide as your hand and a little deeper, say 4″ wide and 6″ deep. Then stuff a 3″-deep layer of vegetable trimmings from the kitchen into it and chop this coarsely with the trowel. On top of it sprinkle a little blood meal, about 1 tablespoon per square foot of surface. Then refill the trench to ground level with earth, patting lightly. Make a row by pressing the edge of a board ½″ deep into the middle of the fill, dampen with water, drop radish seeds 1″ apart into it and refill the row with earth, patting it down firmly. This will quickly give you a flourishing sample organic garden nourished largely by vegetable wastes that in most households end up in the garbage can. In the next chapter we'll go into this method more completely. We mention it right away, though, because it is nice and simple, and so natural. Organic gardening needn't be complicated.

Now, for the garden itself.

Because we have lived here and there about the country a

good deal during our lives we have made a lot of gardens, and this experience has helped us to think in pretty basic garden terms. So we can tell you in two words what we look for whenever we start to make a garden: convenience and climate. Convenience means such things as having the garden easily accessible from the house, near a tool shed, and so on. Climate covers sun, air, and water.

Here are the points to consider:

Site

Close to the house. Try to have the garden near enough to the house so you can treat it as a living pantry. That way, you can whisk out for a handful of herbs or stalk of celery any time you need them, and can put off harvesting vegetables for a meal until the last minute, to keep all the sweetness and vitamins and tenderness intact.

Nearness to the house also makes for better attention to the garden by you. If you don't have to walk a country mile to get to it, you'll know what is going on in the garden nearly all the time. You can nip a lot of problems before they get well started, keep an eye on new plantings, harvest crops at their peaks of perfection. A garden is a living thing, changing every day and even every hour.

Sunshine. Try to locate your garden where it will have all-day sun. Impossible? It will settle for less. The practical minimum is 6 hours of sun. If you live in a canyon and don't have even 6 sunny hours per day, try planting leafy vegetables such as lettuce, cress, chard, mustard. The fruiting vegetables, such as tomatoes and peppers, are pretty hopeless if they don't get plenty of sun, and most root crops are somewhere in between. See Chapter 10 for more information on this. In a canyon garden that we had a few years ago we managed to grow a good variety of crops despite scanty sun. The vegetables included most of the leafy greens, nearly all the root crops including Jerusalem artichokes (which grew 12′ tall reaching for more sunshine), squash, leeks, and so on. By putting some planters on a deck that received an extra hour or two of sun, we grew bush beans and midget tomatoes.

Trees. Locate the garden far enough from trees to prevent their competing with it for food and water. Tree roots usually extend out at least as far as the branches reach, sometimes twice as far. One way to keep them in their place is to dig a trench 2′ to 4′ deep between tree and garden, line it with galvanized sheet steel, and refill it. The digging will prune the tree roots too.

Air. Most plants do not grow well if the movement of air about them is much hindered, as by buildings or thick shrubbery. A slope is a help here since cooler air will move down it, setting up a circulation. If the slope is a gentle one, run plant rows crosswise to the direction of the slope to keep water from rushing downward and eroding your soil. A steep slope, say one of 10 degrees or more, should be terraced into a series of broad steplike beds to control erosion. Set a board on edge to serve as the riser of each step, and fill in earth behind it. Two or three stakes will hold the board in place and it can be left there permanently. Don't use creosoted boards. Plants cannot survive close to them.

Underground drainage. Most plants hate wet feet, as gardeners put it, and if your site is soggy, wet feet are what they'll have. Instead of laying a tile drainage line—the classic, expensive, and fairly permanent remedy when properly done and maintained—we suggest you plant in raised beds. This usually means bringing in earth and raising the level of the whole garden by about 2′. You can build bottomless boxes and fill them with earth, or simply make a flat-topped pile of earth to cover the entire site. If you had a vast amount of raw plant material you could build a giant compost pile over the entire garden site and raise the level in that way. More realistically, bring in earth and keep adding to it the compost you make year in and year out.

Access to deliveries. If you do bring in earth, or anything else, you'll need a way to get it in. If your garden is so located that a truckload can be deposited alongside it, this will save hours of hard work. We used sand in a big Belgian endive bed in one of our gardens, and lugging buckets of sand 50 feet nearly wore us out, but we couldn't get a truck any closer. See Chapter 10 for an easier way to grow this exotic and expensive crop, and for pennies.

Soil. Most gardeners must get along with whatever soil they have. This means you usually must keep on adding organic matter to your garden, as the great majority of soils need it and plants keep using it up.

Mostly for purposes of comparison with whatever soil you happen to have, here is what you'd have if you had a perfect garden soil: a loamy combination of sand, silt, clay, and a lot of organic matter; good structure, neither sticky nor loose, but rather spongy; high in all plant nutrients, earthworms, and micro-organisms; neutral or slightly acid; and, finally, plenty of depth so that roots could go down to 4' in it.

Since we go into this subject in Chapter 4, we won't pursue the matter of soil further here except to say: Don't be discouraged by poor soil. You can do something about it. And although it takes Mother Nature a thousand years to make a single inch of topsoil, her organic gardening children know some shortcuts.

Non-organic residues. If there had been a garden where you are now about to start your garden, you may be worried about the residual effect of chemical fertilizers and poisons used against pests by the previous gardener. We have seen figures running to $75,000 per acre as the cost of restoring farm land to organic ideals, though we haven't heard of anyone spending that kind of money, nor do we expect to.

Here's what we suggest: Keep in mind that most chemical insecticides and pesticides are decidedly short-lived. By and large, they lose potency within from a few hours to three weeks after application. A few do linger on in the soil, but the chance of your running into high concentrations is small and grows smaller as you reinforce soil with compost.

As to chemical fertilizers, there is still less to concern yourself with. Nearly all of them leach away rapidly, and even a strong build-up of salts from heavy applications will be largely carried off by a season's rains. If you follow a gardener who depended entirely on chemical fertilizers, supposing there are any such gardeners, the thing to do is to rebuild the soil with additions of organic matter. See Chapter 4, with particular reference to green manuring.

WATER

Next to a good site, water is the most important thing your garden needs. Mulching will help here, as described in Chapter 6, but you'll still need *some* water. With several of our gardens we had to depend on rain, but where we could run a sprinkler we did so. We worked out a system we recommend to you, to wit:

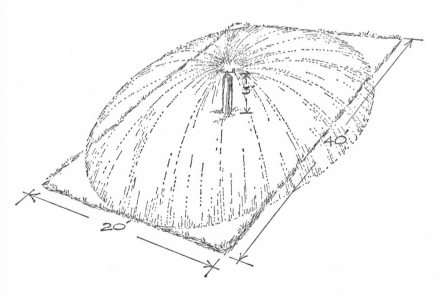

Sprinkler. When we decide where the garden is to go, we put a sprinkler in the middle of the site and turn it on. The area it covers is where we make the garden. By setting the sprinkler a few feet above ground level we can cover a larger area, and if we have space for a still larger garden we set two sprinklers. After that, all we have to do to water the garden is to turn a handle.

A general rule for the amount of water a garden needs is, 1″ per week. If you have a 1″ rain, that takes care of it. You can measure how much a sprinkler is raining down by placing a few empty tin cans here and there in the garden to catch the water. After the sprinkler has run for 30 minutes, measure the water in the cans with a dip stick and you'll learn how long the sprinkler has to run to give the garden 1″ of water.

Trench irrigation. To water your garden by trenches, make them on a slight slant in a gridiron pattern between rows, about 6″ deep. This system doesn't work well in sandy soil, and is too rigid an arrangement for our taste anyway. We would rather be free to change the pattern of the garden on short notice if we want to. But from an organic-gardening standpoint it makes no difference how you water, so do what comes naturally.

Additives in water. Gardeners who distrust the purifying materials in city water sometimes worry about their effect on the garden. We agree that rain is the best water, if it doesn't absorb pollutants on the way down. But though we have endured some pretty poor-looking city water for household use, we have never thought it bothered the garden. The earth itself is an excellent filter, and by the time water gets down to the roots, it has passed through a good deal of earth.

TOOLS

Some gardeners seem to attract tools. You need very few, really, and if you haven't gardened before, try getting along with just the essentials at first. Here are the essentials: a spade, a fork, a trowel, a knife, a 3-pronged cultivator, a rake, a hoe, and a file to keep edges sharp.

You do big digging with the spade and little digging with the trowel. The knife is mainly for cutting when you harvest and for transplanting in cutting out blocks of earth with each plant in flats. The fork is for some digging and to turn compost. The cultivator can be a small hand tool for a small garden, or one on the end of a long handle for a larger garden, or a wheel hoe for a still larger garden. We find we use a small one 90 percent of the time. The hand hoe is for weeding and some cultivating, and the rake is for smoothing seedbeds and for general garden grooming.

If you can call them tools, there are a few other conveniences we keep on hand. One is an old kitchen fork for tiny cultivating and for hunting cutworms just below the soil surface. We keep a small board in the garden for making seed rows in flats, and another board 3' long for making rows in beds, for a straight edge, and for leveling and hilling up earth. It is marked off with crayon into feet and inches for convenient measuring. A soft pencil for marking labels and seed packets with planting dates is kept in the garden, and so is a pair of scissors and an old spoon or two, for harvesting and for transplanting small things.

You need a place near the garden where you can keep tools. Otherwise you'll walk needless miles every season. If we find it impossible to locate a garden near tool storage, we compromise by installing a small storage place inside the garden for trowels and the other small tools. A rustic weatherproof box set on bricks serves nicely, and so does a parcel post rural mailbox, painted dark green, set on a post, and with a vine running up the post.

GARDEN PLAN

Even if you don't follow it faithfully, making a garden plan is a good idea because it tells you things you ought to know ahead of time, such as what you don't have one speck of room for at all. Our own garden plans are informal—just casual maps of what is probably going where this season. An engineering-minded gardener would writhe at such flippant designs.

Our taste is for a garden divided into beds of various sizes. A typical bed might be 10' long and 4' wide. Not very wide, you see, so we don't have to step into it to cultivate or harvest. or at least not very often. We could plant this whole bed with one crop, say beans, but we usually don't. More likely it will have quite an assortment. To give a for-instance, we have just checked on the occupants of one bed in our present garden. It covers about 60 square feet, and in it are: 18 celery plants, 2 catnips, a few Chinese cabbage seedlings, 6 small marigolds, a row of parsley, some oregano cuttings being rooted, a dozen basils, 3 garlics, and 2 dozen snap beans. Most of these plants are repeated elsewhere in the garden.

Now, in a typical farm garden there would be long rows, well spaced, and a good many home gardeners prefer this plan, with vegetables grouped by species. It takes more room than a bedding arrangement, but it can be cultivated quickly and it is a good way to raise a large quantity of vegetables, with a single crop ripening over a short period in some cases.

In the space most home gardeners have, the bedding garden is a flexible and attractive arrangement. We used to make wide paths between beds, but later narrowed them to save space. If you think this isn't a significant saving, measure your garden for square footage. In one of 500 square feet, we found, three paths were taking 100 square feet. We eliminated one path and spotted a few stepping places instead.

A bedding garden is as easy to alter as a row garden, and by numbering the beds you can more easily keep track of where and when plantings are made. Which brings us to the matter of keeping track.

GARDEN RECORD

Climates differ, even the climates of your garden and your neighbor's garden. So the general rules you get from books on gardening must remain general. This is one of the best arguments for keeping a garden record. From it you will be able to find out what happened in *your* garden the past season, and the seasons before that, after you have been keeping track for a while.

This is immensely helpful. It will save you effort, time, money, and even embarrassment. From your record you will learn when you planted something too early or too late, how near the average maturity time a vegetable took to ripen, what problems befell it and what helped with them, and all sorts of other facts.

We keep a record like this in a loose-leaf notebook, one page for each variety of vegetable, fruit, and herb. At the top of each page is the year, the name of the plant and the variety. The one on zucchini squash, for example, shows that we seeded a hill of Burpee Hybrid under a wire-and-plastic cover April 3 in Bed No. 5, using a method we call instant compost, described in the next chapter. The sheet also mentions that we sank a clay flowerpot in the center of the hill to provide extra summer watering. We are in a dry climate, but this is a good way to water squash anywhere.

The next entry on the sheet is dated April 10, when we looked under the cover and noted: "Sprouting well." We removed the plastic the next day, laying a few leaves on the wire to temper the small plants to the sun. The entry of June 5 notes that many bloom buds had formed, and a June 16 entry records fruits forming. On June 20, the record states, we ate the first squashes.

This 11-week gap from seeding to harvest is slow for the variety but fairly normal in our cool climate. Had we been gardening in the Midwest we would have seeded a month or so later and still had squash on the table at about the same time as we were eating these.

The only problems these zucchinis had was an attack of cutworms along with some stray cabbage worms, and the record states we got control by hand picking and then by sprinkling the plants with compost tea, a method we take up in Chapter 9.

The record closes with a notation on when we ate the last of the zucchinis, November 22.

For some vegetables and fruits we keep a record of the total harvest by weight or count. Other items often jotted on the record are: transplanting dates, if any; when mulched and with what; any unusual fertilizing; comments on growth; any experimental procedures we may be trying; companion plantings used.

When we set up the sheets for the next season's garden we use the experience gained from past seasons and write at the tops of the pages the planting times that have seemed best, the actual maturity times, the days it takes to sprout seed, and any special requirements or problems. We may not write all of this on every page, as we know some of it by heart, but we mention it here to show the value of a personal garden record. It could be much more elaborate and detailed, perhaps including photographs as well as the sketch of the garden layout and some general comments that we do include, but a fairly brief record is more apt to be kept up to date.

REFERENCE SHELF

Most gardeners, we suppose, have a garden handbook of some sort to consult when they need information. We suggest you take this a step further and set up a reference shelf. On it should go the garden record we just described, along with any books on gardening. Other useful references are: government bulletins, both federal and state, seed catalogues, supplier literature, and gardening magazines. See Appendix II for listings in each case.

We also find that a file folder or large envelope to hold clippings, leaflets, labels, and such oddments is a handy thing. We could make a scrapbook of these, but by keeping them loose it is simpler to go through them quickly, and also simpler to discard now and then those we no longer need.

The place for such a reference shelf is not in the garage or garden tool shed, convenient as this may be. We have seen more than one garden handbook ruined by moisture from this kind of storage. Better give your references house room.

3

CompShifts

IT IS NO ACCIDENT that we are talking about composts so early in this book. Vegetable compost is the life of a garden, and especially of an organic garden. It is for most of today's home gardeners what manure was for past generations of gardeners. It is the organic matter, that dark cushiony stuff in the earth that plants insist on if you expect them to do well. It is a superb and balanced fertilizer, teeming with trace elements. It is a soil-structure improver of a high order. It is also something of a mystery, and nobody knows all the reasons why compost is a food, conditioner, and even a medicine for plants. But we do know that whether you spread it on the surface of the soil around plants, or dig it in, it helps enormously to make things grow and to flourish.

In this chapter we take up, in this order, these points about compost: what compost is and does, what compost looks like, how you use it, what you make it out of, what goes on when compost is being formed, and eight different ways to make compost.

The U. S. Department of Agriculture has said compost is "not greatly different from average farm manure in chemical composition or in crop responses." The USDA was speaking here of composts that incorporate some manure, but this is not a necessity, as demonstrated by a research project at the University of California and described fully later in this chapter.

Like manure, compost remains in the earth a long time, so that more than one season's crops benefit from it. It does not dissolve away as chemical fertilizers do. And by adding compost to your garden soil you restore organic matter that plants keep using up—burning up, by oxidation, chemically similar to a log burning in the fireplace.

There isn't much use asking the dictionary what compost is, if your dictionary is as terse as ours: "A mixture of various substances, as dung, dead leaves, etc., undergoing decay, used for fertilizing land." It adds that the Latin root is *compositus*, for compounded. Anyway, it is easier, and more satisfying, to make compost than it is to define it.

Although we have never had all the compost we could use, we have been making it longer than we sometimes care to dwell on. But it was during World War II that we began getting really serious about it. Those were the food-scarce days, as we said in Chapter 1, with red and blue stamps, and military service had brought us to the East Coast. We rented a cottage in Arlington, Virginia, with a back yard that had a beaten-earth look. In desperation we set to work building a huge compost pile with leaves, weeds, straw, and nearly everything else in sight, all of it inoculated with some herbal stuffs we bought.

It turned out excellent compost, making us a garden about three months later, and while it was composting we got acquainted with another method that was going on in the next-door garden. We describe it in this chapter under the title The Kuyper Method, named for Mrs. Kuyper, the next-door gardener. She was Dutch, her garden was cushiony with compost and an Eden of plenty—trellis walls of lima beans, rows of cabbages, hedges of tomatoes, beds of endive, strawberries, and blueberries, a towering Tartarian cherry tree in front, and flowers everywhere, from the fragrant *Ismene calathina* to the flamboyant fritillaries, and of course tulips and jonquils in waves of color.

Mrs. Kuyper was one of the most successful gardeners we have known, and utterly organic. She neither bought nor used chemical sprays or fertilizers—and until we started a chicken project, the only manure she had was an occasional horse dropping she noticed on roads. With her, compost was just about everything, and her little back-yard garden literally supplied her and her husband with about four-fifths of their food the year around, even in that fairly cold-winter climate.

After the war and when we were living on our Midwest farm, we for once had a lot of manure, so we composted some of it alone and mixed the rest into vegetable compost piles. We needed all we could get and then some, as we were doing everything at once—planting fruit trees, starting herbaceous borders, shrub borders, and constantly enriching the vegetable garden.

On that farm we found what could be done by mulch composting, or at least that is the name we gave it for convenience. It came about when we added a screened porch to the house and were advised by a friend: "The afternoon sunshine blazing in here is going to blind you in the summer. I'll bring you a vine."

She did, a feeble looking little *Clematis paniculata* she had pried from around her own big plant. The earth alongside our new porch was of hard, tight clay, and sage was the only thing we'd tried to grow there, but we didn't want to seem ungrateful, so we dug a hole with a pick, popped in the little clematis and wished it luck. But since it was only a few steps from the kitchen, we encouraged it with coffee grounds and also dropped at its base such kitchen trimmings as radish tops and lettuce leaves. As this little blanket of mulch built up, watered from the cistern pump nearby, it began turning into compost on its own, softening the ironlike clay as it did so, and holding moisture.

Pretty soon we had to string up a hasty binder-twine trellis for the clematis, it was growing so. In a few more weeks it had woven a leafy screen, and by the time it blossomed it was like a bridal veil. It smelled delicious, the bees adored it, and when summer was over, it obligingly retired for the season and let the sunshine in all winter.

The next summer it grew bigger and better, a frothy green-and-white waterfall of a vine, and it had established itself as a summertime fixture. We gave most credit, correctly, to the mulch compost and to the earthworms and bacteria it had attracted.

Among composts we've made since the farm days, there were some we enriched with fish—gar from a bayou we lived on in the Mississippi Gulf Coast country; there were some mostly pine straw composts there too, varied with live oak and pecan leaves; another time, we had two immense compost bins that went with a house we leased on a mountainside; and there have been so many other composts, from Virginia to California, we have to look at old diaries to recall some of them.

We once heard a European woman say that she had had to abandon her home three times in the face of war, and the first things she did each time in the new country was to learn the language and start a garden. We have never been forced from our homes, but we think we understand this war victim's need for roots, in both senses. Over the past several years we have many times left a flourishing garden, often one we had started, and gone on to start a new one somewhere else. And one of the first things we did each time was to start composting, to nourish the garden we were planning.

Now let's get down to the how-to:

We used to say (and still do) that if you wanted two different opinions, all you needed was two experts on the same subject. When it comes to compost, this, to make a small pun, is true in spades. Everybody has his own idea of how to make compost and some methods are pretty involved. However, the differences are all variations on a theme. We're not going to say that most of the systems don't have merit, but we would like to make something clear before we go any further: *Making compost is easy.*

Making compost is so easy that you'd have to work *not* to make it. If you so much as drop a panful of potato peelings on the ground and don't pick them up for a few days, you've started a compost pile. A heap of leaves would do the same thing, or grass clippings, or last week's party's flower arrangement.

Here, now, are some answers to questions new gardeners have often asked us and others about compost:

What does compost look like? This won't seem an overly simple question if you are very new at gardening. We remember a new gardener who said one day in pure frustration: "My garden book says to thin my little lettuce plants. For God's sake, *how* do you thin?" We told him to pinch them off at ground level, or use a pair of scissors, until those left standing were about a foot apart, and he was limp with relief. So . . . what *does* compost look like? It is black or dark brown, feels moist but light in the hand, and is crumbly like the soil from a forest floor. If you pour water over it, it holds the water almost like a sponge. And it has the nice woodsy smell of moist earth when ripe—and before that, it has a good barn smell.

How do you use compost? You use compost to grow plants in, for one thing. They will grow in compost alone, but if you mix it with your garden soil, it will go farther.

You also use compost to feed plants. This is called top-dressing them, and is done by spreading compost on the earth around the plants. Spread it an inch deep if you have enough, working it into the soil gently with a 3-pronged cultivator or a little stick.

You can mulch plants with compost. Chapter 6 gives details on mulching. Using compost as a mulch will also feed plants, and this is a mulch that will not borrow nitrogen from the soil, so you don't have to remember to add extra nitrogen. If you mulch only with compost, it will take a good deal of compost; but if you have a big compost pile and a small garden, you'll have a lot of happy plants.

Compost is also used to condition soils. Adding it to clay soil makes the clay less tight, and adding it to sandy soil is just as helpful, binding the loose grains into larger groups that will hold moisture.

Compost is used as part of potting mixtures. A general rule is: 1 part of builders' sand, 2 parts of compost, 2 parts of garden soil. This mixture is also good for covering seeds.

And, compost is a tonic for plants, a kind of medicine for some of their troubles. Very little is known on this subject, but it has been suggested that compost contains an antibiotic for plants. We mention some of our own experiences in Chapter 9.

What do you make compost with? People who should know, say you mustn't put diseased plants into compost, or even plants infested with insects. Others, who also should know, say you can. We have tried it both ways and we can't see any difference in results. We have a strong suspicion, however, that if a compost pile does not heat up properly, diseased plants in it would harm the finished product. Further along in this chapter, under The California Method of composting, note the death points of some well-known disease organisms; if your compost heats up sufficiently, no disease organism or insect will survive.

In theory, anything that will decompose can go into a compost pile. In practice, though, you usually have to draw the line somewhere. Where you are living has a good deal to do with this. In a crowded residential area it is advisable to check with the health department, to see if it is legal to dispose of your waste products by composting.

Our farm compost received the discard when we dressed out chickens, and even once, as an experiment, when we butchered a steer, but we have ruled out even fish trimmings or eggshells when we could not protect a compost pile from persistent animals such as raccoons. A well-run compost pile doesn't have any offensive smell, but meat in it will interest animals anyway. Even too many snails in it will attract raccoons, surely among the nosiest creatures in existence.

The basis of compost is vegetable matter, "vegetable" in the Vegetable Kingdom sense. That is, you can put into it your kitchen waste—orange peels, onion skins, cabbage leaves, coffee grounds, and so on—your raked-up leaves, weeded-out dandelions, discarded plant parts from the garden, leafy prunings, faded flowers. No end of things. Woody material such as tree limbs take too long to become compost, but rotting wood is acceptable. If you have a shredder, though, you can run pruned tree branches through it and compost the result.

Ehrenfried Pfeiffer, spokesman for a well-known method of gardening and farming, the Bio-Dynamic one, advocated putting a great variety of materials into compost, and we think this is right. It always pleases us when we can give the compost something a little different, such as faded orchids or pomegranate rinds. Like a party, compost thrives on an interesting mix, it seems. Dr. Pfeiffer's reasoning was that different plants mine the soil for different substances, such as magnesium, calcium, iron; and so "An imitation of this process can be accomplished in a practical way by making compost of *everything*. The greater the variety of plants used in making compost, the richer and more useful it is in its nutritive potentialities." (From *Bio-Dynamic Farming and Gardening*, by Ehrenfried Pfeiffer, Anthroposophic Press, New York, 1938.)

Having put your vegetable matter to composting, you can stop right there if you wish, merely piling the material on the ground and letting it alone except to keep it damp, though even this is optional. In time it will inevitably decay and turn into the woodsy-smelling earthy material we have described. You can speed this up a great deal, though, and get a richer compost by adding earth, manure, and conditioners. Here's how:

Earth. Nearly everyone adds some earth when making compost. Fertile soil is used, and the reasons for using it are to quicken the bacterial action that makes compost and to act as a deodorant. Earth is not vital to composting, however.

Manure. If you can get it—a big if—any manure is welcome in the compost. It can be fresh or rotted or dried. The amount you add is the amount you can get. In fact, rotted manure is a compost all by itself.

When you add any manure to your compost pile you add some of the nutrients plants need, making the finished compost a little richer. In Chapter 4 we list the manures and their average nutrient percentages. These percentages always come as a shock to those who assume manure must be terribly high in nutrients because plants do so well with it. The most needed nutrients in quantity are nitrogen, phosphorus, and potash, and a 100-pound sack of dried blood, a well-known fertilizer, has about 15 pounds of them. But 100 pounds of any dried manure has only from 2½ to 7½ pounds of them, and 100 pounds of fresh manure has less. So the idea of adding manure to compost is important for reasons other than nutrient, to wit: beneficial organisms, which is a way of saying that nobody knows everything that manure does for plants, but they are sure it does it.

Conditioners. The most usual conditioner added to a compost pile is nitrogen, and phosphorus is next. Since manure contains both, there is no other conditioner needed if you add manure. The alternate is to use a fertilizer, and it can be any garden fertilizer. The dried blood mentioned would be good, say ¼ cup for each bushel of vegetable matter.

Some gardeners add lime to compost piles, or wood ashes (which, like lime, contain calcium). The general idea is that lime will keep the compost pile from being too acid, as micro-organisms work better under only slightly acid conditions. But not every authority recommends lime, some saying quite positively that if you use it you'll waste a lot of nitrogen through chemical reaction. We have added lime (enough hydrated lime to just whiten the surface of the compost each time the pile was built up by about one foot), and we have added wood ashes (roughly, ten times as much as the hydrated lime), and we have added neither. Each time, the resulting compost was a pleasure to use. Maybe the only thing this proves is that we were lucky, but it suggests that compost isn't as fussy as it is made out to be.

Some other conditioners are on the market, in fact quite a few of them. We used some of them years ago when we came across them for the first time. If they helped make compost faster or better, it wasn't obvious to us, nor have we seen any impartial evidence that they do. The fact is, the fastest composting method we ever heard of—the one we've called The California Method, invented at the University of California and described at the end of this chapter—operates on the conviction that all the needed micro-organisms are present when you have assembled the chopped-up raw vegetable materials for compost, and nothing more than air and possibly water are needed. The only thing they add is energy—they turn the compost frequently.

What goes on when compost is being formed? A compost pile that is working right gets hot, exactly the way manure to heat hotbeds gets hot. This heat is due to the action of certain bacteria, and a thermometer in the center of the compost would run up to as high as 160° F. or a little more. This is enough to break down soft materials in a hurry, to kill any disease germs (pathogens), and to multiply at a great rate the bacteria that prosper at these high temperatures.

Fungi also appear after the heating has been going on for a week or two. Since compost can be made without earth, or even without touching the earth, these fungi appear to be airborne or carried on the raw compost material. In any case, they do their work in the less-warm areas of the pile, co-operating with another kind of bacteria that want the same temperatures. The two of them are able to break down tough, woody stuffs—though not so fast that you won't still recognize it in the finished compost if it is too tough and woody.

As decomposition goes on, the compost pile is a kind of microbe city, teeming with one population explosion after another as the work proceeds. In addition to organic matter, these tiny living millions require moisture, which is why water is added to dry composting material. They also require air, which is why a compost pile should not be packed tightly. In fact, if a compost pile gets to smelling bad, the chances are excellent that it needs air. The way to give it air is to poke holes through the pile, or restack it. Adding some garden earth at this time is also often helpful.

Eight Ways to Make Compost

Of the many ways to make compost, we have selected eight to describe here. Among them they pretty well cover the field, and they all end up with good compost. They differ mainly in the time required—both of the compost and of the gardener—and in the equipment, and somewhat in the variety of ingredients.

The California Method

This method, worked out in 1953 at the University of California, produces finished compost in 2 weeks, faster than any other method we know of. The researchers used mu-

INSTANT COMPOST

MULCH COMPOST

KUYPER METHOD.

LLOYD METHOD

INDORE METHOD

ROCK
MULCHING

PAPER MULCH

HAY AND STRAW
MULCH

TRASH
MULCH ON
COW WALK
DOWN A
SLOPE.

SAWDUST
MULCH

nicipal waste—meaning garbage—handling tons of it at a time and turning it every day. They also ran home-garden-sized tests, turned every two days, and got the same results. Here are some of the significant things they found out about compost—and remember, this was done with the facilities of scientific measurements and controls, which makes the findings especially illuminating:

1. Adding various stuffs such as inoculants, earth, manure, and old compost to the new heap neither helped nor hindered the composting.

2. The more succulent the raw organic matter was, the faster it became compost.

3. Adding lime to the heap resulted in a serious loss of nitrogen.

4. Grinding or shredding the material before composting, helped. The shredded pieces should not be smaller than about 1″ long. Pulping the material slowed the composting greatly.

5. Turning the compost made it decompose uniformly, and was a much better way to aerate it than blowing air into it, which was too drying. The turning also exposed all disease germs and insect larvae to the killing temperatures that develop inside a compost pile.

6. This inside temperature ran up to 163° to 167° F. Here are the thermal death points of some common disease organisms:

Salmonella typhosa	death within 30 minutes at 131°–140° F.
Trichinella spiralis larvae	death at 144°–162° F.
Brucella abortus or *suis*	death within 3 minutes at 142° F.
Streptococcus pyogenes	death within 10 minutes at 129° F.

7. The moisture content for good composting was around 50 percent. If the pile is too wet it will cool off and smell

bad. The best remedy is to turn it daily. Next best is to add straw, soil, or paper such as torn newspaper.

Here, now, is how the home-garden-sized compost was made by The California Method:

A wooden 3-foot-square bin with a removable front was filled with grass clippings and garden weeds to a depth of 3½'. Nothing was shredded, no water was added, and the mixture was turned by hand with a spading fork every two days. In exactly a week the temperature reached its peak, 167° F. By the twelfth day it had declined to 140° F. and the compost was ready for use. An analysis showed it had 1.97 percent nitrogen, 2.79 percent phosphorus, and 5.03 percent potassium, or nearly 10 percent of the three major nutrients.

In a second trial a wider variety of materials was used—whole dahlia plants, grass clippings, dry garden weeds and sycamore leaves, whole heads of lettuce and cauliflower, avocada seeds, and some kitchen refuse. Because of the dry weeds and leaves, some water was added. Otherwise, the only difference between this and the other pile was in the variety of materials. The compost was ready in 13 days. It analyzed half as high as the other on the three major nutrients, since the raw materials were lower in them than the grass-and-weeds mixture.

It may be of interest to refer here to our garden record on a compost pile we made according to The California Method this past summer. We made it for a friend, intending only to start it and then let her continue it after the first turning. As the record reveals, things worked out a little differently. We quote:

This compost heap is being made in Ellen's garden. Started August 10. Used two bushels dry horse manure gathered from pasture in valley, 1 peck dry chicken manure, dry and fresh grass clippings, iceplant [a succulent], kitchen and garden refuse. Made a pile approximately 3' square and 3' high. Since manures were dry, set a sprinkler on top of pile and ran it about 1½ hours.

August 11. Ellen reported pile heating up. Warm to the hand.

August 12. Phone call: Ellen suddenly in hospital, emergency.

August 13. Turned pile. It was quite hot, probably near peak heat. Much steaming as we forked it.

August 16. Turned pile again. Hot, and breaking down well.

August 18. Turned pile. Still as hot as on August 16, we judge. Continuing to break down, though there are some stems and still-green bits that haven't been inside the pile yet. Repiled in a lower and longer shape, about 6' long, for convenience. A bin would be a timesaver here.

August 20. Turned pile. Breaking down well, so much so that we took a bucketful from center to use in transplanting some small thyme plants from flat to garden. Pile still warm, but heat is reducing. Some stems, in fact a good many, but no green.

August 23. Final turning. Drove 4 grape stakes in ground and wrapped rabbit wire around them to form a bin. Forked compost into it. Still warm, but looks finished. Good dark brown color, nicely moist, clean smell.

We used compost from a pile much like this one, made in our own garden, on a new asparagus bed that had been doing poorly, due to inferior roots, and which we had considered digging out. Our record notes that we spread the compost August 6, that 10 days later the asparagus was looking thrifty for a change, and a month after spreading, the record comments: "Excellent new growth of asparagus has continued." Prior to that, no other feeding had had much effect.

We would add this footnote to The California Method: Although valuable measurements were made of several aspects of composting, notably the final nitrogen-phosphorus-potassium values, it was neither practical nor possible for the researchers to tell this compost's *total* garden value. We refer to trace elements and to as yet unknown benefits plants receive from compost. Nor, of course, could The California Method compost be compared to other composts in these respects. We mention this so that no one will be so impressed by The California Method that he thinks no other composting method worth trying. We don't know all the answers yet, by a long shot.

The Lloyd Method

This procedure carries the recommendation of Gordon Baker Lloyd, a widely respected and experienced gardening consultant on the West Coast. Mr. Lloyd reports the method makes compost in just about 6 weeks.

He uses a bin, a 4-foot-square box 30″ to 40″ high, with no top or bottom. It is made of light boards, with gaps between them ranging from 1″ on the lower third, to 1½″ on the middle third, to 2″ on the upper third.

The raw materials consist of 4″ layers of succulent vegetable matter and 1″ layers of garden soil, alternating until the top of the bin is reached. When this layering is begun, a stake such as a broom handle is placed upright at each of the four corners, 18″ from the sides of the bin. These stakes are frequently wiggled as the pile grows, and are removed when it is finished. Their purpose is to admit air and water to the pile's interior.

The layers are dampened as they are made, and the finished pile is kept damp and shaded.

In cold climates this method will most probably take longer than 6 weeks, but will be faster than non-aerated methods.

The Kuyper Method

This system, used by the Dutch neighbor we spoke of, is essentially pothole composting. Perhaps its greatest advantages are its economies of space and labor. Here is how Mrs. Kuyper did it:

She put the household vegetable garbage in a covered 5-gallon container she kept on the back porch, and added a little water each time she added vegetable trimmings, coffee grounds, etc. When the container was full, she emptied it into a hole she dug in the garden. She added no nitrogen supplement, but merely filled the hole to ground level with a few inches of earth and paid no further attention to it.

Over the years, every foot of her garden was enriched in this way, probably several times. She did not plant over these filled potholes immediately, but did so within two or three weeks, as we recall, during the growing season.

The Kuyper Method gives the compost a running start by beginning the decomposition in the 5-gallon container. Because it is an anaerobic procedure, covering the container is needed to keep odors confined. The earth covering takes care of this when the container is emptied into the hole. It is the only anaerobic method we know that we approve of, since its small-unit arrangement gives it enough speed in handling to overcome some objections.

The Indore Method

A pioneer in working out organic procedures, and in getting them widely known, the Englishman Sir Albert Howard developed this system while in India. He turned his compost only once. The time needed to produce a finished product will vary with the climate. From 3 months upward is the general experience.

Like The Lloyd Method, this one aerates the pile by inserting stakes during the layering and removing them when the pile's construction is completed. No bin is used, however, and the mix is more varied. A heap that narrows slightly toward the top is built 5′ high, 5′ to 10′ wide, and any convenient length.

This is the way it is layered:

1. About 6″ of vegetable matter.
2. Then 2″ of manure.
3. Next, about 2″ of earth.
4. Finally, a sprinkling of ground limestone and of rock phosphate.

These layers are repeated 6 or more times until the right height is reached, when the pile is patted firm, the stakes are removed, the top is slightly dished to hold rain, and the whole thing is covered shallowly with earth.

The Bio-Dynamic Method

Dr. Ehrenfried Pfeiffer, and before him, Rudolf Steiner, who originated this school of thought in horticulture, insisted on the use of certain semisecret herbal preparations in compost making. These additives are available from the Bio-Dynamic organization listed in Appendix II. No bin is used, and the procedure for composting is:

First, a pit 5″ to 10″ deep is dug and a thin layer of ripe compost is spread on the bottom. Then, layers of up to 8″ of vegetable matter, a sprinkling of unslaked lime, and 2″ or more of good garden soil, are repeated until a 5′ to 6′ height is achieved. The Bio-Dynamic preparations are added at the 3′ level.

Layers are moistened as they are made, if necessary, to a damp-sponge feel, and the pile is made in the shade or is covered with mats or brush if in the open.

The pile is turned once, after 3 to 5 months. In cool, damp climates it is ready in 8 to 12 months, and in warm climates in about 3 months.

Mulch Compost

This is the method we described earlier in this chapter in connection with the clematis vine alongside a porch. Mulch composting is the simplest of any. All it amounts to is letting any organic mulch that you place around a planting go to pieces on its own—as it will do anyway. When the plant you are mulching is fast-growing and shallow-rooted, you usually need to add some nitrogen along with the mulch. This is because the bacteria decomposing the mulch need nitrogen to function and will compete with the growing plant for it if there is less than enough in the soil to supply both. To add nitrogen, sprinkle about 1 tablespoon of cottonseed meal over each square foot of mulch, or half as much blood meal or hoof-&-horn. This will supply enough nitrogen for a mulch of up to 4″ thick. One application a season is usually enough, even if you add more mulch later on.

Sheet Composting

Sheet composting consists of spreading organic matter over any size area of soil in a layer a few inches thick (from 1″ to about 6″) and mixing it with the soil by spading or with machinery such as a rotary tiller or a disc plow.

As you can see, this is a way to put a large amount of organic matter into the soil in a hurry, to improve the soil's fertility and structure. It is also a way to dispose of organic waste if that is an object. Both reasons were present in an agricultural experiment made in the summer of 1970 in a farming area near us, close to Gilroy, California, under the direction of the University of California.

There on 500 acres, tomato peelings, other cannery waste, and cull fruit were spread ankle-deep on plowed and smoothly harrowed ground. This amounted to 5 or 6 pounds of organic waste per square foot of ground. After drying for 2 days the waste material was plowed in. Two days later the land was plowed again.

The experimenters, a group of canners, thought a fly problem might develop, but none did. Summing up the test, the magazine of the industry, *American Vegetable Grower*, reported:

> There was little, if any, odor of decomposition. There was, of course, some fresh-fruit smell—which is one reason the disposal site was relatively isolated. Other potential problems, including soil compaction, are being studied.
>
> By the end of the season, each acre of the field had absorbed more than 120 tons of wet waste. Soil scientists William Flocker and William Wildman and microbiologist George York claimed, after intensely studying test plots in the field, that the waste material put on last July, August, and September apparently was completely recycled into the soil by midwinter.
>
> The soil's ability to consume waste has not been determined. But the scientists guess it could be as much as 200 to 400 tons per acre per year.

Although the test was for commercial purposes, it has significance for some home gardeners, especially those with large land areas and with access to considerable amounts of vegetable waste. And it has significance to all of us as a welcome development in a sensible, conservation-minded disposal of waste.

Instant Compost

This is a method we worked out. We wanted to see if we could adapt the technique of green manuring to composting, for the sake of simplicity and speed. In green manuring, a crop of a grass or a legume, usually, is sown and when half-grown it is plowed under. It begins decomposing swiftly, providing nutrients for whatever crop is planted. Some nitrogen is usually added just before the green-manure crop is plowed under, to feed the bacteria doing the decomposing.

Our system of instant compost was this: We dug down about 12″, threw in waste vegetable matter of all kinds, and chopped it coarsely with a spade. As we chopped it, we added some earth and some fertilizer high in nitrogen. When the chopped-up material had been built up to within 4″ of ground level, we filled in with soil. We then seeded or transplanted *immediately* in this bed, and carefully avoided compacting it thereafter by stepping in it, as it was quite cushiony and porous.

The results were dramatic. We seeded beets, broccoli, carrots, cress, lettuce, onions, summer squash, tomatoes, and witloof chicory and transplanted celery and lettuces. Every crop seemed to get what it wanted from the instant compost. The root crops grew lustily and were well formed, the fruiting crops developed properly (and though tomatoes do not always ripen satisfactorily in our location, the plants set fruit prolifically), and the leafy crops were lush and healthy.

In succeeding experiments we dug down less than 12″, trying depths of 8″, 6″, and 4″. The 4″ depth was too shallow, but the 8″ and 6″ depths worked about as well as the original 12″ one. For these shallower depths, we used only 2″ of soil on top.

Blood meal is a good fertilizer to add to the chopped waste, about 2 tablespoons to each square foot of bed. If you use cottonseed or soybean meal, double this amount. Out of curiosity, we tried adding no fertilizer to one bed, transplanting bibb lettuce into it. The lettuce promptly began turning bronze on leaf tips, and we promptly added nitrogen.

We continue to make compost in the more usual way because we need it for other purposes, but for speed and good results in poor soil such as we are currently cursed with, this instant compost was as good as anything we ever used, and better than most.

4

Soils and Nutrients

YOU MAY HAVE HEARD that what a plant gets from the soil is a mere 10 percent of its total nutrient needs. The rest comes from air and water. Yes—but the 10 percent is vital. Also, gardeners cannot do much to change the air or water, but they can do a good deal to the soil.

In this chapter we take up soil profile, soil analysis, pH values, major and minor plant nutrients, organic fertilizers, foliar feeding, heavy and light feeders, the C/N ratio, cover crops/green manuring, tillage, and earthworms.

In Chapter 2 we said that a home gardener has small choice as to soil. He must accept what he has, level or sloped, sunny or shaded, stony or stone-free, clay, loam, or sand, soggy or dry, and so on and on. And if yours is a new house, it is likely to be surrounded by grounds plagued with buried fragments of roofing, sheet metal, masonry, glass, and worse.

A good way to get acquainted with your soil quickly is to dig a hole about four feet deep. The sides of the hole will show a cross-section of your soil, or a soil profile, as soil scientists say.

The two big divisions of soil are mineral and organic, and

all soil traces back to rock, though it is sometimes a very long and involved journey. If you dig far enough down you'll hit broken rock and then solid rock. On the way, you'll dig through a kind of layer cake of soils, each layer produced over a geologic time span by the action of weather and plants on rockstuff and by the addition of organic matter from the plants and from animal life. If your soil has no such layer-cake structure, you can be sure it hasn't been there long but has been deposited mechanically, as by wind, water, or dump truck.

Digging such a hole will tell you five important things about your soil: depth, texture, structure, drainage, and trash content, if any.

Depth. This is the thickness of topsoil, the top and darkest colored layer; the thickness of the next layer, subsoil, which ends where the weathered or broken rock begins; and finally the total depth from earth level to solid rock. You can hope for a foot of topsoil, though you will probably have less. Three feet of topsoil and subsoil combined gives most roots reasonable room to forage in, though they may go on down to solid rock before they stop.

Texture. Each layer of soil will have its own texture, made up of varying proportions of sand, silt, and clay. You can tell what kind of soil you are handling by squeezing a moist handful. A sandy soil won't hold its shape, a sandy loam will feel nearly as gritty as a sandy soil but will hold its shape fairly well, and a clay soil will squeeze into a gooey, shaped mass that even retains the imprint of your fingers. Of these three big groups (and there are many in-betweens), the sandy loam is the best garden soil for water holding and cultivation.

Structure. This quality, closely related to texture, refers to the grouping of soil particles into larger, though still tiny, masses. A soil's structure affects the movement of water and roots through it. The extremes are sand, which is without structure, and clay, which has too tight a structure.

Drainage. The rule of thumb for finding out if your soil drains off excess water to a plant's liking is to fill your hole with water when you have dug down 2′, and then time the disappearance of the water. In a well-drained soil it will take up to an hour. There is some leeway, but drainage in 10

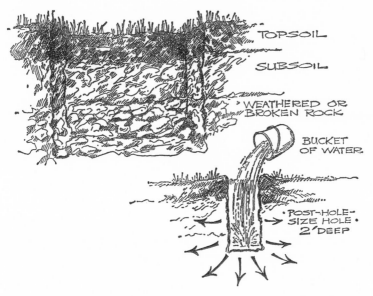

minutes would be too fast for the soil to have good moisture-holding properties, and drainage that took 6 hours would indicate much too clayey or too soggy a soil for a garden. Both kinds of soil, the too-fast and the too-slow, need more organic matter.

Trash. Digging a hole is also an excellent way to find if you are trying to garden on top of a former dump or trashy fill, or if a builder has got rid of waste by burying it. If possible, remove the trash. If this isn't possible, bring in topsoil and make raised beds 1′ or more high. Gardens made on top of dumps have often done amazingly well.

Once we discovered an old concrete walk about 8″ under

where we were making a garden. Breaking it up and hauling it off would have been more work than it was worth, so we let it stay, and located a garden walk right above it.

Should You Have Your Soil Analyzed?

On paper, having your garden soil analyzed—which means finding out how acid or alkaline it is, how rich or how lacking in plant nutrients, and what its texture and make-up are—seems a good idea. In practice, not many home gardeners do so, unless we've been talking to the wrong gardeners all our lives.

Perhaps the reason for this is the willingness of most fruits and vegetables to get along wherever they are planted, or at least to try. Climate is a far more limiting factor than soil.

Unless you live in such alkaline country as the western Great Plains, your garden soil is apt to be on the acid side—and nearly all vegetables and fruits prefer a slightly acid soil. Since well-made compost is normally a little acid, and is also a complete fertilizer, it is the answer to most garden needs. With a good and continuous supply of compost you should be able to raise just about anything your climate will let you raise.

But if, in spite of everything, you still cannot grow some crops that ought to do well where you live, a soil analysis may tell you why.

(Before pursuing the matter much further, you might consider making a rough test for acidity by buying a little litmus paper at a drugstore and touching it to a moist sample of your soil. If the paper turns red, the soil is acid. If it stays blue, the soil is alkaline.)

Two ways to get a more thorough soil analysis of your garden are: Buy a do-it-yourself kit; or ask your county agricultural agent for an analysis (see Appendix II). The kit will cost from about $5 to about $40. The county agent's test will cost you nothing. We aren't telling you this to discourage your doing your own soil testing. To do so may give you much satisfaction. Also, you can repeat it every season or oftener if you wish. And a county agent is a very busy man, so he may not be able to give you service fast enough to suit you. (There are also independent soil-testing laboratories the county agent can refer you to, and we list another in Appendix II; also, soil analyses are usually available without cost from your state agricultural experiment station, which you'll also find listed in Appendix II.)

If a soil analysis shows a deficiency of some nutrient, the remedy is simply a matter of adding it through a fertilizer containing it. A more usual finding is one calling for decreasing a soil's acidity. Here the ordinary remedy is to add lime.

There are several forms of lime, including that from snail and egg shells. We have usually used hydrated lime, which is carried by hardware stores and builders' suppliers, as well as garden centers. Hydrated lime is a powder, easily sprinkled on the soil. One pound to 20 square feet is a general rule. This is enough to whiten the soil.

If you have a fireplace you can use the wood ashes as if they were lime, but use 5 to 10 times as much for the same effect. They also contain some phosphorus and potash.

But don't add lime or ashes at the same time you are adding a fertilizer containing nitrogen, as the lime will cancel out some of the nitrogen's effect. To be on the safe side, if you fertilize, do so a month before liming, or a month after.

YOUR SOIL'S pH

You will come across, in a soil analysis and elsewhere, references to a soil's "pH." All you really need to know about pH is that it measures the degree of soil acidity or alkalinity.

This is indicated by a number, usually somewhere between 4.5 and 7.5.

The "p" means "power" and the "H" means "hydrogen ions," which is another way of saying "acid," since all acids contain hydrogen, and the strength of an acid is determined by the number of hydrogen ions it has (an ion being part of a broken-up hydrogen molecule).

If your garden soil had a pH of 7, it would be neutral—right in the middle of the pH scale, which runs from pH 1 to pH 14. The reason for this 1 to 14 instead of, say, 1 to 10, is that the pH scale is a logarithmic one, so that, starting at pH 1, each whole number up the scale represents 10 times the one just below it. It goes like this: pH 1 stands for a degree of acidity in which the concentration of hydrogen ions is very high, one to every 10 parts of the volume of whatever is being tested—soil, water, etc. Since pH 2 is 10 times pH 1, here there is one part hydrogen ions to every *100* parts of the material being tested. For pH 3 the proportion is 1 to *1,000*, and so on until when you get to pH 7 it is 1 to 10,000,000, which isn't acid enough to matter. In mathematical shorthand this fraction, one ten-millionth, is 10 raised to the 7th power, 10^7, which is how it happens to be 7 on the pH scale. By the time you get to pH 14, the fraction is the figure 1 followed by 14 zeros, or 100 trillion. This is terribly alkaline, just as pH 1 is terribly acid.

To get back to garden facts of life, a pH of about 6 is acceptable to most vegetables, and nearly all are quite tolerant of some variation from their ideal pH, whatever it may be. Also, lots of organic matter in the soil makes them even more tolerant.

The following chart, adapted from the U. S. Department of Agriculture, is a good guide to suitable pH values for some of the popular vegetables. Note that a pH of 6.0 is acceptable to every vegetable listed.

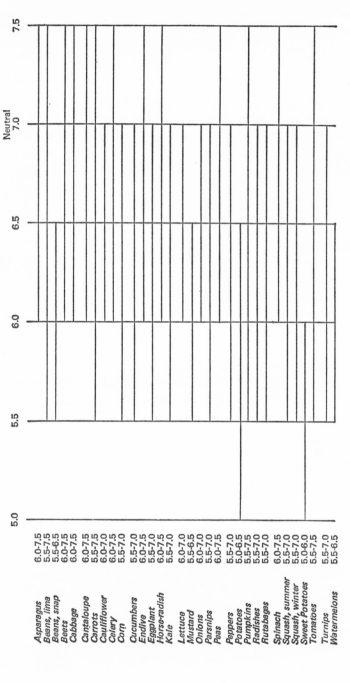

pH Requirements of Vegetables

	5.0	5.5	6.0	6.5	Neutral 7.0	7.5

Vegetable	pH Range
Asparagus	6.0-7.5
Beans, lima	5.5-7.5
Beans, snap	5.5-6.5
Beets	6.0-7.5
Cabbage	6.0-7.5
Cantaloupe	6.0-7.5
Carrots	5.5-7.5
Cauliflower	6.0-7.0
Celery	6.0-7.5
Corn	5.5-7.0
Cucumbers	5.5-7.0
Endive	6.0-7.5
Eggplant	5.5-7.0
Horse-radish	6.0-7.5
Kale	5.5-7.0
Lettuce	6.0-7.0
Mustard	5.5-6.5
Onions	6.0-7.0
Parsnips	5.5-7.0
Peas	6.0-7.5
Peppers	5.5-7.0
Potatoes	5.0-6.5
Pumpkins	5.5-7.5
Radishes	5.5-7.0
Rutabagas	5.5-7.0
Spinach	6.0-7.5
Squash, summer	5.5-7.0
Squash, winter	5.5-7.0
Sweet Potatoes	5.0-6.0
Tomatoes	5.5-7.5
Turnips	5.5-7.0
Watermelons	5.5-6.5

PLANT NUTRIENTS

For proper growth, plants need 13 elements from the soil —and probably others that scientists aren't as sure about. The 13 are classed as 6 major and 7 minor or trace elements (so called because only small amounts of them are needed by plants).

In addition, plants need three elements—carbon, hydrogen, and oxygen—which, however, they get from air and water, not from the soil.

Here are the 13 needed from the soil:

Nitrogen. This is the most important element. Without it, plants cannot manufacture the proteins that are needed to make protoplasm, the vital life-stuff of all living tissues, both vegetable and animal. Yellowish or off-color leaves may show a nitrogen lack.

Phosphorus. Next in importance to nitrogen, phosphorus is vital to the movement of energy in plant tissues as the plant grows. Without phosphorus, plants could not mature. Yellow margins on leaves can indicate a need for more phosphorus.

Potassium. Third in the major-element group, and often called potash, potassium's role in growth is known but not well understood. Plants use a lot of it, especially root crops, and it has a part in adapting sugars needed in the growth of plants. It makes stems stronger, and improves the size, looks, and flavor of some crops. Yellowing of leaf tips and edges, and yellow mottling, are symptoms of potassium deficiency.

Calcium. Fourth in the group of six major elements, calcium is a part of lime and of wood ashes, correcting a too-acid soil, but calcium is also a plant food essential to proper root growth and to cell health generally.

Magnesium. In some way, magnesium is indispensable to photosynthesis, that function of the leaves in which they manufacture sugars.

Sulfur. The final element in the major group is sulfur, as important as is nitrogen in making protoplasm. Sulfur also forms a part of amino acids, as does nitrogen. Most soils have enough sulfur for plant needs.

The 7 trace elements are these:

Iron. This is needed in the formation of chlorophyll, the green coloring in leaves. A deficiency of iron causes chlorosis, which shows up as a yellowing of leaves. Most soils have enough iron.

Manganese. Enzyme activity in cells requires manganese. A lack of it can show up in yellowing of leaves, as with a lack of iron or nitrogen.

Zinc. Enzyme systems also need zinc, and a shortage of it may show up in the form of thick, stunted leaves too closely spaced, with some yellowing.

Copper. Another enzyme need is copper, and many plants must have copper in order to breathe properly. Soils at two extremes—very sandy, or very high in organic matter—may be low in copper. Stunted plants are a symptom.

Boron. For normal, continuous plant growth, a little boron is required, but very little. A lack of boron may show up as a cracking of root crops and of celery.

Molybdenum. Also needed in tiny amounts, molybdenum is another mineral needed in plants' enzyme systems.

Chlorine. Plant health requires chlorine, and in sizable amounts for a trace element, but how plants use it is not clear. Rain adds chlorine to soil, and most soils have enough chlorine.

Fertilizing Values of Some Organic Materials

The same organic fertilizer will be judged different in nutrient value by different analyses, though the differences are not usually great. We have tried to strike averages in the table that follows. In the case of compost, we give a range of values because compost is peculiarly subject to alteration by handling. How good it is depends on what goes into it and how well it is processed.

Also, remember that when you put a fertilizer into soil *you are feeding not the plant but the soil micro-organisms*, which then convert the nutrients in the fertilizer to forms that plants can use.

And finally, keep in mind that these fertilizers, along with most other organic fertilizers, benefit the soil with trace elements and in other ways not well understood, or understood at all, but plain to be seen.

Material	% Nitrogen	% Phosphorus	% Potash	Total
Ashes, wood	—	2.0	5.0	7.0
Blood, dried	13.0	1.5	1.0	15.5
Blood Meal	15.0	1.0	0.5	16.5
Bone Meal, raw	3.5	15.0	—	18.5
Bone Meal, steamed	2.5	15.0	—	17.5
Castor Bean Meal	5.5	1.0	1.0	7.5
Compost	1.5–2.0	1.5–3.0	1.5–5.0	4.5–10.0
Cottonseed Meal	6.5	2.0	1.5	10.0
Fish Meal	10.0	4.5	—	14.5
Greensand	—	—	6.0	6.0
Hoof-&-Horn Meal	13.0	1.0	—	14.0
Linseed Meal	5.0	2.0	1.5	8.5
DRIED MANURES				
Cattle	1.0	0.5	1.0	2.5
Horse	1.5	1.0	1.0	3.5
Poultry	4.0	2.5	1.0	7.5
Sheep	1.5	1.0	1.0	3.5
Rock Phosphate,	—	30.0	—	30.0
Sewage Sludge, activated	5.5	4.0	0.5	10.0
Soybean Meal	6.5	1.0	2.0	9.5

How to Use Organic Fertilizers

There is a chasm of disagreement between organic gardeners and non-organic, but both use their favored fertilizers in the same general way. That is, they broadcast the fertilizer or spread it along a future row or hill before seeding, working it into the soil, or they side-dress growing plants with it by gently working the fertilizer into the soil 2″ or 3″ from the plants.

The amounts used are quite flexible, mainly since soil fertility is different in different gardens. And there is another reason in the case of organic gardeners. It is the use of compost. Compost is a fertilizer in itself, and it also helps other fertilizers do a better job for plants. If you use enough compost, you will need little if any other fertilizers. How much is enough is something you judge by an ever-increasing familiarity with your own soil and crops. In our own present garden soil, which is sandy, a dug-in bushel of compost per square yard each season would be wonderful—if we could make that much compost. A heavy clay soil could use as much, too. Most soils fall somewhere in between.

For a rule of thumb in estimating how much fertilizer to use, figure on about ¼ pound of dried manure per square foot unless it is poultry manure, which goes three times as far. Use cottonseed meal, linseed meal, castor bean meal, soybean meal, and activated sludge at a rate of about 1 pound per 15 to 20 square feet. Use dried blood or blood meal at a rate of about ½ pound per 20 square feet. Each of these is a balanced fertilizer, as you can see from the preceding list. The others on the list, except compost, lack one or two of the three elements cited and are for use where plants need more of a particular nutrient. In using them, observe the rule of moderation, a good rule for using any fertilizer. As an example, 1 teaspoon of rock phosphate would be nearer right for a plant than would 1 cup, though the ideal amount might be neither. When in doubt feed lightly. And then observe how the plant responds, for this is the best and surest guide for your particular garden.

Foliar Feeding

A few years ago there was a flurry of interest in feeding plants through their leaves with so called foliar fertilizers. These were, of course, soluble fertilizers (though not every soluble fertilizer is for foliar feeding).

The best thing we heard said for foliar feeding came from a distinguished horticulturist, the late B. Y. Morrison, who told us he felt it helped in re-establishing a transplant during the period when it lacked some feeder roots.

In organic gardening, "compost tea" makes a foliar fertilizer, and, as mentioned, also has the virtue as well, some think, of providing plants with an antibiotic to combat pests. You can make this natural foliar fertilizer by putting 3 or 4 inches of well-made, finished compost in a bucket, filling the bucket with water, and letting it stand for an hour with occasional stirring. Strain off the liquid through burlap and sprinkle it on the plants. If you prefer to spray it on, strain it a second time, through coarse muslin. In our opinion you should make this product just before you use it, for best results.

Heavy Feeders vs. Light Feeders

It is a good idea to have a working knowledge of which vegetables want lots of nutrients (heavy feeders), and which want but little (light feeders), or come in between.

For the heavy feeders, give them first chance at a compost-enriched bed, and then if possible follow the crop with a lighter feeding one. Heavy feeders include these: virtually all the cabbage group (cabbage, kohlrabi, cauliflower, broccoli, Brussels sprouts), the vine plants (squash, cucumbers, melons), celery and celeriac, most onion types, tomatoes, corn, and most leafy and salad crops.

The in-between feeders are the legumes (peas, lima and snap beans, other beans).

Light feeders are pretty largely such root crops as turnips, rutabagas, carrots, beets, and radishes, and most herbs. None of these will refuse heavier feeding, but neither will they refuse to grow without it. In our experience, witloof chicory is an exception here, as, though it is usually grown for roots to be resprouted in winter, it needs good, rich soil while growing those roots.

THE C/N RATIO

In addition to pH, another bit of shorthand you will run into in the matter of soils, and also compost, is the "C/N ratio." Here, C means carbon and N means nitrogen. All living matter contains both these elements. Carbon supplies energy, in the form of carbohydrates such as sugars, starches, cellulose; and nitrogen provides growth, in the form of proteins. Living organisms use about 30 parts of carbon for each part of nitrogen. This applies also to the microbes that decompose compost. On the average, the plant material that goes into a compost pile has about 50 parts of carbon to 1 part of nitrogen, or a C/N ratio of 50 to 1. For convenience this is shortened to C/N 50. As the material decomposes much carbon passes off in the gaseous form of carbon dioxide. This changes the proportions, so that by the time decomposition is finished, the C/N ratio may be 15 or 20. A good, normal soil will have a C/N of about 10, though it fluctuates as plants grow, or as humus and other material is added to the soil.

The thing to remember here is that such non-juicy materials as sawdust, straw, and dry leaves, are high in carbon, with a C/N of 40 or much more—so if you should dig a lot of them into your soil or use them as a heavy summertime mulch, you may throw your soil's C/N out of balance unless you also add nitrogen. Another way is to compost these dry, high-carbon materials first, and then use the compost as a mulch or a soil conditioner. (Using straw or leaves as a mulch for winter protection, however, is not the same thing and is standard practice in cold climates.)

Here, from sanitary engineers at the University of California, are some typical nitrogen percentages and C/N ratios of materials you might reasonably be using in a compost pile:

Material	% Nitrogen	C/N
Cabbage	3.58	12.0
Carrots	1.57	27.0
Green Peppers	2.56	15.0
Onions	2.63	15.0
Raw Garbage	2.15	21.0
Tomatoes	3.33	12.0
Turnips	1.00	44.0

Cover Crops/Green Manuring

A cover crop is one grown to be turned under to help the soil. Fall is when most cover crops are seeded, a secondary purpose being to protect the land from wintertime erosion.

So far as home gardens are concerned, cover crops are more talked about than planted. When we were gardening in the Midwest most home gardeners we knew preferred to rough-spade their gardens in the fall and expose the clods to freezing and thawing all winter. This helped tame the clay, as we can testify. However, there was no question the clay needed organic matter to improve its structure, and cover crops supply this. Also, for a garden on a slope, a cover crop is sensible erosion protection in any climate.

When a cover crop is turned under it becomes what is called green manure, a suitable name because of its fertilizing value for the following crop. Farmers use this method more than do home gardeners, but it is good garden practice. It is most effective in climates having at least 20″ of rainfall per season.

Rye grass is a popular cover crop, making a good start in the fall and growing along through the winter so that there is a lot of it ready to be turned under in spring. Hairy vetch and crimson clover are both favored, and being legumes they put more nitrogen in the soil than rye does. Some grains, such as winter wheat in the northern Midwest, and oats in the South, are used as cover crops. Some other cover crops are alfalfa, cowpeas, and lespedeza, all of them being legumes.

Though cover cropping on a garden scale is a far cry from the usual farming operation, it is a good idea to ask your county agricultural agent for suggestions on what cover crops are used in your area. You'll need 1 pound of most seed to cover crop an average-large garden, say 30'×30'. Some home gardeners make a virtue of necessity and get rid of old vegetable seed by broadcasting them on the garden when the season ends, and raking them in, thus getting a cover crop of sorts. To do much good, they must make more than a token growth. A cover crop's value is also below ground, and you want strong-growing plants that will make thrifty root systems to add organic matter along with the top growth and to mine the subsoil for nutrients that the next crop will use.

In the colder climates, a cover crop can slow up spring planting by delaying the warming of the soil, and by adding the extra chore of thorough spading-under before any planting can start. So do this spading as early as the soil allows in spring—meaning when a handful of soil will not quite hold together after squeezing. Early spading should give the cover crop time to decompose in the soil before you do your spring seeding. If not, it will tie up nitrogen that your new seedlings need. A common remedy, or preventive, is to spread a nitrogen fertilizer before turning the cover crop under. Two pounds of cottonseed meal or 3 pounds of dried chicken manure would take care of 100 square feet for this purpose. You can then proceed at once with spring seeding, the Lord and the weather willing.

A final word on green manuring: If your soil is already high in organic matter, green manuring will probably not be a good idea. This is because turning under succulent, easily decomposable material can set up so much activity on the part of the soil micro-organisms that they will burn up some of the existing organic matter and actually leave the soil worse off instead of better.

To Dig or Not to Dig?

The trend in gardening is toward less spading than in years past. Since spading is harder work than nearly any other garden job, this trend pleases a lot of gardeners. The reason behind the no-digging idea is that you lose organic matter when you disturb the soil; the digging apparently speeds up the resident microbes at their business of decomposing organic matter, in which they change some of it to gas (carbon dioxide) that escapes into the air.

However—and there is always a however in gardening—this loss of organic matter is alarmingly large only when the soil is regularly and intensively disturbed, as in plowing for row crops in a big farm garden. Not many home gardeners are apt to duplicate this with a spade in a small garden.

In any event, you must nearly always spade when first starting a garden, in order to turn under whatever is already growing on the soil and to make a bed in which seeds will grow easily. Nature drops seed on the untilled earth and is satisfied with one or two plants from a thousand seeds, but gardeners expect at least nine hundred.

After that initial spading, though, some gardeners never spade again—merely scratching the soil lightly when seeding, or spreading screened compost on the soil and seeding in the compost. Both ways have worked satisfactorily for us, especially in sandy soil. If we had to settle on one way from now on, we would take the spread of screened compost. We prefer to keep our options open, however, and spade if we think it is needed, as when turning under a crop or exposing pest-ridden soil to the sun and air.

The same controversy regarding spading, applies to cultivating, but here it pivots on mulching, and we cover this matter in Chapter 6.

EARTHWORMS

Earthworms are welcomed by the great majority of gardeners, only a few regarding them as troublesome. We have never thought of earthworms as anything but allies, and are always rescuing stranded ones after a rain and hurrying them to the garden.

Their chief value seems to be that of underground cultivating. Most of their work is done in the top 6″ or 8″, but they go down as far as 8′, pulverizing the soil and making it less acid by means of a glandular secretion. They shun soil that is too acid, in fact, or too alkaline, and if you have no earthworms although you have plenty of organic matter in your soil, have it checked for its pH reaction.

The work of earthworms lets air into the soil, a necessity to plants, and allows water to penetrate soil more easily. Like most matters in gardening, not everything is known about how earthworms help plants, but when they were introduced into soil, nursery trees planted there have doubled their normal rate of growth, it has been claimed, and strawberries doubled their usual production.

The value of earthworm castings (digested waste) is a moot question. Some gardeners believe this waste product of the worms' digestion greatly increases soil fertility. Others feel, along with some scientists, that this would be nice if true, but they see no proof that castings are any better nutritionally than the raw material they are made from. Our own opinion is that we'd rather have the castings than not have them. We don't think anyone can determine the castings' full value as plant helpers by measuring their known nutrients against those of the raw material, any more than one can measure the full value of cow manure to a garden by comparing its nutrients with those of the feed the cow ate.

The easiest way to encourage earthworms is to work plenty of organic matter into your garden soil and don't cultivate deeply (they prefer that you use mulch instead). Burying bits of suet or some sugar will also please some of them, but will attract ants, too, very likely. We have found earthworms attracted by coffee grounds. The same materials you put into compost also appeal to most earthworms—waste vegetable matter and manure.

5

Seeds and Transplanting

IF YOU MADE A LIST of what you could grow in a vegetable garden *without* planting seed, you'd be finished very soon. Asparagus, chives, garlic, Jerusalem artichokes, horse-radish, onions, potatoes, rhubarb, shallots, sweet potatoes . . . that's about it. To grow the 40 or more other vegetables popular with home gardeners you need plants from seed or seed itself. So seeds are basic.

In this chapter we cover these points about seed: how to save your own seed, how to read a seed catalogue, the packet, germination, flats, soil mixtures, starting seed indoors, and transplanting. For seed life, see the table in Appendix I.

How to Save Your Own Seed

We started to head this part of the chapter: *Should* you save your own seed? and then reflected that a gardener who wants to save his own seed is going to do it no matter what anybody says. If this sounds as if we don't advise saving seed, that is

NOTE: In Appendix II you will find names and addresses of mail order seed houses.

about 90 percent right. But there's still that 10 percent of agreement.

The argument against saving your own seed is based on the good quality, health, and vitality of most commercially produced seed, the wide selection available, convenience, and labor saving. Also, varieties are not nearly as unchanging as they may seem, so that planting the bean you save from this year's garden doesn't guarantee you'll raise the same good old bean next year. Professional seedsmen are only too aware of this and other hazards and are usually able to avoid them.

The argument in favor of saving your own seed is based on independence, satisfaction of accomplishment, control of seed-growing conditions (mainly fertilizers and pest measures), the continuation of favored varietal strains, economy, and sport.

When you decide to save some seed, say from a plant that has endeared itself to you by defying a wilt that killed all others, here are the points to consider, in the order of importance:

1. Is it a hybrid variety? If so, forget it. The seed you save won't come true. Today's hybrids are first-generation hybrids (F_1), and plants grown from their seed would be second-generation hybrids (F_2); they might be interesting to you, but they wouldn't be as all-around good as the F_1's.

2. Is the seed likely to grow plants true to type, or is it apt to have been cross-pollinated? Vegetables most inclined to cross between their own varieties include corn, melons, squash, cucumbers, and pumpkins; cress, spinach, onions, and beets; Brussels sprouts, cabbage, cauliflower, collards, kale, kohlrabi, mustard, radishes, and turnips. To be sure that seed from any of these vegetables will grow the same variety as the seed parent, it must be grown well apart from other varieties of its kind. Seedsmen consider a quarter-mile separation necessary to

avoid cross-pollination by bees, and a mile if pollen is wind-borne, as with corn.

Vegetables that *can* cross-pollinate but aren't so likely to, include carrots, celery, eggplant, peppers, and tomatoes.

Vegetables that are usually self-pollinated, and therefore safest to save seed from, include lettuce, okra, peas, and most beans except limas.

3. Is the plant an annual or a biennial? If a biennial, you'll have to give it garden room an extra year to get seed.

Annuals include beans, cantaloupes, corn, cress, cucumbers, eggplant, lettuce, mustard, okra, peas, peppers, pumpkins, radishes, spinach, squash, tomatoes, and watermelons. And perennial vegetables that produce seed do so annually. (Strictly speaking, tomatoes are tender perennials, treated as annuals.)

Biennials include beets, Brussels sprouts, cabbage, carrots, celery and celeriac, chard, collards, kale, kohlrabi, leeks, onions, parsley, parsnips, rutabagas, salsify, and turnips.

Either annual or biennial, according to how and where they are grown, are broccoli, Chinese cabbage, cauliflower, and endive.

4. Is the entire plant an outstanding one? This is the basis on which to choose. The wrong way is to select an especially good fruit, say a tomato, no matter how poor-looking a plant produced it. Seeds from a good fruit on a poor plant are likely to grow poor plants; good fruits on poor plants are usually flukes.

To save seed from fruits—melons, tomatoes, peppers, etc.— let the fruits ripen on the plant, then squeeze or scrape seeds onto a dinner plate and dry them in the shade, stirring them a few times during the drying. Tomato and squash seeds are sometimes let stand about 24 hours in water until fermentation frees them from the pulp.

Podded seeds such as bean, pea, and okra, are no problem,

except possibly to keep them from insect damage and animal or bird depredations while they ripen on the plants.

The chanciest seed crops are those that form clusters in heads, such as carrots and salsify, and shatter easily or ripen unevenly. They must be watched for changes to a darker color, then clipped off by clusters as they ripen. Dry them on sheets of paper indoors. Blow away chaff, when they have dried, and remove stems.

Root vegetables can be left in the ground over winter, to seed the next year, protected with a straw mulch in cold climates. However, by digging them you can choose the best roots for growing the seed crop. Cut off all but an inch of stem, and store the roots right in the garden, in the earth; lay them side by side in a hole about 1' deep, refill the hole with earth, and mark the place with a stake at each corner. In the spring dig them up and plant them, in the normal upright position, with the tops of the roots just below ground level.

Envelopes are convenient containers for your saved seed. You can make your own out of the paper from brown paper grocery bags. We have done this, matching the size of commercial seed packets, which lets us keep all seed packets filed together in a box we take to the garden. Mark each of your own packets with the name and variety of the seed in it, and the year it was grown.

Heat and moisture are the enemies of stored seeds. To keep seeds properly, store the packets in closed plastic bags, in the refrigerator. Another good method is to store paper packets of seeds in a coffee can with a few tablespoons of fresh wood ashes in the bottom of the can. Put the lid on the can and store in the refrigerator. This storage also applies to any seed you are holding from one season to the next. As you can see from the seed-life table in Appendix I, it is quite possible to make a single packet of seed last you for several years in most cases—saving a tidy sum when you consider that yesteryear's dollar's worth of seeds now cost about five dollars.

How to Read a Seed Catalogue

Ordering garden seed by mail, from a catalogue, is not only a good old-fashioned way to buy garden seed but also gives you leisure to meditate on choices, and offers a great variety of those choices, sometimes a stupendous variety. We once counted 88 kinds of tomatoes listed by one seed house (Stokes).

Seed catalogues are not at all consistent about where they carry indexes, some being at the front, some at the back, some in the body of the catalogue. Some even omit an index entirely. If the index page isn't printed on the cover of the catalogue, we write it there for future reference.

Price is usually a sales appeal in a mail order business, but this is not universally true of the mail order seed business. Per-packet prices are often as high or higher than at rack displays in stores, and virtually every mail order seed house today adds a service charge, amounting to about the cost of one packet, to each order or to orders below some minimum total such as $5.00. This charge is shown on the order blank. It is an industry custom to pay the postage on seed, however, and state sales taxes are not charged on interstate business. Many seed houses also sweeten the transaction a bit more by including a packet of gift seed with each order.

One way to cut costs on a catalogue seed order is to take advantage of assortment offers. The saving ranges from about 10 percent to about 25 percent. If the assortment is close to what you'd choose as separate items, it is a clear saving. And since you can store seed, the saving can often be stretched over more than one season.

It is also a good idea to make a garden plan, showing where you are planting what, so that you won't overlook something and have to reorder; with a service charge added, a small order can be too expensive.

Some years ago we needed to go through a great many old seed catalogues, some of them dating back to the 1870s. They were enchanting, chock-full of chatty informality, household advice, and details of the seed business. Today's catalogues are not as personal but they have managed to keep a good deal of the helping-hand aspect the old ones had, even though they don't carry on at such lengths as this old catalogue description of the interesting luffa gourd: "A natural dish-cloth, and a most admirable one, is furnished by the peculiar lining of this fruit, which is sponge-like, porous, very tough, elastic, and durable. Many ladies prefer this dishcloth to any prepared by art. The fruit grows about two feet in length, and the vine is very ornamental, producing clusters of large, yellow blossoms, in pleasing contrast with the silvery-shaded, dark green foliage. . . . The dried interiors of these gourds have already become an article of commerce." As a matter of fact, they still are being sold in drugstores for a dollar or more each, and they also make good bath sponges. And you can still order luffa gourd seed from many catalogues and grow your own.

Many catalogues mark in some way the varieties they con-sider most outstanding. Some use a larger type size for the headings or a darker type face, and others employ an asterisk-like printer's mark or something similar. This is a service worth paying attention to, as seedsmen do not knowingly risk their reputations on duds. Do not, however, take it for granted that every vegetable so honored is the best one for you. It may be that its merits have made it ideal for commercial use (short harvest span, tough skin, storage tolerance, etc.) and these qualities aren't necessarily even wanted in a home-garden veg-etable. So read the descriptions of these starred varieties care-fully, to see why they are being touted.

A year or two ago we were so taken with the color photo in a catalogue of an unusual blue flower, we ordered seed, only to discover when it came that the plant demanded shade which we couldn't give it, and grew twice as tall as we wanted. We turned back to the catalogue to find out what had gone wrong. Nothing had, except we. The catalogue plainly stated shade requirements and ultimate height. We had simply skimmed over them, bewitched by the color picture. The moral might be: Skip the color shots in the catalogue and concentrate on the words. Maybe you wouldn't want to go that far, but profit by our example, at least, and check off these make-or-break items in the descriptions:

Maturity time. Allow for a week longer on the fast crops, and 2 to 4 weeks longer on slow crops, if you want to play it safe. Also remember that maturity times for transplants (tomatoes, celery, peppers, cabbage . . .) date from when *plants* are set in the garden. Maturity times are based on performance in test plantings, and since vegetables perform differently in different areas, one seedsman's "40 days" will be another seedsman's "55 days," for the very same variety in some cases.

Size of plants. A variety you want may grow too large for the space you can give it. Catalogue descriptions almost always give a range of sizes of plants if this is considered a significant point (though sometimes they take too much for granted in the case of beginning gardeners, who may not know that a sweet pepper plant grows to 1½' or 2' high, or that a hill of summer squash will need a very minimum of 25 square feet to roam in).

Special purpose. Some varieties are grown more for freezing or canning than for eating fresh, or are drought resistant, etc. If you need these qualities, well and good, but check descriptions for the features *you* want.

Disease resistance. This is so important that catalogues always shout about it if the variety has it. However, if you aren't troubled with the problem in your area, you may do better with a non-resistant but perhaps more epicurean variety.

Hybrids. A modern hybrid vegetable isn't a chance cross between two different varieties, as the old-time hybrids were. It is the result of a mating of two parents rigorously selected for certain good qualities and then inbred for several generations to purify these qualities, or characters, as geneticists say. This may produce an indifferent-looking plant—but when it is mated with another that has been treated in the same way to purify a complementary set of characters, the resulting offspring combines the good characters of each parent in an unusually husky, healthy framework. "Hybrid vigor" is the term that arose as a result of this huskiness. Hybrids usually bear big crops—and as a result, need extra feeding and watering. Quality of the crop is ordinarily very good. If you are having trouble growing a standard variety of some vegetable, try a hybrid if one is offered. Hybrids are not necessarily tastier than good non-hybrids, and may not even grow as well in some areas as well-performing non-hybrids. Some organic gardeners object to hybrid vegetables, though we have never seen any grounds for these objections that we consider valid, other than the ones we have already cited for specific cases. It is true that hybrid seeds cost more, the reason being that a hybrid takes much more attention and delicate hand labor for a seedsman to produce.

One other general point about seed catalogues: Look at more than one. Seed houses differ in the number of varieties they list, in the areas they try to appeal to, and in other ways, some specializing in certain lines or in being particularly helpful to home gardeners. And there are price differences. Most catalogues are free, and you'll find them advertised in the January–April issues of gardening magazines, and to some extent in other months. A list of these magazines will be found in Appendix II. Or write directly to the seed houses listed there.

THE PACKET

Some gardeners pay no attention to the information on their seed packets, and are the poorer for it. We urge you to study the packet and to use it as a running record. Its information includes culture of the vegetable or flower whose seed it contains, and some packets cover climatic information, seed count, viability data, and suggestions for crop use.

To make the packet a record as well, write on it the date and place where the seed was sown. We often have six or more such notations on a packet, stretching over three or more years. Such use of a packet is a better one, we think, than impaling it on a stick as a row marker.

GERMINATION

Did you know that the most critical period of a plant's life so far as water is concerned is when the seed is germinating? To germinate, a seed needs moisture, heat, and oxygen. Cold and lack of oxygen will slow germination, but if a moist seed dries out, it dies.

Most seeds can germinate at a temperature of about 70° F. Lettuce, peas, and spinach will germinate at as low as 40° F. The warmth lovers—eggplant, cucumbers, cantaloupes, lima beans—prefer nearly 80° F. but ordinarily respond to the 70° F. level.

FLATS

The shallow box called a flat is almost a must for raising plants to go to the garden. It is only about 3″ deep, so the plant roots can't go down to China and make transplanting hard. And a flat is compact, perhaps 12″ wide and 18″ long, so that even filled with soil it isn't hard to carry. Also, the bottom boards are spaced so that excess water can drain out. This is a standard nurseryman's flat, and the best way to get it is from a nurseryman, who can usually be persuaded to sell one or more used ones. Or if you buy a flat of plants, the flat comes with them and is yours forever, until you wear it out.

We use flats as little nursery gardens. We keep a few going all the time the regular garden is going, seeding in the flats to save space in the garden, then filling a whole bed at once with transplants from the flats, or spotting them in open places here and there.

A flat full of assorted plants is also a nice way to give someone a running start on making a garden.

Soil Mixtures

Though there are many formulas for soil mixtures when seeding flats, the best we know of is: equal parts of good garden soil, builders' sand, and compost. Screen the soil and compost through ¼″ hardware cloth.

Some gardeners sterilize the soil that goes into their flats. To do so, you can bake it in the oven 1½ hours at 350° F. in old coffee cans. Don't sterilize the compost, by the way— just the soil. The object of sterilizing is to prevent damping-off, a fungus disease that kills seedlings. It is sometimes claimed that good compost in the soil mixture prevents this, and we think this is probably right. Another way to prevent damping-off is to spread ¼″ of shredded sphagnum moss on top of the filled flat and plant the seeds in the moss.

Starting Seed Indoors

When we find ourselves living in a cold-winter climate we bow to the inevitable and start seed indoors in flats, in early spring or even late winter, to give the long-season vegetables such as tomatoes and peppers enough time to grow. We drag our feet a little over this particular procedure because it takes more attention than we sometimes care to spare, but not every gardener feels this way, and for all we know, some may adore this indoor sport.

To do it, first decide on where you're going to put the flats. This is the absolutely No. 1 priority matter. If you have a greenhouse, that's the most convenient place because you can control the temperature to the plants' desires (instead of having to compromise on a temperature they will accept and you can bear to live with), and a greenhouse is an ideal place for messing around with earth and water, which homes usually aren't.

But you probably don't have a greenhouse.

The basement is usually the next place to consider if you have a basement. To suit your seedlings, the basement must be on the cool side, somewhere in the healthful 60s except for the germinating period, when 70° F. is right. To play it safe, take your basement's temperature. Many basements are warmer than the 60s in winter.

If it passes the temperature test, the next question is your basement's light. Most are fairly dark. If you can give your flats light from a south window, they'll be all right. Next best is an east window, with west and north windows running poor thirds and fourths.

If you don't have any available windows, or any at a convenient height, you can use artificial light. Fluorescent tubes give evener light and are cool, but a regular incandescent light bulb will also make plants grow. If fluorescent, use 40-watt daylight tubes. An 18″ one located 12″ to 15″ above the flats will light two flats side by side. A 60-watt incandescent bulb about 2′ above the flats will perform the same service. You can let the lights burn continually, though some gardeners prefer to run them on a daylight schedule.

This artificial lighting arrangement can also be used elsewhere than the basement, of course. If you do start seed somewhere else in the house, put the flats on something moisture won't hurt. A few clay pots are more manageable than flats in a house, though they hold fewer seedlings. If plants get spindly and yellowish, take it as a sign they aren't getting the kind of lighting and temperature they want, and try a few variations.

As a general rule there are two kinds of vegetables and flowers you start indoors: 1. Those that take a long time to reach maturity; 2. those with seed too small for convenient or economical handling in the garden. Vegetables usually started indoors are celery, eggplant, peppers and tomatoes (start them 6 to 10 weeks before the warm-weather outdoor planting time), and broccoli, cabbage, and cauliflower (give them 4 to 6 weeks).

Before these indoor-grown plants go to the garden they must be "hardened off." This means to toughen them after their sheltered life inside, and it is done by putting them outside for a while each day, starting about 2 weeks before they are due to move to the garden. Make the airings short at first, and not in bright sun or brisk wind. If you have a coldframe, you can harden the seedlings more simply by putting them in it, still in their flats or pots, and gradually increasing the ventilation as weather permits.

Another way is to move the seedlings from indoors to the garden at once, transplanting them and putting a paper Hotkap over each plant. "Hotkap" is a trade name for a waxed-paper dome. Keep an eye on the plants by cutting a peek slit in the paper after a day or two, and when the weather is behaving itself, tear the paper away over a period of a few days, until the little plant is exposed entirely and on its own.

TRANSPLANTING

You can transplant any vegetable. This doesn't mean it is always a good idea to transplant, though. Vegetables not ordinarily transplanted are beans, carrots, peas, radishes, spinach, and corn. Either they don't care to be moved, or you save no time by transplanting. But if it is more convenient for *you* to transplant than to direct-seed, the plants will humor you, we've found.

Transplanting does slow plants somewhat, though it may also make them grow a better root system, as with celery. However, the big reasons for transplanting are: to protect plants, and to save space.

Protection. This is usually thought of in connection with tender vegetables such as tomatoes and peppers. They would be frost-killed in the open garden in early spring.

We also use transplanting as another way of protecting seedlings, in this case from pests. If slugs, earwigs, or some other scourge mows down a stand of young plants in the garden, we repeat the seeding in a flat. One row in the flat can accommodate a great many little plants; you can fill a medium-sized garden with the contents of one or two flats of certain vegetables. We don't mind crowding these seedlings if we have to, as we often transplant them quite young, sometimes before they have their second set of leaves. This isn't standard practice, but if done carefully it works. And the younger the plant, the quicker the recovery. Just handle them gently, watering first, then loosening a group of them by running a knife blade under the roots and jiggling it; lift one plant at a time, holding it by a leaf, not by the stem (a plant can grow replacement leaves, but if its stem is hurt, it is a goner). Next, make a wedge hole by stabbing a trowel in dampened earth in a flat or in the garden, and leaning the trowel to one side. Remove trowel, lower plant into hole, seeing that roots are hanging loosely, not bunched. Close the hole by again inserting the trowel in the earth an inch away, and pushing slightly toward the plant. Don't push too hard, but be sure the pressure is firmest lowest down, to settle the roots. Then settle them still more by watering at once. When transplanting into another flat, space plants 2″ apart each way so that cutting them apart later for moving to the garden will provide each with a good block of soil.

A transplant can use some mild shading for two or three days, unless the weather is cloudy. Invert plastic berry baskets over small plants to shade them. A rabbit-wire cover with a few leaves over the top is effective, too. If you can't offer shade, wet the plants with a fine spray of water several times over 2 or 3 days.

We seldom remove leaves from young transplants, feeling that the gain in lessened wilting by doing so is offset by the loss of food-manufacturing capacity. But after the transplants seem happy, we trim off any leaves that failed to recover well.

Can you transplant big vegetable plants? Even ones that are already producing? Some you certainly can. We've moved lettuces, chard, celery, tomatoes with compact plant habits, endive, and a few others. We wouldn't advise moving squash or corn (unless you were moving from a pot to the open ground).

To move a large plant, wet the earth an hour beforehand; then dig the plant with a ball of earth as large as you can sled across the garden on the blade of your spade, and ease it into a hole about 2″ deeper than would bring the plant to its original ground level. Have some compost at the bottom of the hole, and pack some more around the earth ball. Water well and give the plant a fine spray of water whenever it looks droopy for the next few days. It isn't always practical to shade large plants, and the water spray will substitute for this.

6

Mulches

MULCHING, like composting, has the tremendous example of nature to point to in its favor. Trees mulch the soil around them with leaves. Dead plants become a mulch for living plants. And most gardeners follow nature's example, especially organic gardeners.

In this chapter we take up: depth of mulches, shredders, additives, trash-mulching, and these mulches: compost, weeds, hay and straw, grass clippings, boards, sawdust and shavings, peat, paper, plastic, foil, dust, shade, and rocks.

A mulch is anything that you carpet the earth with to control erosion, keep weeds down, keep vegetables clean, hinder moisture from evaporating, and help provide a favorable environment for roots. A mulch may also speed ripening and increase the size of the crop—usually a quick spring crop or a warm-season one. In hot weather a mulch may lower the soil temperature by 10° F. or more (but this is not true of plastic mulches, as discussed further on).

There are all sorts of mulches, too numerous to mention. What this means to you as a gardener is: The mulch to use is the mulch you can get. For example, spoiled hay (hay that was rained on while it was curing, spoiling it for use as live-stock feed) makes a good mulch, but don't waste time trying to find some if you don't live where someone in easy reach might be raising hay.

When putting mulch on your garden, start by stirring the soil—spading, or cultivating it. Then lay the mulch on, nestling it right up against the plants. They should look as if they are growing out of mulch instead of earth. If you happen to have fruit trees in your garden, keep a 1′ space around the trunk clear of mulch so as not to give a haven to bark-eating field mice.

If a mulch packs down tightly, as grass clippings will, combine it with a springy mulch-stuff such as twigs.

Mulches are ordinarily put on after the plants are a few inches high—at least high enough to show over the mulch.

How Deep?

A mulching question that has aroused a great deal of argument is how deep it should be piled. Short of burying the plants you're mulching, there seems no limit to the depth—if you are gardening where deep mulching works well. This can be a big if.

In a terribly wet climate, heavy mulching can encourage soggy soil unless the soil is porous enough to maintain proper drainage, and plants will suffer an oxygen lack.

In a terribly dry climate, heavy mulching can rob the soil of what scanty rainfall does come, soaking most of it up before it can work its way down to ground level.

Pests are also a factor in heavy mulching if your pests include some that thrive under cover of mulch. Some that do are slugs and snails, earwigs, sow bugs and pill bugs, cutworms, garden centipedes, some destructive beetles, and mice. Heavy mulching can also permit moles and gophers to go undiscovered by you for a time, sometimes a most destructive period.

So consider your own situation on climate and pests if you are uncertain whether to mulch heavily. Non-heavy mulching, meaning from 2″ to 6″ deep, depending on the material, is not as critical as to the moisture situation in wet or dry climates and is easier to handle when you need to inspect the soil surface for pests. Since experience is always the surest guide for the future, you can learn a good deal in even one season by mulching different parts of your garden at different depths and seeing how the plants respond. If you have the same general mix of plants for each depth of mulch, the results will be more informative.

SHREDDERS

Machines that chop up tree prunings and other plant waste have become popular among some gardeners in the past few years. These shredders, or compost grinders, will make mulch nearly as fast as you can keep them supplied with the raw material. This is, in fact, the only practical way to make much garden use of woody tree and shrub trimmings.

The shredders do their work with blades, tines, or hammers, and are powered by gasoline engines or electric motors, like power mowers. They cost more than most mowers, running from about $150 to about $350. The history of popular gardening accessories indicates these prices will gradually drop.

A branch 2″ thick is as big as the strongest such home-garden shredder will take, and 1″ is easier on the works. Gasoline engines are husky, at least 4 horsepower, and a heavy-duty 1 horsepower is fairly standard for electric-motor shredders.

If you can justify the expense, a shredder can save you much hand work and time. Its output makes a neat mulching material, and if you use the shredded product in your compost pile instead, the compost will be ready sooner than with un-shredded material. You can also run finished compost through the shredder.

In using a shredder, keep in mind that there are hazards involved.

ADDITIVES

When undecomposed plant material used as a mulch begins to decompose under the action of microbes, as it will, the microbes need nitrogen to do their work. They get it from the mulch, and often partly from the soil. If from the soil, this may deprive the growing plants you are mulching. Therefore, some gardeners automatically add some nitrogenous fertilizer when they apply mulch. The list of fertilizers in Chapter 4 shows which are high in nitrogen, such as blood meal.

But not all gardeners do this. Some say their gardens grow quite well under mulch without added nitrogen, thank you. You may as well try it both ways. If you find you don't need to add nitrogen, you save work and money. The way you can tell if you need to is to keep an eye on mulched plants and see if the leaves are keeping their green. If they turn yellowish or off-color, add nitrogen. There is no fixed rule on how much to add, but if we are using a high-nitrogen fertilizer such as blood meal, dried blood, or hoof-&-horn meal, we sprinkle 1 tablespoon or less over each square foot of mulch. The mulches most likely to need this nitrogen treatment are those of fairly succulent, juicy organic matter, such as fresh weeds; this is because the microbes go to work on them most vigorously.

Given the choice, we prefer to mulch with compost, and compost provides nitrogen rather than requiring it. However, we don't always have enough compost to go around, as who does?

TRASH-MULCHING

Outside the boundaries of the garden we have used what we call trash-mulching, to save work in transforming an unattractive area. We recommend it to you. Like any mulching, you use what you have, like this:

On our Missouri farm we wanted to phase out what had been an eroding cow walk down a slope and make it a wide border on that side of the vegetable garden. In the fall we started piling leaves, small red cedar branches after they had served their Christmas-decorating purpose, and coarse refuse from the vegetable garden, sandwiching in some matured basil and French marigold plants loaded with seed.

The next spring, we removed any heavier branches or vines, for a smoother appearance, and that summer we had a heavenly smelling basil hedge all along the garden fence, spangled with golden marigolds.

The next time we used this labor saver was on the sandy soil of the Mississippi Gulf Coast. This time it was a 750-foot-long stretch of unattractive fencing along the road that we wanted converted, and we were already pretty well occupied with frontage nearer the house, hedged with gardenias and azaleas and needing lots of mulching, watering, and care.

To get the other started, we set euonymous cuttings in a trench, much closer together than prescribed. Then, being well acquainted with the good points of multiflora roses from farm experience, we were delighted when a neighbor offered us a dozen plants. We put them in—and then mulched the whole stretch with pine straw, fallen pear leaves and branches, and loads of weeds from other parts of the property.

A large percentage of the euonymous cuttings rooted and grew, the multifloras flourished and then sowed their own seed, and after three years we had added greatly to our bird refuge and had much improved the looks of the place with comparatively little work and no expense.

Later, on a steep mountainside in California, we had a soil erosion problem, and here we trash-mulched with acacia branches, eucalyptus branches, live oak leaves. We trampled them into the ruts and topped them with bushels of borage plants full of ripe seed. Volunteer borage plants by the hundreds that next summer made a lovely sweep of blue blossoms down the mountainside for fifty feet.

The most recent trash-mulching we have done was done in our present garden, or alongside it. There we had an old, unused driveway of hard, compacted soil mixed with rocks and some broken concrete. We were pruning cypress branches and an escalonia hedge, so we cut the trimmings in 1′ lengths and piled them on the old driveway. We added leaves and vine trimmings, then harvested dried alyssum plants and dropped them upside down on the trash mulch, with their myriads of seeds.

We let this whole thing remain undisturbed during the winter rains, and by May we had a wide, white flowery path, sweet-smelling and loud with bees. And just last week a friend who could never get alyssum started though she planted packet after packet of seed, reported that she now had all sorts of alyssum seedlings popping up; we had given her a bushel of our "alyssum hay" and she had treated a stretch of her adobe soil in the trash-mulch way.

SOME MULCHING MATERIALS

Don't regard the following as even close to a complete list of mulches. There is no complete list. Gardeners are an ingenious lot and they'll try anything, it sometimes seems, for mulching.

Compost. Especially if shredded, compost makes an ideal

mulch. If not shredded, or not chopped well, it isn't as neat but it is still everything else. We make a compost mulch about 2″ thick, and it can be thicker. If we don't have enough compost for a 2″ mulch, we sometimes spread 1″ of it as a bottom layer and put some other kind of mulch on top. Or we put all the compost on the beds that most need it and let the others wait for the next compost pile.

Weeds. Chopped-off weeds make a good mulch. Don't use weeds that are carrying mature seed, though, or you'll be giving aid and comfort to a Trojan horse that will populate your garden with weeds. You can use freshly cut weeds or wilted ones. Fresh ones, chopped into finger-long pieces with a sharp spade and piled 3″ or 4″ deep are best, we think. You may need to add nitrogen, as suggested earlier.

Importing weeds to your garden from vacant lots is a way to get a lot of mulch quickly. Just be sure about those possible seeds.

Hay or straw. Both make good mulches. Both may also bring weed seeds with them, and both will need some nitrogen added by you, especially hay. Use plenty of either of these mulches, piling them about 1′ deep, as they'll settle to a final 2″ or 3″. Stir this mulch now and then to make sure it hasn't packed so solidly that air and water cannot easily get through. If it has packed, work in some twiggy prunings between layers of the straw.

Grass clippings. These pack too tightly in time to make an ideal mulch by themselves. Mix them with twiggy stuff. Better yet, compost the grass clippings instead. They are high in nitrogen and make excellent compost.

Boards. We've never thought much of boards as a mulch, though they are sometimes used. Short lengths are best, say 3′ to 4′, to make them easily movable. And you'll have to peek under them frequently to catch pests hiding there.

Sawdust and shavings. A friendly lumberyard lets us scoop boxes of sawdust or shavings from their catch bins, free.

Some lumberyards charge a little, such as 10¢ a sackful. We use these materials mostly to mulch strawberries, to keep the fruit clean. They make attractive mulches wherever used, but are apt to be blown about in windy locations. Sawdust, particularly, is acid, but not excessively so for most vegetables, and it makes a fine mulch and soil additive for the acid lovers, such as blueberries and watermelons. Don't expect much in the way of plant nutrients from either sawdust or shavings. Either one will last for a whole season in most places, however, and they break down so slowly that they may need no nitrogen added.

Peat. Peat in its various forms (see the Glossary on this) is too expensive to use as a mulch, we think. Aside from that, it makes an attractive and long-lasting mulch if it doesn't get blown away, and it needs no nitrogen added. If shortage of water is a problem, peat would do you a better job in the soil than on top. It holds water well, but when used as a mulch it may withhold water from the soil if rainfall is scanty.

Paper. Here is one area where organic home gardeners and truck-crop commercial vegetable growers agree, which makes it a pretty rare area. Commercial growers have been using paper for mulching for years. However, where home gardeners use newspapers and other wastepaper, commercial growers use rolls of special paper that looks like heavy wrapping paper and is usually treated with a fungicide to keep it from decaying quickly. This paper is spread by a machine that anchors the paper in the same operation by throwing earth over the edges with a couple of angled disks.

The anchoring is an important point for home gardeners, too. If you decide to try a paper mulch, a layer of earth completely over it will also hide it, making a better-looking garden. Some gardeners cover the paper with compost or with a light mulch of strawy material. Both serve to dress up the garden. The compost also provides some plant food and will hurry up the decomposition of the paper—a desirable process in the home garden.

Most home-garden paper mulching is done with newspapers, since there are plenty of them around most homes. The ink in the paper has been regarded fishily by some gardeners who think it may hurt plants. Printers' ink is a thick, oily liquid, most frequently having a mineral-oil base and colored with mineral-derived pigment. You wouldn't want your plants exposed to excessive amounts of either, but the amount of ink in newsprint is so small that it is absorbed by the paper instantly as the roll zips through the press. Some think the ink helps plants by supplying minor nutrients.

Though commercial growers use a single sheet of paper, home gardeners ordinarily lay down from 3 to 8 or more newspaper sheets. You can lay these sheets after the plants are up and growing, or lay them before seeding and then seed through holes you make in them. In either case, newspapers decompose too slowly to need added nitrogen.

Laid in the thicknesses mentioned, a newspaper mulch will gradually break down and contribute cellulose, which is a carbohydrate, to the soil. Complete this process at the start of the next season by spading the garden before laying down a new mulch.

One other point before we leave the newspapers: Some gardeners tear up the papers or run them through a shredder before mulching with them, or add water to paper pulp and make a semi-liquid mulch. If you have much wind, torn or shredded paper will be a problem to spread and hold in place. The wet pulp would certainly avoid this; it requires three operations: shredding, soaking, and churning.

Plastic. So far, we haven't cared for plastic mulches, nor do we know of many home gardeners who use them. Organic gardeners seem hostile to plastics' refusal to decompose, but we suspect the reason for the hostility stems from the plastics' link with factories and all their synthetic works.

We have seen plants grow well with plastic mulching, and we have also seen a few plants mysteriously dying while alongside them, plants without plastic were thriving. But these were casual observations, not careful studies.

The plastic used is generally polyethylene, either clear or dark colored. The clear kind lets sunshine through and warms the soil more than the dark kind does—10° F. or 12° F. for clear, against 2 or 3 degrees for the dark. The extra warmth may be a help, especially early in the season, making the clear plastic seem to offer more. However, the dark plastic keeps weeds from thriving.

Plastic mulches are also praised by satisfied users for retaining moisture (it evaporates from the soil, forms drops on the lower side of the plastic, then falls again on the soil like a small rain) and reducing leaching of nutrients by rainfall or excessive watering. In fact, some gardeners have found it almost unnecessary to water when using plastic mulch.

On the other hand, some commercial growers have been horrified to find some injurious soil insects and diseases encouraged by the plastic-mulch-induced climate under the soil, and also pretty hard to get at with the plastic mulch protecting them. Moles, however, have been repelled by a plastic mulch.

Plastic-mulched plants often show a nitrogen deficiency. Foliar feeding has been used to correct this, though many home garderers aren't going to see much point in a mulch that makes problems, when the idea is to solve them.

As undercoatings for garden paths, or as spot fumigants for soil infestations, the plastics presently in use have something to be said for them, and they are unquestionably handy as coldframe covers—but none of this has anything to do with our subject, mulching.

If you decide to try plastic film for mulching, cultivate the soil first, smooth it, apply the mulch, and anchor it to keep the wind from flipping it about. The best anchor is earth.

Next best: bricks. Round rocks are apt to roll if the wind gets under the plastic.

Foil. Like plastic, foil as mulch has its supporters, both home-garden and commercial. Sheets of foil on the earth prevent loss of moisture and discourage weeds, just as dark plastic does. But foil does something else—it reflects some sunshine up into the plants. Even on overcast days it throws a little more light onto the leaves. If a shortage of sun is a garden problem for you, foil may help. You can cover pieces of thin plywood with it, to keep the foil from getting crumpled, and use them flat on the ground as reflector mulches. They can also do a job when stood up, but they aren't being mulches in that case, of course. Squash has responded well to this reflector-mulching, and the reflected sunshine has had a curious and welcome side effect—it has repelled aphids and, consequently, the virus diseases they may carry.

But so far as looks go, foil in a garden is even worse than plastic. And if you cover foil you lose its reflecting advantage.

Dust. By shallowly cultivating the soil you produce a dust mulch. It is supposed to keep water from escaping, on the principle that earth acts as a wick up which water climbs, if the earth is sufficiently compact; you make it uncompact on top by cultivation, and halt this wicking action.

However, dust mulching has been falling out of favor over the past several years. It encourages wind erosion, may cut feeder roots near the surface during the cultivating, can cause puddling on clay soils, and must be done all over again after every rain or watering. It does look good, but beauty is as beauty does.

Shade. It may seem to stretch the definition a bit, but shade is a kind of mulch, too. This refers to the shade plants throw on the soil they are growing in. Shade slows down weed growth, helps moisture retention, and keeps roots comfortably cool in hot weather. And since shade is a do-it-yourself mulch for a plant, all you have to do about it is be grateful.

Rocks. Here we are going to refer again to the gardening authority Gordon Baker Lloyd, who has had much experience with rock mulching. His system is simple and organically sensible. He developed it for tree fruits and shrubs, but it can be used in the garden, too.

First he removes a few inches of earth from the area to be mulched. Then he nearly fills this basin with dried leaves, and tops the leaves with about 1″ of rotted redwood sawdust. The rocks go on top of this, roundish creek rocks between 4″ and 6″ thick. Finally, he soaks the area thoroughly with water.

"In the first three months," Mr. Lloyd says, "the mulches will disappear rather quickly. Raise the rocks and add more leaf material. By the way, avoid grass clippings. Peat and manures are of little value in this operation."

No nitrogen is added when using this mulching for trees and shrubs. For vegetable-garden use, ½ tablespoon of dried blood per square foot of mulch, sprinkled over the sawdust, would be in order.

7

Companion Planting

WE APPROVE of mixed plantings in a vegetable garden, and we have always practiced it. This way of doing things is also referred to as companion planting, and it has the blessings of authorities on natural gardening. Among them was the Dr. Ehrenfried Pfeiffer we referred to before in connection with Bio-Dynamics.

Dr. Pfeiffer felt that plants can affect other plants they are growing near, helping or hurting them. In his book he cited a number of combinations he had tested. Herbs make excellent companions for other plants when used for borders or for interplanting, he believed, and leeks and carrots helped each other, as did early potatoes with corn or beans. On the other hand, he found kohlrabi hard on tomatoes, fennel hard on bush beans, and cucumbers and tomatoes hard on each other.

Though we have thought well of the Bio-Dynamic approach, and followed it for some years, we didn't often find their companion plantings behaving the same way in our gardens. Nor have many *non*-Bio-Dynamic combinations either.

What we say in this chapter is based entirely on our own

experience except where noted, since in Chapter 9 we go into reports and studies of others on the subject as it relates specifically to pest control.

We can understand the appeal that companion planting has to new gardeners. It sounds like the answer to everything. Last year, for instance, a young woman in Carmel Valley, near where we are living, grew a vegetable garden for the first time, and announced that by planting a half-dozen little French marigolds she had kept every pest away. So this year she said she was enlarging her garden and was going to grow her own marigolds, to have plenty. She did, lining every path with them as well as interplanting with all the vegetables. Then she happened to go out of town for a few days, and when she returned, a plague of pests had almost cleaned out her garden, marigolds included.

We weren't terribly surprised. It had happened that three years ago while we were on a trip, a friend staying in our house had decided to do us a favor by planting some marigolds from a nursery along a dry rock retaining wall. (We might say in passing that dry rock walls are often pretty much of a nuisance offering a haven to pests galore, including rattlesnakes if they are around. And loose rocks are a hazard, too, especially if your hands are full or if you are in a hurry.) At any rate, when we returned from our trip, the gift marigolds had already gone. Earwigs had crawled out of the dry rock wall and had shredded the little things. So much for marigolds as universal pest repellers. But they do control certain nematodes, and we usually plant a few among the vegetables just because we like their cheerful flowers.

A friend on the Mississippi Gulf Coast writes us that she has no rose bed problems because she interplants with garlic. Now, from experience in our own Gulf Coast rose garden years ago, we know there are few more pleasant places than a Southern rose garden on a sunny morning, or a hot afternoon

—or just at sundown when the Bourbons, the old teas, and the noisettes release such a lovely fragrance that we suspect our friend spends, as did we, a good deal of time in this delightful spot. So . . . when a touch of black spot, a speck of mildew, a worm or bug show up, they are seen and banished at once. Here, the most effective companion "plant" is the gardener himself—a point we cannot emphasize too strongly.

Other gardeners have assured us that any of the onion family make fine companion plantings, keeping pests far away from themselves and all nearby plantings. Yet, a Spanish onion that grew magnificently for us last year was a failure this year, unable to protect even itself. And our leeks may have a poor year after many good ones. Garlic does usually do well, but may be damaged by maggots if they do not have enough other food, and the same is true of shallots; as companion plants, neither has a great deal of effect in our garden.

This year we interplanted bibb lettuce and Florence fennel, and we noticed that no slugs attacked the lettuce. We tried the combination again, and this time slugs did attack the lettuce. Had we stopped with the first trial, we might have been gulled into thinking we had found the answer to keeping lettuce free of slugs. And maybe the fennel did keep the earlier planting free of them, perhaps helped by a different day-length, or phase of the moon, or vibrations we knew nothing of, but we don't know what the combination was, whatever it was.

Also during this year we transplanted some lettuces to a new asparagus bed as a catch crop to take advantage of a heavy dressing of compost we had just given the asparagus. And again, no slugs attacked the lettuce, and if we had harvested it just at maturity we could have credited the asparagus with being an anti-slug companion plant. But in the rich compost, the lettuce had grown so fast it was ready before we were, and

when we finally started harvesting it, there *was* slug damage
—not much but some. Plainly, compost and timing were
important factors as regarded slug damage. Maybe the asparagus was a factor, maybe not.

Though it didn't work in the lettuce-asparagus case, ordinarily companion planting helps keep you from sowing too
much of any crop because you tend to spot small plantings
here and there about the garden. This also helps space the
harvest, avoiding an unmanageable surplus of any one crop.

Herbs are highly popular with many gardeners as companion plants, and popular with us, too. Is there any blue in
the botanical world more appealing than that of borage blossoms? (And to charm a child with a pretty tidbit, dip the
blossoms in slightly beaten egg white, then in sugar, and dry
them on waxed paper.) But as companion plants, we can't
take an oath that herbs are effective.

For a while a neighbor of ours thought they were. She had
decided to start a garden and she planted an herb wheel in her
yard; very pretty, full of culinary herbs. Then she added a
few salad plants and had a great season, not a pest to speak
of, and she gave the herbs the credit. Well, she repeated this
garden the next year, and by then the pests had got the word.
Every day from then on our neighbor found it advisable to
visit her garden, checking for earwig damage, scratching for
cutworms, peering for caterpillars. The real reason for her
first-year success, like that of our marigold friend, was once
pinpointed for us by a gardener whose hobby was also his
job, as he worked for a seed house. We had asked him what
advice he could give someone trying to start a garden in the
yard of a just-built house, where earth is cluttered with
building waste and no garden has ever been grown. To our
surprise he was optimistic. "Much of the soil may be excellent," he declared roundly. "Furthermore, it hasn't been subjected to overplanting, many soil diseases and insects haven't

become established, and there is no competition from shrubs and lawns." Since then we've seen him proved right more times than not.

But . . . what do you do after that first pest-free interlude? we can hear new gardeners asking. Well, experiment with companion plantings, by all means, and use other and more provable practices such as nourishing your garden with good compost. But, more than anything else, keep in mind that the best companion for any plant in your garden is you, your care and attention. "The foot of the owner enricheth the land," is one version of an old and true saying. Though gardens do sometimes survive and even thrive under neglect, they are the exceptions. We try to visit ours every day, and

when trouble shows up, we go more than once. Is a broccoli wilting? Dig alongside it and see if maggots are after the roots. Black droppings on chard leaves? Look for green worms. Kale leaves sliced off and lying on the ground? Stir the earth shallowly around the plant and you'll probably find a cutworm curled there. You can't stop every pest, but you can break many a breeding cycle with this kind of checking and keep damage from becoming catastrophe.

Our old Dutch gardening friend in Virginia, Mrs. Kuyper, nearly lived in her garden during the growing season. This was because she enjoyed being there, but the only pest we ever heard her complain much about was a plague of Japanese beetles—and then her close attention revealed that they were bedding down at night on a *Clematis paniculata*. Early the next morning she harvested the beetles into a can of kerosene, and reduced a serious invasion to a trifle.

This summer we found that our foot-of-the-owner inspection could be helped by keeping sections of zucchini squash on the earth here and there about the garden. They attracted cutworms, garden centipedes, slugs, and some harmful beetles. For those gardeners who do not have squash available when cutworms are troublesome, we suggest using fresh vegetable leaves instead; broccoli and chard are good.

Though it pains us to mention it, we have this final comment on being a companion to your plants: We were running a feeding experiment this summer with three hills of zucchini outside our regular garden. One hill was getting a commercial soluble fertilizer, the second was planted over a bushel of the instant compost we describe in Chapter 3, and the third was being fed with a commercial chemical fertilizer.

All had been started July 19, and for the first month there was hardly any difference among them. Then the instant-compost hill began spurting ahead, and after nearly another month it was so outstanding we decided to take its picture for possible use in this book.

On September 15 we cultivated it and gave it a light mulching, for better color contrast in the photograph, and decided to take the picture on September 19, exactly two months after planting.

The next day we noticed that a leaf of one plant in this hill was droopy. "Gopher?" one of us said. But we hated to mess up the planting now that it was ready for picture taking, and argued that the leaf stem had probably been hurt when we were cultivating, and could be cut off without harm if it didn't recover.

The day after, we had a lot of errands to do in town, and when we looked over the squash plantings in the late afternoon we found the entire plant of the damaged-leaf plant was now flat, broken off at ground level. Though it was typical of gopher damage, we elected to put the blame on raccoons because they had been swarming over the house roof the night before.

But we still had two plants left in the instant-compost hill, they looked fine with the new mulching, and we could still take the picture, we thought. We should have known better. Raccoons had never destroyed a sizable plant, but gopher damage was an old story to us. We should have dug around the planting at once, regardless of the upset to our photography arrangement. And so, the day following, we found the two surviving plants surviving no longer, their roots eaten away and the tops dead.

We did dig then, found the gopher tunnel we knew would be there, and trapped a big gopher an hour later. But if we had followed our own advice and gone into action when we saw the first wilted leaf, we could have saved the whole enterprise.

8

To Love a Weed

IF OUR WEEDS COULD READ they would think we titled this chapter with our fingers crossed, because though we regard many weeds amiably, we still kill them. Still, that's not the same as the pure unmitigated hate most gardeners direct at weeds. What we really want to do is to reconcile you to weeds, gardening's inevitables, by exposing what few good points they do have.

Our Glossary says a weed, though usually meaning a wild, persistent, nuisance plant, can be any plant where it isn't wanted. For present purposes, though, we don't mean a volunteer cucumber popping up in a broccoli bed, but a weed everybody knows is a weed, like pigweed or plantain, bindweed or dock, even if they don't know the weeds' names.

In the first place, we *aren't* suggesting you let any weeds go to seed. They are marvelously quick to do so, and they'll get out of hand before you know what's happening. In this chapter we cover weeds as cover crops, companion plants, anti-pests, mulch, soil improvers, compost material, food; and finally, how to get rid of weeds.

WEEDS AS COVER CROPS

By keeping something growing in your garden soil throughout the year, you will reduce erosion and loss of plant nutrients by leaching. But during the growing season, a bed may often be vacant for only a short time between crops—too short a time to mature a catch crop. This is where weeds can do you a favor.

Merely turn your back, and up they'll come with no effort from you at all. Let them grow along in happy ignorance for the two, three, or four weeks until you are ready to plant the bed. Then spade them under, and they will decompose rapidly and enrich the soil. This is green manuring, as described in Chapter 4, and since you turn the weeds under while they are still immature, there will be no weed seeds to germinate and make a problem for your cultivated crop. The fertilizer you normally add when seeding or transplanting will also take care of any nitrogen requirements of the weeds' decomposition.

We will add one caution here. There are some weeds to which you can give no quarter, and which you should not consider for green manuring. These are the weeds such as crab grass, that roots at the joints; bindweed, with deep and persistent rootstocks; and quack grass (also called witch grass), which spading will merely multiply, as each broken underground stem will grow a new plant. You most probably already recognize your local persistent weeds and understand our warning here. And in no case are we recommending weeds as a long-term cover crop. But for short-term use, a succulent crop of weeds benefits the garden when turned under. In a commercial experiment some years ago in the South, weeds as a green manure grew a higher quality crop of tobacco—a very demanding plant—than anything ever tried, including any other fertilizer.

WEEDS AS COMPANION PLANTS

In his book *Weeds, Guardians of the Soil* (Devin-Adair, 1950), Joseph A. Cocannouer tells of questioning the Pawnee Indians near his Oklahoma boyhood home about their practice of maintaining weedy fields instead of practicing the clean cultivation of the white man. Among the corn and pumpkins grew pigweeds, sunflowers, milkweeds, wild lettuce, and purslane. It turned out that the Indians did not weed their fields because the weeds were part of the crop (they used some leaves as cooking greens), and they also helped the corn and pumpkins grow.

Cocannouer had noticed the excellence of the corn and pumpkins. He found this same pattern of using weeds as companion plants when he investigated the mountainside agriculture of Indians in Mexico years later. There, weeds among corn, beans, peppers, and squash were encouraged because they anchored the soil as well as helping the vegetables in other ways the Indians perceived but could not explain.

The author is partial to pigweed as a companion for potatoes and some other root crops, and also for tomatoes, peppers, and eggplant. Lambs' quarters, which is also called pigweed, was a native on our Missouri farm, and was a companion plant for all these vegetables. We chopped the lambs' quarters out when we weeded, but the garden was so large and our time spread so thinly that we now suppose the lambs' quarters had the opportunity to do our crops some favors in spite of us.

Pumpkins and watermelons often surprise gardeners by doing well in the midst of weeds, and this is true of some other crops, even globe onions in some cases, though onions are notorious for needing a lot of weeding. In such cases it is clear that the weeds in some way help the cultivated crops.

One caution here: When using weeds as companion plants, space them, using as a rule of thumb the same or wider spacing that you are giving the vegetables growing with them. Letting the weeds grow at will is too much of a good thing, and will choke out the vegetables in most cases.

WEEDS AS ANTI-PESTS

Since weeds are themselves usually regarded as problems, how in the world can we call them anti-pests, the good guys? Well, we can call *some* of them that, and in two ways.

For one, some weeds are trap plants for injurious insects. You can tell this by noticing the damage done to the weeds that grow in your area. When a bad insect prefers a weed to a crop plant, your cup of luck runneth over. Also, you can dispose of such insects for good while they are eating the weeds, if they are not bugs that can fly off and escape.

The second way weeds sometimes serve in pest control is as a haven for beneficial insects. We quote a biological-control insectary, Rincon-Vitova in Rialto, California, on this point: "Even the natural weeds can effectively provide a protective niche for predators and parasites and keep them in the area during times of stress; they will also suppress the plant-feeding insects before their populations can rise to pest status."

WEEDS FOR MULCHING

We had clay soil in Missouri and one of the best ways to keep it from baking during summer was to keep it mulched. For this we used weeds whenever they were there to be used. We sharpened the hoe and sliced the weeds off at ground level. To do this with the least effort, work close to your toes, backing into the weeds as you hoe. Held close to the vertical in this way, a hoe blade meets the weeds at about the angle a razor makes with the skin while shaving.

Some years ago the American Farm Association experimented with weeds as a mulch for corn, letting the weeds grow along with the corn for four weeks, then knocking the weeds down and letting them remain on the ground as a mulch. Not only did corn production go up, but an analysis of the soil at the end of the season showed such an improvement that another crop of corn could have followed at once.

You can also mulch with weeds you cut elsewhere and bring to your garden. But don't use weeds carrying ripe seeds.

Weeds as Soil Improvers

Most weeds have excellent root systems, fitted to delve deeply and mine subsoil much more efficiently than do most cultivated vegetables. This habit has at least three benefits for the vegetables: 1. It taps a source of nutrients including some hard-to-get trace elements. 2. The deep rooting brings underground water up into the root region of the vegetables, if they are growing nearby, the water ascending the weeds' root channels, on the outside of the roots, by capillary action. 3. The strong weed roots cultivate the soil, in a sense, and are especially helpful in loosening tight soil, so that a companion-planted root crop can grow to better size.

Weeds for Compost

By composting weeds you take advantage of the good they have stored up for themselves and release it in a form your cultivated plants can use. Mulching with weeds will also accomplish this in time, as will turning them under.

Succulent weeds are high in nitrogen. In fact, a ton of mixed weeds averages about 18 pounds of pure nitrogen, or close to 1 percent by weight.

You can compost weeds carrying ripe seeds if you run a good compost pile that heats up properly, as described in Chapter 3. The heat germinates the seeds prematurely. However, it is safest to compost immature weeds, and they also break down faster and do more for the compost.

WEEDS FOR FOOD

Certainly some weeds are good to eat. Dandelions, chicory, and lambs' quarters are outstanding examples of nutritious cooking greens. In some parts of the country you find the Jerusalem artichoke considered a weed, but its tubers are as edible as the Jerusalem artichoke you plant in the garden. Having said this much, though, we'll have to admit that as for food, we feel about most weeds the way we do about wild mushrooms—we leave them strictly to the experts. We admire Euell Gibbons' ability to live off the bounty of the land, but we don't try to compete. Many innocent-looking plants are mildly poisonous, and some are violently so. Pokeweed, for instance, is popular as a spring green, for which the young shoots are used, but its roots contain a deadly poison. Children are much inclined to experiment at nibbling strange plants, and dangerous weeds are often of interest to them, so consider this before setting them an experimenting example with weeds.

BUT WHEN YOU MUST GET RID OF WEEDS . . .

Yes, when they become a pest, weeds must be scourged out, so in recent years an industry has grown up based on making weed killers, commonly called herbicides. Some work by overstimulating the weed. In effect, it starves.

Organic gardeners take a dim view of herbicides. The feeling is, a herbicide interferes with nature. True. Witness the defoliants of warfare.

In our own gardens we have never used herbicides—and have never used them anywhere else except for spot treatments of poison oak and poison ivy, because one of us is highly susceptible. And we have preferred to let even these plants live when they are not in our way. A far corner fence post of our farm garden was so beautifully wreathed with poison ivy—a quite lovely plant if you can divorce your mind from the villainous aspects—that we kept it as an ornamental, admiring from a distance.

Keeping a weed chopped off with a hoe will kill it eventually if not at once. You starve the roots by depriving them of nutrients the foliage manufactures. If a weed is too persistent for you, though, try this: Boil a cupful of water and dissolve in it all the rock salt it will take. Put a few drops of this saturated solution on the exposed cut end of the weed after hoeing.

Here is a U. S. Department of Agriculture recommendation for weed control: Cover the weed with tar paper, or similar light-proof material, and seal down the edges of the material with earth. The weed should die of overheating and lack of light.

At Michigan State University a field technique called the stale seedbed has been developed recently to get control of early-season weeds. It goes this way: The grower gets his field ready for planting, but then lets it alone from 10 to 14 days while the weed seeds in the top 2″ of soil sprout. He then kills these weeds, plants his crop, and it is so well established by the time the second flush of weeds come along, they are often choked out. And although the growers use a herbicide to kill the early weeds here, in a home garden a sharp hoe is more natural and will do a more satisfying job.

9

How to Handle Garden Pests

IN THIS CHAPTER we are covering a great many harmful insects and diseases that will probably never bother your garden, for the most part. But by doing so, we hope you will be able to find any of the pests that may cause you trouble.

At any rate, don't feel discouraged by the number of pests. Like the ills that flesh is heir to, very few of them will happen to any one individual—or here, to any one garden.

We cover pest management from these aspects: prevention, sanitation, mechanical controls, predators, household materials, botanical controls, and biological controls.

PREVENTION

Preventing trouble is always better than having to cure it. Here are eight ways to do so in your garden.

NOTE: At the end of this chapter is a list of vegetables and their possible pests, and a list of fruits and nuts and their possible pests. Following each of these lists are descriptions of the insects and diseases mentioned, and organically safe controls. Beneficial insects are listed in a separate group at the end.

Resistant varieties. Many vegetables have been bred to thrive under conditions others cannot cope with. This resistance is a built-in physical character that keeps the disease from getting a foothold. Choosing resistant varieties will often prevent a problem from occurring, and seed catalogues stress this. Since a virus disease, mosaic, attacks snap beans, a defense is to plant Improved Tendergreen, Topcrop, Wade, or Tendercrop. All are resistant to mosaic. A purple snap bean, Royalty, repels bean beetles by its color, which is a form of resistance. Several good cabbages are resistant to a difficult virus disease, yellows, and though tomatoes are prey to several ills, there are excellent varieties that resist many of them.

Timing. An often overlooked technique for avoiding pests of some crops is simple timing. Many home gardeners plant certain vegetables a little too soon in the season, in their eagerness to get them going, and plant others a little too late. We do it ourselves, taking chances that often don't work out. The fact is, the too-early eggplant or pepper, say, is apt to mope along in weather too cool or days too short for it, an unthrifty plant and liable to attack. The too-late onion or bean is likely to be checked in growth by shortening daylengths and cool nights, so also is an easier victim than it would be in its proper season of robust growth.

Timing is also a factor in escaping insect damage, since many insects appear at definite periods and then are gone. By planting after they leave—or protecting plants until they do leave—you can outguess them. This is one of the rewards of keeping the kind of garden record mentioned in Chapter 2; you learn the habits of the insects that frequent your garden.

Site. Another way to prevent some trouble is to locate your garden so as to get good air circulation and good water drainage.

Some air movement, as on slopes, is good for plants. A very

poor site, by contrast, would be a basin surrounded by a dense hedge. Chapter 2 has further details on this point.

If your site has poor water drainage, some plants will not grow at all, and others will grow poorly. See Chapter 2 for ways to correct poor drainage.

Succession plantings. Since pests are worse at some times during the season, you can avoid having a crop wiped out if you make smaller plantings at intervals. You may still lose some plants to the pests, but you aren't likely to lose all. We do this with radishes, lettuce, and mustard, for example, partly for this reason. You cannot do it with something that takes all season to grow, such as pumpkins, but you can do it with most vegetables.

Spot planting. Separating plants of the same kind within the garden is also a preventive measure that sometimes works well, especially in a large garden. By dividing a chard planting between three or four places, for example, you can avoid being wiped out by a concentration of cutworms when the plants are small. And though flying insects get around more easily, even they may overlook some spot plantings of their favorite foods.

Trap plants. A trap plant is one you grow to *attract* insects. The object is to so beguile them with the trap plant, they will patronize it exclusively. Then you swoop down and kill them, along with the trap plant in some cases. The trap plant can be the same kind as the ones you want to protect, except that it is planted sooner and thus gets a monopoly on the pests. Or it can be any plant the pests will flock to.

Gladiolus will attract thrips, harlequin bugs swarm to mustard, and we have used butterhead lettuce as a trap plant for slugs when we wanted to keep them off a planting of cos lettuce.

Keep in mind that the insects you want to attract must be those that settle down and stay on a plant.

Guard plants. A guard plant is one that repels pests, thus protecting nearby plants from those pests. This is something like companion planting, covered in Chapter 7, but specialized for guard duty.

Marigolds are the best-documented guard plants. Scientific experiments in Connecticut during the 1960s demonstrated that marigolds killed meadow nematodes so effectively that a field planted to marigolds was then free of nematodes for the next 3 years. The experiment drew on experience in the Netherlands and elsewhere, and this suggestion was offered to gardeners: "Interplanting with marigolds may not greatly benefit during the first season, but benefits become apparent the following year. . . . Marigolds must be grown all season to give lasting control."

The control is a chemical in the marigold roots. When released as a root diffusate it kills the nematodes. This effect extends about 3' out from the plant, so by spotting marigolds about 3' apart in your garden you can build a nematode barrier by the second year. Marigolds are annuals, so plant them each year for best results, using either the small French marigolds or the large African or American ones. Our own preference is for semi-dwarf hybrid Americans, as they don't shade everything around them, and have spectacular blooms by the dozens.

If you suspect nematodes (the usual symptom is a stunted, weak plant, especially if a cucumber, tomato, or okra), check the roots for swellings. These may be tiny, or up to 1" thick. Pearly white specks inside them will be nematode eggs. Burn them.

Marigolds also have an effect on some above-ground pests, many home gardeners say. This varies in different parts of the country, and the marigolds seem most effective in this way where summers are warm. It has been reported that in the Southeast they have even warded off the persistent Mexican bean beetle.

Many aromatic herbs are interplanted with vegetables, to

act as guard plants. Evidence of their effect is not verified as well as that of marigolds on nematodes. Rosemary, sage, and peppermint have been used against the maggot fly in plantings of cabbage and other brassicas. Basil is interplanted with tomatoes as a general guard plant, one basil to each 3 or 4 tomato plants.

Garlic is a popular guard plant, and we have found aphids sometimes less troublesome to broccoli if garlic is near. Other gardeners say it chases Japanese beetles, ordinarily a hard pest to move.

Painted daisies (*Chrysanthemum coccineum*) are one of the plants from which the insecticide pyrethrum is obtained, and the daisies are also used as guard plants by some organic gardeners. The insecticide is obtained from the flowers.

Tansy is also planted as a general insect repellent.

If you find that insects leave a plant strictly alone, it is probably worth testing as a guard plant.

Gophers and moles may be repelled by surrounding a garden with bulbs of squill (*Scilla*) as a border planting. Squill is not a demanding plant and has attractive spring flowers.

Good health. One of the best of all insect repellents is a healthy plant. This is one growing strongly and normally, looking as if it were posing for a catalogue picture. Some say that insects attack sickly plants and shun healthy ones alongside. In our experience, the insects will attack any plant, but the weak ones falter and the healthy ones shrug off the effects.

SANITATION

Like a clean house, a clean garden does not invite pests, and if they come, makes it easier for you to strike back. Here are the more important points in good garden housekeeping.

Weeds. As discussed in Chapter 8, a weed may have merits

as a companion plant, a trap plant, and in some other ways, but when in doubt, chop it out.

Fall spading. If you are being troubled by pests that live snugly in the soil over the winter, exposing them to cold weather by spading the garden is good sanitation. Even a permanently mulched garden may need this treatment at times. When spading for this purpose, leave the surface rough until spring planting time.

Hand-pick insects. Caterpillars and some beetles are easily caught by hand. So are snails and slugs. We kill such captives and drop them into the compost pile to add nutrients.

Trash. Trash piles offer cover to pests and look poor in a garden. Set such materials to composting or get rid of them.

Rotation. If you grew beans in a bed last year, grow them in some other bed this year, and plant a root vegetable or a leafy green where the beans were. This is called rotating crops. The idea is to starve out any disease or soil insect by removing their favored fare (and also to equalize the drain on available nutrients in the soil, as different plants have different requirements). Though rotation is more practical in a large garden, it helps in a small one too.

Cultivation. Like fall spading on a smaller scale, loosening the top inch or so of soil can discourage some pests, and it admits needed air. Cutworms are a notorious example of pests found near the soil surface.

Digging. A spot inspection by digging is sometimes the best way to nip trouble in the bud. When a plant looks sickly and no reason for it is in sight above ground, dig carefully around it. Burrowing animals may be exposing roots to air, or eating them. Air pockets may have formed after a transplanting. And ants, nematodes, and maggots are all underground enemies that digging can expose.

Old plants. Prompt harvesting will help keep some pests down. When a plant passes its peak of maturity it gradually becomes a potential victim to insects and diseases, besides being less acceptable on the table.

Unhealthy plants. Sick plants are best removed from the garden and destroyed. We hate to do this, but like a sick chick, a sick plant never catches up with the rest, and may become a menace to healthy ones—as when a sucking insect spreads a virus disease the sick plant has contracted. When you pull up a diseased plant handle it gently so as not to scatter any fungus spores or other detachable pests.

MECHANICAL CONTROLS

Fences and cages. If your garden pests include animals, a fence is often the only remedy, especially against rabbits, dogs, and deer. In one area where we lived, deer were so persistent, the best remedy was a wire cage for the entire garden.

We use a small version of this by bending down an 8″ strip along each side of a sheet of rabbit wire to form a box, then setting it upside down on a bed of small plants. Such a box made of screen wire will also keep maggot flies off, and taller growing plants can be protected by cheesecloth over a wooden frame.

By turning the rabbit-wire box, open side up, and burying it about 10″ deep, moles, gophers, and chipmunks are usually turned aside on their way toward plants growing inside this underground basket. In parts of California no one would dream of planting anything without this protection from the persistent gopher.

Traps. Boards laid in the garden can trap a good many insects such as sow bugs, pill bugs, earwigs, and slugs. Look under the boards each morning and kill the insects. Vegetable matter on the ground, such as a broccoli or chard leaf or a squash half, are also effective, and will attract cutworms, garden centipedes, and some other pests. There are some commercial traps for flying insects, though some take more attention than they are likely to get from many gardeners.

A simple form of slug and snail trap that received much attention in 1970 is a shallow pan half filled with beer. At the Beltsville, Maryland, station of the U. S. Department of Agriculture such a trap proved ten times as effective as regular metaldehyde bait, killing 300 snails in 4 days. This was in a greenhouse, though, not a garden. The slugs and snails are not poisoned by the beer, but get tipsy and then drown in it. Happily, we suppose.

To make a bait holder that will protect metaldehyde baits from the effects of rain and watering, cut the bottom of a coffee can enough to fold back a half-circle for the entrance of slugs and snails, put the lid on the other end for a back wall, put a spoonful of bait inside and set the can on its side in the garden. A rock inside it will anchor it, and if you paint the can dark green it will not be noticeable.

The best trap we have found for gophers is a brand called Macabee. To use it, expose the animal's tunnel with a spade and set two traps, one facing down one side of the tunnel and the other facing the opposite way, since you don't know which direction the gopher will be traveling. Tie strong cords to the traps, tie the other ends onto sticks pushed into the ground. Cover the hole you have made, using a piece of fresh sod, and check the traps at least once a day, resetting after each catch until no more animals show up.

Though this is still in the experimental stage as we write it, recent research at Cornell University showed good results in trapping black flea beetles in cabbage-family plantings by using an oil obtained from mustard. A control trap baited with plain water also caught flea beetles, but the one baited with the mustard oil trapped ten times as many.

Others. Lights in or near the garden may frighten raccoons. Those used to being fed by people will not be bothered.

Strips of foil hung from strings are occasionally effective in keeping destructive birds from a young seedbed.

Cheesecloth pegged down over a strawberry bed will protect it from birds. So will a lightweight netting sold for the purpose and good for more than one season. One gardener we know uses it all over her small garden to keep out cats.

Pea-eating birds can be kept away from the peas by sticking twiggy branches into the row every foot or two and stringing strong black thread along them.

Predators (Allies)

Besides various insects and other forms of life that prey on pests of the garden, we often get some help from other predators, wild and domestic. Here are several you can call allies.

Birds. Although some birds eat plants and seeds, they also eat a great many injurious insects. Feeders will lure some birds to you, and water for bathing and drinking will bring more. Trees, vines, and bushy shrubs are all of interest to birds as nesting and hiding places.

Bats. Bats, the flying mammals, are friends of the garden, too. Insects are their food, usually caught in the air. You might not want bats in an attic, a place they sometimes favor, but outside they can be highly useful.

Cats. Cats and birds seldom coexist peacefully, although an Audubon Society official told us that cats tend to catch sick or injured birds. In any case, some cats are helpful in the garden. We knew a pear grower in Missouri who kept an enormous tomcat for controlling rabbits and mice, which kill young trees by eating the bark. A dog can keep rabbits down, but this pear man objected to their habit of burying bones, which attracted rats.

Cats can be efficient at catching moles and gophers, and they don't wreck the garden doing so. It will help the cat if you dig a hole to expose a gopher tunnel. When the gopher shows up to plug the hole, the cat can catch it. Cats are also interested in chipmunks, but chipmunks are much faster than gophers, and may outrun the cat in a short sprint. Some gardeners go after both chipmunks and gophers with guns, a method that takes a good deal of patient waiting and a fast trigger finger. And may be against your state game laws for chipmunks.

If you have a mole but no cat, try this: Watch for the earth to start heaving into a low ridge, usually in early morning, at noon, or in late afternoon. Quickly drive a spade into the ridge 1' behind its front point to cut off the animal's retreat. Then dig it out fast. In fairness, we should add that moles do some good by eating grubs and other insects in the soil, for moles are meat eaters, while gophers are vegetarians. Chipmunks eat nuts, seeds, berries, and insects.

Toads, lizards, snakes. A toad devours more than 100 insects a day, especially cutworms and caterpillars, so is highly useful. They eat earthworms, too, but will have to be forgiven this for their other merits.

Lizards, if you are lucky enough to have them in your garden, are also superb insect catchers.

Snakes seem to many a gardener a dubious blessing, since they scare many persons as much as they scare insects. They also eat mice and moles, though, and gopher snakes eat gophers. Except for venomous snakes, we live and let live.

Skunks. An excellent ally for a garden is a skunk, though not many gardeners seem to know this. Skunks eat meadow mice and a great variety of insects such as white grubs, cutworms, grasshoppers. Weasels also eat some insects and are terrors to rats and mice.

Shrews. Looking like small, short-tailed mice, shrews are enemies of both mice and insects. They are nearly incessant eaters, doing a good deal of their work at night. Cats will catch them, but the shrew does have the defense of glands that produce a smell the cat dislikes.

Poultry. Ducks eat slugs, snails, and certain insects. Chickens and guineas eat many insects. Geese are good weeders in orchards. But none of these birds belongs in a garden, if you ask us. All are too apt to damage the garden. The only exceptions we have made were for young chicks and for broody hens with a flock of guinea chicks we had assigned to her.

HOUSEHOLD MATERIALS

Many ordinary things around the house are death to insects though harmless to people. Here are several.

Soap. An effective weapon against some insects is plain soap. Make a strong solution with a cubic inch of soap to 1 gallon of water, and spray or paint it on plants. Aphids are quite vulnerable to this. You can also dissolve 1 cup of soap flakes in 1 gallon of water, and there are special soaps of fish oils and coconut oil made for this purpose. Follow the soap with plain water, as soap left on a plant may hurt it.

Sulfur. When you were young, sulfur and molasses may have been given you as a spring tonic. Sulfur is also used in skin ointments, and our bodies contain sulfur. Though it is usually thought of as a garden fungicide, sulfur used as a dust is also a control for some mites, some scale insects, and young caterpillars. Ask for dusting sulfur or wettable sulfur. It will damage squash and other cucurbits such as cucumbers and melons, however, and should not be used on any plants if the temperature is above 80° F.

Molasses. This partner of sulfur in tonics is also an insecticide. Use it as a spray, mixing ⅓ cup of molasses with 1 gallon of water. Used as a contact spray (you must hit the insect with it) it has been found effective against many injurious pests.

Water. Water alone is an effective weapon against some slow, soft-bodied insects. Aphids can often be washed off a stiff-stemmed plant with a hose. This water treatment received the approval of researchers in the Canada Department of Agriculture Research Station at Summerland, British Columbia, in 1969 when they found that a strong stream of water on apple trees knocked off and drowned small insects, including mites, that are not affected by most insecticides. We find aphids hard to drown, incidentally, but they are easily damaged by the force of water, and perhaps they then drown.

By flooding a seedbed before planting it, thrips and aphids present can be drowned. And if you can put 3″ or 4″ of water on your entire garden just before spring planting, root aphids and garden centipedes will be drowned. Do this a day or two before you plant, so the garden can dry out enough for soil to be workable.

Wood ashes. We spread wood ashes around plants of the cabbage and onion groups to discourage maggots, repeating this several times while plants are young. It isn't completely effective, but it is worth doing. Ashes are said to control some sucking insects, such as aphids, when sprinkled on plants the insects are attacking. A spray for cucumber beetles is ½ cup each of wood ashes and hydrated lime stirred into 1 gallon of water. Strain it and use at once.

Paper. Paper is a barrier against some pests. A stiff paper collar around stems of young plants can keep cutworms from hurting them. The collar should reach 1″ underground and 4″ above, and be about 1″ wider than the stem all around. You can use foil instead of paper for better weathering, though paper has the advantage of eventually going to pieces and requiring no further attention.

Moth balls. If dropped into mole runs every 6′, moth balls may drive moles away, though they seldom go far, and sometimes merely dig alternate runs.

Oil. Ordinary mineral oil will kill corn earworms if applied at the right time, which is *after* the silks go limp and their ends start to turn brown. Squeeze 5 or 6 drops of the oil from an eyedropper onto the silks where they enter the ear tip. The oil coats the worm and smothers it, and it is also almost impossible for insects to build resistance agains a mechanical control such as this.

Others. A simple spray that usually keeps plants free from rabbit damage for a while is made by dissolving ⅓ cup of Epsom salt in 1 gallon of water. Rabbits are also repelled by blood, 3 or 4 tablespoons in 1 gallon of water. The fertilizer dried blood can also be sprinkled about for the same purpose, and small cloth bags of it hung on shrubs that deer fancy will more or less repel them.

Crushed eggshells have been used against cutworms, the shells being sprinkled around plants and then lightly covered with earth. If you have raccoons visiting your garden, they would give you trouble by digging up the eggshells, so keep this in mind.

A spray of ordinary table salt, 2 teaspoons to 1 gallon of water, is used against cabbage worms and some mites.

Skim milk, used straight as a spray, has given control of mosaic affecting peppers and tomatoes. Skim milk can be bought cheaply in the dry form, which keeps indefinitely.

Botanical Controls

There are a number of controls for garden pests that come from plants themselves and so are more acceptable to organic gardeners than chemicals are even though some of the botanicals are poisons.

Rotenone. This useful product is produced by several plants, chiefly by derris, cube, and timbo. Rotenone is a stomach poison to insects, a contact poison, and a repellent. It is harmless to warm-blooded animals. It lasts about a week after spraying or dusting, and is a slow killer, taking as much as two days to take effect. It works in cool weather, which some controls do not. It is often combined with pyrethrum, described below, because they are compatible and they complement each other.

Pyrethrum. Pyrethrum is a natural combination of four plant toxins called pyrethrins. Pyrethrum is found in three species of chrysanthemums. It is a stomach poison and a contact poison, like rotenone, and also like rotenone it is harmless to warm-blooded animals. It works much faster than rotenone but lasts for only a short time, from less than 1 hour to a day or so. It should be applied, when used as a spray, very soon after being mixed. This is good advise for any spray but especially for pyrethrum.

There are also synthetic forms of pyrethrum, though our personal preference is for the natural ones.

Nicotine. The active ingredient of the tobacco plant, nicotine kills some insects when it touches them. It is also a stomach poison for insects. You can make a nicotine spray by steeping a handful of smoking tobacco in 1 gallon of water. When fresh and mixed with 1 cup of soap flakes it will work fairly well on some pests. However, you run a risk of spreading mosaic by doing this, so a better way is to use nicotine sulfate. A well-known brand is Black Leaf 40.

Nicotine residue on a plant is poisonous to humans, but the residue is no longer harmful after about 2 days. To be on the safe side we don't use nicotine on leafy greens at all, and we give it 3 or 4 days to wear off any other plant before harvesting. For best results with nicotine, use it in warm weather.

Nicotine dust is also available (ask for tobacco dust), and in addition to being a mild insecticide it has fertilizing value.

Garlic. Here is an insecticide you can grow for yourself. During 1970, research at the University of California in Riverside proved what many a gardener had long suspected: Garlic just naturally smelled as if it ought to be a powerful menace to bad bugs. The university scientists used it to spray mosquitoes, with startling success, killing even tough pasture mosquitoes that strong solutions of chemical insecticides had not harmed. The oil in the garlic contains the effective ingredient. So dilute a solution is used—10 or 12 parts per million parts of water —that for home use a drop of garlic juice squeezed from a garlic press into 1 gallon of water would be potent.

The researchers, by the way, suggested two organically interesting reasons why the garlic worked on the mosquitoes, and why such natural insecticides may have a bright future. First, mosquitoes had been able to build up an immunity to chemicals after years of treatment with them. Second, few insects have been able to build any such immunity to plant-derived insecticides.

Sabadilla. The seeds of a tropical plant, sabadilla, are the source of another insecticide, used against leaf hoppers, squash bugs, cabbage worms, and some other pests. Sabadilla is not as widely available as the other plant controls mentioned above even though it is not a new control. See Appendix II for sources.

Hellebore. Another seldom met, and plant-derived, insecticide is hellebore. Also an old product, it is expensive but harmless to man and a stomach poison for insects. It comes from the root of the Veratrum, or false hellebore. (Note: The true hellebore, commonly seen in the species called Christmas rose, *is* poisonous to man, its root containing the toxic substance.)

Ryania. A newer but also not easily found insecticide, ryania comes from a Latin American shrub. It is used against insects such as squash bugs, corn borers, corn earworms, cabbage worms, onion thrips, Japanese beetles, and some aphids.

Tomato leaves. A spray made by steeping tomato leaves in water is somewhat effective against pests of the tomato. Crush the leaves first. Cherry tomatoes are considered by gardeners to be better here than others.

Hot peppers. One of the more effective ways to make a spray from hot peppers is to run them through a blender with an equal volume of water, using about 1 cup of each. Let this mixture steep for a day. Then strain it through cloth, to make a stock solution, stirring ½ cup of it into 1 gallon of water. It is a general insecticide but should not be used on tender young plants.

Herbs. A number of herbs have been used against fungi, and bacterial diseases. Herbs tried for this include mints, lavender, sage, savory, and wormwood. You can steep the herbs in cold water, but a faster way is to pour boiling water over them, 1 quart of water to 1 quart or less of herbs. Let it stand for 15 minutes, then drain, add water to make 1 gallon, and use at once.

Compost. How it works is not clear, but a compost solution (compost tea) appears to act as a systemic insecticide at times. Put a 4″ layer of ripe compost into a bucket, fill the bucket with water, stir it and let it stand for 30 minutes with occasional stirring. Strain it through burlap and sprinkle it on the leaves of the plants being treated. We have got an excellent control of some worms on squash and celery with this treatment. Chard and broccoli have hardly responded at all, however, perhaps because their leaves would not absorb the solution.

This treatment has the added advantage of feeding the plant—which can also be a help in combating insects and diseases.

BIOLOGICAL CONTROLS

Biological control of pests is the act of setting one form of life against another. This may be insect vs. insect, bacteria vs. insect, or some other combination. This form of control is nature's own and is present to some extent in your garden without any effort from you. You can also introduce some beneficial predators into your garden. Suppliers are listed in Appendix II.

This kind of pest control is getting more attention lately from commercial growers. In addition to public criticism of many chemical pesticides, one big reason for this commercial interest in biological controls is the decreasing effectiveness of many pesticides due to the appearance of resistant strains of insects, a survival of the fittest. Some have been known to withstand a dosage 1,000 times as strong as that which had killed previous generations.

But no matter how resistant to insecticides such insects become, they are still vulnerable to their natural enemies. Importation of such natural enemies is being used on a broad scale against such pests as alfalfa weevils, which a small wasp can control; greenbugs, which are devoured by ladybugs; and lygus bugs, killed by lacewing larvae.

This is not a brand-new way of fighting pests commercially. It has been going on, frequently with government aid, for at least ninety years. The control of a type of mealy bug on citrus in California in the late 1920s through importation of parasites from Australia is famous. It was also in Australia that a moth became the biological control of prickly-pear cacti, which had become a strident nuisance. The moth larvae invaded the cacti and rotted them. In 7 years, starting in 1926, millions of acres were cleared solely in this way.

Though about 100 parasites and predators of this beneficial kind have been imported to the United States since the 1880s, it may seem mysterious and exasperating that biological controls have not been more encouraged commercially *instead* of pesticides. Some reasons are, they don't always work, or may work only partially, or work in some places and not at all in others. Also, finding the right control is often a slow and uncertain search. Add also, human impatience to find fast solutions, whether or not they are the best solutions.

And, to be honest about it, biological controls sometimes have their own unpleasant reversals. Some years ago, mongooses were brought from India to the Caribbean islands where rats and mice were rampant, but the mongooses cleaned house so thoroughly that they ran out of rats and mice and had to start killing all sorts of other small animals that no one wanted killed. Another difficulty in biological control is that there are some pests we have no such controls for at all.

Nevertheless, biological controls are gaining new interest. Entomologists are breeding control insects on a mass basis, and some are in business as consultants for harried growers. An interesting point here is that the cost of this control to growers is often dramatically lower than for spraying.

Biological control does not necessarily eliminate every member of the pest being fought, by the way. To do so would leave the beneficial insects without food. The object is more likely to be similar to nature's own arrangement: holding down insect populations to an acceptable level.

In our own garden the usual beneficial insects are ladybugs, some ground beetles, assassin bugs, dragonflies, syrphid flies, some lacewing flies, and spiders. It is a good idea to make such an insect inventory of your own garden, to see what help you can expect. Possibly you may decide to introduce a new beneficial insect. Those most available are aphid lions (larvae of lacewing flies), ladybugs, praying mantids, trichogramma wasps, some fly parasites, and scale parasites. See Appendix II for suppliers.

Such an introduction of a beneficial insect will cost from $5 to $10 on the average, on a garden scale, and the supplier will include instructions on when and how to release the insects or eggs. An important point is that the enemy be present, as an immediate source of food for the beneficial predaceous insect. Ideally, some of the beneficial insects will become part of your garden's permanent insect population, but this is not always so.

This introduction of beneficial insects can be very successful. It can also be disappointing. Not every insect group will stay where you want it to stay, or it may be killed by other insects, or by the weather. This is why we suggest you make an inventory of your insect population first, as it may reveal that you already have some insects you may want.

Here is the work some beneficial insects do. Each is described in the list at the end of this chapter.

Aleochara beetles are parasites of maggots, a hard pest to control. *Ant lions* are one of the few insects that keep ants down. They are most widely distributed in the South but are also found here and there throughout the country. *Aphid lions* are larvae that eat not only aphids but also a wide range of other injurious insects. *Assassin bugs* specialize in destroying the immature forms of many insects. *Centipedes* eat slugs and some insects. *Damsel bugs* eat some of the same fare as assassin bugs, plus aphids and flea hoppers. *Dragonflies* catch other flying insects in the air. *Ground beetles* feed mostly at night, on caterpillars and some other insects. *Hornets and yellow jackets* keep down caterpillars and flies. *Lacewing flies* are the adult form of aphid lions. *Ladybugs* and their larvae live on aphids, spider mites, scales, and mealy bugs. *Pirate bugs* and their larvae eat mites and the eggs or larvae of several insects. *Praying mantids* are quite long, up to 5″, so are able to eat all sorts of things too large for others in this list. *Spiders* also come in large sizes, and prey on a large assortment of other insects. *Syrphid flies* have sluglike larvae that eat aphids and some other damaging insects. *Wasps* of some species hunt caterpillars. Others such as *trichogramma wasps* lay their eggs in the bodies of some other insects which are then killed by the larvae when they hatch.

The other form of biological control, in which a disease is given to some pest, can be illustrated by two examples. One is a control for the Japanese beetle, the other a control for many caterpillars or worms.

The Japanese beetle control is a spore that is plugged into the soil in infested areas, 1 teaspoon of the material to each 10 feet. It causes the beetle grubs to die of what is called the milky disease. A 90 percent kill is not unusual.

The caterpillar/worm control, generally available to home gardeners since 1971, but with a success record before that with commercial growers, is called *Bacillus thuringiensis*. It causes a fatal internal paralysis in the victims and seems to be harmless to plants and to other life. Kills have run over 95 percent. The effect takes hold in a few hours, and an application lasts about a week.

If these controls are not available locally, see Appendix II for suppliers and trade names.

As a matter of interest, though not home-garden practical, we should mention three other biological controls that are under test. One reduces the numbers of one sex of an insect species, usually males, with some artificial attraction so that they can be destroyed in quantities. The result is to reduce the reproduction rate.

Another control involves treating adult insects with a juvenile hormone or hormones, a condition fatal to the insects at certain periods of their lives.

Third, there is a technique of synthetically extending daylength with lights over a field during the fall of the year. By doing so, scientists have caused larvae of corn borers and of codling moths to mature early and thus die that winter of cold and a lack of food.

Finally, keep in mind that where sprays or dusts are concerned, a *contact* spray or dust kills by striking the insect, often by smothering it, and is necessary against sucking insects since they cannot be killed by eating a leaf on which a *stomach poison* has been placed by spray or dust.

In using any dusts or sprays, you'll get better results if you change back and forth among various materials, so the pests won't become immune to any one control.

Freshly made solutions are the rule in all sprays. Stale ones may undergo chemical changes and may then even harm the plants they are supposed to protect; in any case, they are not as effective as fresh mixes, and this is fully as true for organically safe controls as it is for any others.

Dusts are stable, however, and can be considered good throughout a season, ready for use as needed. In general, start each gardening season with fresh control materials for best results.

VEGETABLES AND THEIR POSSIBLE PESTS

Artichokes, globe. Aphids.

Artichokes, Jerusalem. Leaf hoppers.

Asparagus. Asparagus beetles, asparagus rust, corn earworms, cutworms, garden centipedes.

Beans. Anthracnose, aphids, bacterial blight, bean rust, corn earworms, Japanese beetles, leaf hoppers, lygus bugs, maggots, Mexican bean beetles, mosaics, rust, seed decay, spider mites, spotted cucumber beetles, stink bugs, weevils, wireworms.

Beets. Beet webworms, blister beetles, cutworms, damping-off, flea beetles, leaf spot, maggots.

Broccoli. (See Cabbage.)

Brussels sprouts. (See Cabbage.)

Cabbage. Aphids, blackleg and black rot, cabbage worms, clubroot, cutworms, damping-off, flea beetles, harlequin bugs, maggots, pink rot, rhizoctonia, thrips, weevils, wilt, yellows.

Cantaloupe. Anthracnose, aphids, bacterial wilt, damping-off, downy mildew, leaf spot, mosaics, nematodes, pickleworms, spider mites, spotted cucumber beetles, squash bugs, striped cucumber beetles, thrips.

Carrots. Leaf hoppers, weevils, wireworms, yellows.

Cauliflower. (See Cabbage.)

Celeriac. (See Celery.)

Celery. Aphids, blights, celery leaf tyer, damping-off, leaf hoppers, pink rot, spider mites, wireworms, yellows.

Chard. (See Beets.)

Collards. (See Cabbage.)

Corn. Bacterial wilt, corn borers, corn earworms, Japanese beetles, maggots, seed decay, smut, spider mites, wilt.

Cucumbers. Anthracnose, aphids, bacterial blight, bacterial wilt, corn earworms, damping-off, downy mildew, leaf spot, mosaics, nematodes, pickleworms, scab, spider mites, spotted cucumber beetles, squash bugs, striped cucumber beetles, thrips.

Eggplant. Corn borers, corn earworms, damping-off, flea beetles, fruit rot, leaf hoppers, potato bugs, spider mites, tomato horn worms, wilt.

Kale. (See Cabbage.)

Kohlrabi. (See Cabbage.)

Lettuce. Aphids, cabbage worms, cutworms, drop, leaf hoppers, mosaics, pink rot, slugs and snails, tipburn, wireworms, yellows.

Melons. (See Cantaloupe and Watermelon).

Mustard. (See Turnips.)

Okra. Aphids, corn earworms, Japanese beetles, nematodes, stink bugs, wilt.

Onions. Maggots, smut, spider mites, thrips, wireworms.

Peas. Aphids, ascochyta pod spot, blights, cutworms, fusarium wilt, maggots, root rots, seed decay, spider mites, weevils.

Peppers. Anthracnose, aphids, bacterial spot, blossom-end rot, corn borers, corn earworms, cutworms, damping-off, flea beetles, leaf spot, mosaics, tomato horn worms, weevils.

Potatoes, sweet. Blackleg and black rot, weevils, wilt, wireworms.

Potatoes, white. Aphids, blights, blister beetles, corn earworms, dry rot, flea beetles, grasshoppers, leaf hoppers, leaf roll, maggots, mosaics, potato bugs, rhizoctonia, scab, tomato horn worms, white grubs, wilt, wireworms.

Pumpkins. (See Squash.)

Radishes. Maggots.

Rutabagas. Aphids, maggots.

Scallions. (See Onions.)

Shallots. (See Onions.)

Spinach. Aphids, blights, cutworms, seed decay, slugs and snails, yellows.

Squash, summer. Bacterial wilt, corn earworms, mosaics, pickleworms, scab, spotted cucumber beetles, squash bugs, squash vine borers, striped cucumber beetles, thrips.

Squash, winter. (See Squash, summer.)

Tomatoes. Aphids, blights, blister beetles, blossom-end rot, corn borers, cutworms, damping-off, flea beetles, fusarium wilt, leaf hoppers, leaf spot, mosaics, nematodes, potato bugs, spider mites, stink bugs, tomato fruit worms, tomato horn worms, verticillium wilt.

Turnips. Aphids, cabbage worms, flea beetles, harlequin bugs, maggots, thrips, weevils, wireworms.

Watermelon. Anthracnose, aphids, downy mildew, nematodes, spider mites, spotted cucumber beetles, squash bugs, striped cucumber beetles, thrips, wilt.

Vegetable Insects and Diseases

Anthracnose. A fungus that causes dark, discolored leaves and pods on beans. Also attacks cucumbers, peppers, watermelons, cantaloupes.

Plant clean-looking, western-grown seed or resistant varieties.

Don't touch wet plants.

Destroy affected plants.

Rotate crops.

Ants. Thousands of species, unwelcome in the garden because they protect aphids and move them from plant to plant. Ants also kill the beneficial aphid lions. Ant tunnels can damage roots.

Put rotenone dust into ant hills.

Pour boiling water into ant hills.

Pour a solution of pyrethrum and soapsuds into hills.

Outside the garden, pour kerosene into hills.

Aphids. Also called plant lice; small, soft, various colors, pear-shaped, working in massed groups. Suck juices, cause leaves to curl, yellow, and thicken. Aphids breed rapidly, particularly in dry, warm weather.

Control ants.

Spray aphids with strong stream of water.

Spray with soapy water.

Spray with nicotine and soapy water.

Spray or dust with rotenone or pyrethrum.

Spray with ryania.

Dust with nicotine.

Place ladybugs on infested plants.

Crush aphids by hand.

Ascochyta pod spot. A fungus disease that damages peas. Shows up as dark-margined areas on pods and dotted patches on leaves.

Burn any diseased vines after harvest.

Plant clean, western-grown seed.

Asparagus beetles. Blue or orange, ¼″ long. One kind is spotted. They feed on asparagus foliage.

Pick stalks every day in season.

Spray or dust foliage with rotenone to kill larvae.

Asparagus rust. A fungus, showing up as a dusty-orange coloring on asparagus stems and foliage, killing tops. Worst in moist years.

Grow resistant varieties.

Dust with sulfur.

In fall cut diseased tops at ground level and burn them.

Bacterial blight. Attacks beans, peas, and cucumbers, discoloring leaves and pods.

Plant resistant varieties.

Don't touch wet plants.

Rotate crops.

Destroy affected plants.

Bacterial spot. A disease of peppers, spotting leaves with yellow and blemishing fruits with corky areas. Bacteria are carried on the seed, and can infest soil.

Plant new seed, and in a different place in the garden each year.

Bacterial wilt. Attacks vine crops except watermelon, wilting the vines. Spread by striped cucumber beetles. Another form attacks sweet corn, dwarfing plants.

For cucumbers, destroy affected plants, control striped cucumber beetles.

For corn, plant resistant varieties.

Bean rust. Like asparagus rust, a fungus. Forms blisters on bean leaves. Blisters are red or blackish; leaves turn yellow and fall.

Remove and destroy all diseased plants.

Dust with sulfur.

Plant resistant varieties.

Beet webworm. A yellow or greenish caterpillar with black stripe and black dots on back. Rolls up beet and chard leaves with webs, eats leaves and buds.

Spray or dust with pyrethrum.

Blackleg and black rot. A fungus causes blackleg, and a bacteria causes black rot. Both attack cabbage and other brassicas, causing spotted leaves, wilting. Black rot also attacks sweet potatoes.

Rotate crops.

Plant clean seed and unblemished sweet potato roots.

Keep garden free of plant refuse.

Weed out any wild mustard near garden.

Blights. Fungus diseases affecting celery, peas, potatoes, and tomatoes. The leaves develop spots, and the crop is reduced or the plants are killed. Worse in cool, moist weather.

Rotate crops.

Carefully destroy affected plant parts.

Plant resistant varieties.

Blister beetles. Gray or black, sometimes striped, up to ¾″ long. They eat leaves, mainly of beet, chard, potatoes, and tomatoes.

Hand-pick. Use gloves; the name of this insect comes from a blistering fluid it discharges.

Blossom-end rot. A tomato reaction to uneven watering and to deficiency of calcium. Causes dark, sunken area at blossom end of fruit. Also affects peppers.

Mulch plants and don't let soil dry out.

Apply enough hydrated lime to barely whiten the soil, or spread a handful of wood ashes around each plant.

Cabbage worms. Three species, really caterpillars. They damage cabbage and other brassicas by chewing. The imported cabbage worm—smooth, up to 1½″ long, and leaf-green—is the larva of the white cabbage butterfly. The same size but lighter green, the cabbage looper humps its back as it crawls; it is the larva of a night-flying moth, and also attacks lettuce, mustard, and turnips. A small green worm is the larva of the diamond-back moth.

Hand-pick worms.

Spray or dust with rotenone or pyrethrum.

Spray with Thuricide or similar biological control.

Spray with 2 teaspoons table salt in 1 gallon water.

Spray with ryania.

Celery leaf tyer. Greenish worm, up to ¾″ long. Chews celery stalks and leaves, fastens leaves together with web.

Hand-pick.

Dust with lime, pyrethrum, ground tobacco, or sulfur, and repeat in 30 minutes.

Club root. Caused by a fungus and results in deformed roots and stunting of plant. Affects cabbage and other brassicas.

Sterilize soil for flats before seeding.

Rotate crops over long period.

Keep weeds down.

Dust infected soil with hydrated lime.

Colorado potato beetles. (See Potato bugs.)

Corn borers. Pink or brown grubs up to 1″ long that bore into corn stalks and ears. Also attack peppers, tomatoes, eggplant, and other plants.

Destroy by hand the egg masses on undersides of leaves.

Spray with rotenone the ear shoots of corn, and leaf axils.

Make succession plantings.

Spray with ryania.

Spray with Thuricide or similar biological control.

Corn earworms. Also called tomato fruit worms. Green, brown, or pink, up to 2″ long, striped. Eggs are laid by a moth. On corn, worms feed on silks, then eat each other so that usually only one per ear survives. Four or more generations each season. Worms bore into young ears of corn. They also eat tomato buds and fruits, attack okra, beans, eggplant, peppers, squash, cucumbers, asparagus, and potatoes.

For corn, apply 5 or 6 drops of mineral oil to silks at ear end *after* silks go limp and tips start to brown. Or squeeze tip of ear at this time, to crush worm.

For other vegetables, hand-pick worms or dust with rotenone or ryania.

Cucumber beetles. (See Spotted cucumber beetles, and Striped cucumber beetles.)

Cutworms. Plump, soft, fairly smooth, usually gray, brown, whitish, or black. About 1″ to 1½″ long. Curl when disturbed. Some climb, some work at ground level. They cut off or eat leaves, or cut plants off at ground level.

Cultivate shallowly around damaged plants to expose worms.

Destroy worms by hand.

Protect young plant stems with paper collars.

Circle plants with wood ashes and water them in.

Trap worms under vegetable leaves laid on ground, or under sections of squash, melon halves, potato pieces, orange rinds.

Spread commercial cutworm bait.

Circle plants with crushed eggshells lightly covered with earth.

Damping-off. Caused by a fungus. Seeds rot or young plants topple.

Coat seeds with a fungicide such as captan.

Sterilize soil before seeding flat. (See Chapter 5.)

Cover seedbed with ¼″ of sphagnum moss before seeding.

Use compost in planting mixture.

Downy mildew. A fungus disease, causing yellowish or brownish spots on leaves that then curl and die. Attacks cucumbers, cantaloupes, watermelons.

Carefully remove and destroy affected leaves at first signs.

Plant resistant varieties.

Drop. A fungus disease that attacks lettuce, causing wilting and soft rot. Worse in wet weather.

Space plants more widely and avoid poorly drained spots.

Dry rot. A fungus disease that affects potatoes, causing yellow leaves, wilting, rot in stored tubers.

Plant resistant varieties, preferably certified.

Rotate crops.

Do not plant any tuber with discolored interior.

Earwigs. Brown to black, up to ¾″ long, with forceps on back end of body. Active when disturbed. Often found in clusters under rocks and in crevices. Not usually seen in the open. They eat plant parts, often destroying many small seedlings. They are also partly beneficial, since they eat aphids and some other sucking insects.

Trap under boards.

Trap in a rolled newspaper laid on the soil overnight, then burn.

Spread earwig bait, under boards or in open.

Protect plants with mulch.

Flea beetles. Tiny, dark, jumping insects. They eat leaves, giving them the appearance of being shot full of holes. They attack beets, brassicas, tomatoes, potatoes, peppers, and several other plants, especially young transplants.

Dust, especially under leaves, with rotenone and pyrethrum.

Keep weeds down, in and near garden.

Dust with fine ashes and tobacco dust mixed.

Fruit rot. A fungus disease that attacks eggplants, causing shrunken stems at ground level, brown or gray spots on leaves, and blistered fruits. The fungi are carried on seed, and persist in the soil.

Plant resistant varieties.

Fusarium wilt. A fungus disease attacking tomatoes and peas. Leaves turn yellow and wilt, plants may die.

Plant resistant varieties.

Garden centipedes. Not true centipedes. White or brownish, ½″ long, about 24 legs. Inhabit manure piles and other damp places. Bore into young stems of asparagus and several other vegetables. (See Centipedes under Beneficial Insects for comparison.)

Control by destroying when found.

Trap as for cutworms.

Grasshoppers. Well known, many kinds, and several colors. Up to 2″ long or longer. Feed on vegetation.

Hand-pick.

Use rotenone on non-edible foliage such as potato leaves.

Harlequin bugs. Shield-shaped, brilliant colors—black, red, yellow. Less than ½″ long. Attack cabbage and other brassicas. Plants wilt, leaves look brown and scalded.

Hand-pick often. Use gloves as these are a species of stink bugs.

Trap under boards.

Keep weeds down.

Plant an early trap crop.

Dust with sabadilla.

Japanese beetles. Oval, ½″ long, metallic-green and brown. They eat leaves, especially of beans, okra, sweet corn. Larvae are 1″ white grubs in the soil; they eat roots.

Dig up and kill grubs, or treat soil with milky disease spores.

Spray beetles with rotenone or ryania.

Dust plants with hydrated lime.

Set commercial traps.

Interplant with garlic.

Leaf hoppers. Wedge-shaped, ⅛″ long, greenish or brown, active. They suck the undersides of leaves. Tips of leaves may turn dark. Leaf hoppers spread the virus disease called yellows. They attack beans, potatoes, lettuce, eggplant, tomatoes, celery, others.

Spray with pyrethrum or rotenone.

Dust with sulfur.

Plant lettuce in sheltered places, near hedges or buildings.

Leaf roll. A virus disease of potatoes, spread by aphids. Lower leaves roll up, plants turn yellowish and are stunted.

Destroy affected plants promptly.

Control aphids and ants.

Plant resistant varieties of certified potatoes.

Leaf spot. A fungus disease causing small spots on leaves, with light centers and dark margins. Attacks beets and chard, cantaloupes, peppers, tomatoes, cucumbers. Not always serious, though worse in warm, moist weather.

Rotate crops, run a clean garden, destroy perennial weeds.

Lygus bugs. Also called tarnished plant bugs. Flat, oval, ¼″ long, tarnished appearance. When disturbed, they hide behind stems.

Spray with pyrethrum.

Dust with sabadilla.

Clean out trash and weeds in the fall, to prevent over-wintering.

Maggots. Several species, looking like ¼″ white grubs without legs. They are larvae of certain flies that deposit eggs on plants or soil. Maggots hatch and kill young plants by tunneling into seeds, roots, and stems. Attack cabbages and other brassicas, onions, radishes, beans, peas, corn, beets, potatoes.

Surround plants with 3″ tar-paper squares.

Dust earth with wood ashes.

Mexican bean beetles. Adults look like large ladybugs—oval ¼″ or more long, copper-colored with 16 black spots. Larvae are larger, yellow, fuzzy. Both eat leaves and pods of beans. Orange-colored eggs are laid in clusters on underside of leaves.

Hand-pick, including under leaves. Crush eggs.

Remove vines immediately after harvest.

Spray under leaves with rotenone or pyrethrum.

Interplant with marigolds.

Millipedes. Slow moving, cylindrical, many (400) legs. Gray or brown, often found tightly coiled. Hard bodied. Harmful to roots of several vegetables. Otherwise, they are merely scavengers.

Control by destroying when found.

Mites. (See Spider mites.)

Mosaics. Viruses that attack beans, cucumbers, cantaloupes, lettuce, peppers, potatoes, squash, tomatoes. Cause mottled, curled leaves, stunting, poor crops.

Plant resistant varieties.

Keep aphids and striped cucumber beetles down; they spread the virus.

Keep tobacco away from susceptible plants, as it may carry the virus. If you smoke, wash hands before entering garden.

Keep weeds down.

Promptly remove first plants affected.

Spray plants with skim milk.

Nematodes. Tiny worms, also called eelworms. Damage roots of many plants, forming knots or swellings.

Interplant with marigolds.

Change location of garden.

Rotate crops.

Plant resistant varieties.

Keep weeds down.

Plant grass, and spade under for green manuring. (See Chapter 4.)

Pickleworms. Yellowish green, up to ¾" long, sometimes spotted. They damage cucumbers, cantaloupes, squash and pumpkins, late in the season.

Hand-pick worms before they get into fruits.

Dust with rotenone or sabadilla.

Pink rot. A fungus disease that causes soaked-looking spots on leaves and a pinkish cottony growth at ground level. It attacks cabbage, celery, lettuce. Fungi persist in soil for years.

Rotate crops and do not plant other susceptible crops at spots where disease occurred.

Potato bugs. Properly called Colorado potato beetles. Yellow, striped with black, ⅜" long. Larvae are brick-red and humped. Both feed on potato, eggplant, and tomato leaves.

Hand-pick.

Dust with rotenone.

Red spiders. (See Spider mites.)

Rhizoctonia. A fungus disease that attacks cabbage and some other brassicas, shrinking and blackening stems near ground level. It is often called "wire stem." It also attacks lettuce, causing injury something like scab. Fungi live in the soil.

Rotate crops.

Remove and destroy any plants that show symptoms.

Root rots. Fungus diseases of peas, causing yellowed leaves, discolored and rotted roots and underground stems. The fungi live in the soil and often kill vines as they start to blossom.

Plant peas in a different spot each season. Avoid poorly drained places.

Rust. A fungus that attacks bean plants and causes discolored blisters on leaves, which turn yellow and fall.

Spray or dust with sulfur.

Plant resistant varieties.

Scab. Diseases caused by fungi, showing up as rough spots on potatoes and brown, sunken spots on cucumbers and summer squash.

Plant resistant varieties (also clean tubers, for potatoes).

Rotate crops.

Do not use lime or wood ashes near potatoes as soil should be somewhat acid to avoid potato scab, about pH 5.0. (See Chapter 4 for pH values.)

Seed decay. Rotting of seed in the soil, caused by a fungus. Most common in moist, cool weather. Most apt to attack beans, peas, corn, and lettuce.

Treat seed with protective fungicide such as captan.

Slugs and snails. These are gastropods, not insects. Snails have shells; both have soft, smooth bodies, and leave glistening trails. They eat plant parts and are especially destructive to small seedlings.

Hand-pick. They also work at night and can be found with a flashlight.

Spread bait.

Trap under boards.

Trap in pans of beer.

Surround plants or beds with bands of hydrated lime, dry sand, or ashes.

Smut. A fungus disease causing black blisters on onion leaves and white growths on corn stalks, ears, and tassels.

Rotate crops, remove and destroy galls on corn. Do not put diseased plants into compost.

Sow bugs and pill bugs. Not insects, but isopods, related to lobsters and crabs. Gray or brown, up to ½″ long, with several pairs of legs. Often found under wood or rocks. Pill bugs roll into tight balls when disturbed. "Wood lice" is another name for these creatures. Both attack seedlings, pill bugs being the more destructive.

Destroy when found.

Trap under boards.

Protect plantings with mulch.

Repel with light dusting of hydrated lime.

Spider mites. Also called red spiders. Several kinds of tiny reddish, yellow, or green mites. They are arachnids, not insects. They have eight legs. They suck juice from leaves, causing speckling and curling. Attack beans, celery, corn, cucumbers, eggplant, onions, melons, peas, tomatoes.

Spray with strong stream of water.

Spray with rotenone or nicotine.

Dust with sulfur, except cucumbers and melons.

Spotted cucumber beetles. Yellowish green with 12 black spots on back; ¼″ long. They eat blossoms of squash and other cucurbits, leaves and pods of beans.

Trap under boards.

Hand-pick.

Protect young plants with screen-wire cages.

Dust with rotenone or pyrethrum.

Spray with ¼ cup each of wood ashes and hydrated lime in 1 gallon of water.

Squash bugs. Flat, brown stink bugs, about ½″ long. They kill squash and other cucurbits by sucking juices. Oval brown eggs are laid in clusters on leaves.

Hand-pick—using gloves—and crush eggs.

Trap under boards.

Dust with mixed wood ashes and hydrated lime.

Dust with sabadilla.

Dust or spray with ryania.

Destroy old vines after harvest.

Squash vine borers. White grubs about 1″ long. They bore into squash and pumpkin vines, eat holes in stems near base of runner.

Open stem at point of damage with a knife, stab grub. Heap moist earth on cut stem to protect it and to induce rooting.

Stink bugs. Several kinds, shield-shaped, brown, black, or green, about ½″ long. Suck juices of tomatoes, okra, beans. Bugs discharge an unpleasant odor when disturbed.

Hand-pick, using gloves.

Keep weeds down.

Striped cucumber beetles. Yellowish, with 3 black stripes. About ¼″ long. Adults eat the upper parts of plants, larvae eat roots. Squash and other cucurbits are attacked.

Trap under boards.

Hand-pick.

Protect young plants with screen-wire cages.

Interplant with radishes to repel beetles.

Dust with rotenone or pyrethrum.

Spray with ½ cup each of wood ashes and hydrated lime in 1 gallon of water.

Thrips. Small, active insects 1/25″ long, brownish or yellowish, with fringed wings. They suck juices from plants, causing whitish splotches and brown tips on leaves. Plants attacked are onions and related plants, cabbage and other brassicas, squash and other cucurbits.

Spray or dust with rotenone or pyrethrum.

Spray with nicotine.

Spray or dust with ryania.

For onions, plant resistant varieties such as Sweet Spanish and Japanese bunching.

Tipburn. A physiological disease of lettuce and some other plants. In lettuce, margins of leaves dry up.

Plant resistant varieties.

Tomato fruit worms. (See Corn earworms.)

Tomato horn worms. Smooth green caterpillars up to 4″ long, with needlelike horn at rear end and slanting lines along sides. They skeletonize leaves and eat fruits of tomato, eggplant, and pepper. Also attack potatoes.

Hand-pick worms.

Verticillium wilt. A fungus disease of tomatoes. Usually, all branches show wilting at the same time. Not always fatal to the plant, but fruits are exposed to sun damage. The fungi live in the soil.

Plant resistant varieties.

Weevils. Beetles of several kinds and sizes, ground colors usually black or brown, with lighter markings. From ⅛″ to ⅜″ long. Some have prominent duck-bill snouts. Adults and larvae feed on plant parts, attacking peas, beans, peppers, turnips, sweet potatoes, carrots, cabbage, and related crops.

Hand-pick weevils.

Dust with rotenone.

Plant seed treated against weevils.

White grubs. Larvae of beetles, often of June bugs. Grubs are light-colored, curved, with dark heads. They feed on roots and tubers, and are common in soil where grass is growing.

Spade up earth and kill exposed grubs.

Avoid planting in newly turned sod.

(See Japanese beetle for treatment of its grubs.)

Wilt. A fungus disease that causes plants to turn yellowish, wilt, and become stunted. It attacks cabbage and other brassicas, eggplant, okra, potatoes, corn, and watermelon. Potatoes develop a dry rot in storage, as from another fungus. (See Dry rot.)

Rotate crops.

Plant resistant varieties.

Avoid sites where wilt was troublesome before.

Wirestem. (See Rhizoctonia.)

Wireworms. Many kinds, usually yellow or white, with dark heads and tails, slender bodies up to 1½″ long, resembling a many-jointed wire. They live in the soil and tunnel roots of beans, beets, carrots, celery, lettuce, onions, turnips, and tubers of potatoes and sweet potatoes.

Avoid planting in infested soil.

Bury half of a potato 4″ deep, dig it up in a week and destroy wireworms found in it.

Yellows. Diseases caused by fungi and viruses. They deform and yellow foliage, stunt plants. The virus type that attacks carrots and lettuce is spread by leaf hoppers. The fungus type attacks cabbage and other brassicas, celery, and spinach.

Plant resistant varieties.

Avoid planting where disease was present before.

For carrots and lettuce, treat as for leaf hoppers.

FRUITS AND NUTS AND THEIR POSSIBLE PESTS

Almonds. (See Peach.)

Apples. Aphids, apple maggots, borers, codling moths, leaf rollers, mites, scale.

Apricots. Borers, brown rot, codling moths, curculio beetles, scale.

Blackberries. (See Raspberries.)

Black walnuts. (See Walnuts.)

Butternuts. (See Walnuts.)

Cherries. Aphids, brown rot, curculio beetles, mildew, mites, scale.

Chestnuts. Blight, chestnut borers, nut weevils, powdery mildew.

Currants. Aphids, anthracnose, cane borers, currant worms, mildew, mites, scale.

Elderberries. No serious pests.

English walnuts. (See Walnuts.)

Figs. Borers, mites, scale.

Gooseberries. (See Currants.)

Grapes. Anthracnose, black rot, flea beetles, leaf hoppers, mildew, mites.

Hazelnuts. Aphids, nut weevils.

Hickory nuts. Leaf blight, nut weevils, walnut caterpillars, web caterpillars.

Nectarines. (See Peaches.)

Peaches. Aphids, borers, brown rot, curculio beetles, leaf-curl, mites, Oriental fruit moth, scale.

Pears. (See Apples.)

Pecans. Blackened limbs, cankers, nut casebearer, scale, shuckworm, walnut caterpillars, web caterpillars.

Plums. Aphids, borers, brown rot, curculio beetles, scale, yellow-leaf.

Raspberries. Diseases are considered incurable. Plant resistant stock, run a clean garden, provide good air circulation.

Strawberries. Leaf rollers, white grubs.

Walnuts, black. Crown rot, nut weevils, twig blight, walnut caterpillars.

Walnuts, English. Canker, nut weevils, twig blight, walnut caterpillars.

FRUIT AND NUT INSECTS AND DISEASES

Anthracnose. A fungus that attacks grapes, spotting fruit and forming small sunken cankers on stems.

Plant resistant varieties.

Space vines for good air circulation.

Keep down weeds near vines.

Aphids. Also called plant lice. Small, soft insects of various colors, pear-shaped, working in massed groups on leaves. They suck juices, distorting and discoloring leaves. Aphids breed rapidly, particularly in dry, warm weather.

Control ants.

Spray aphids with strong stream of water.

Spray with soapy water.

Spray with nicotine and soapy water.

Spray or dust with rotenone or pyrethrum.

Spray with ryania.

Dust with nicotine.

Place ladybugs on trees or plants.

Crush aphids by hand.

Apple maggots. Legless grublike larvae of a fly. They tunnel into the fruits.

Control by destroying the saclike pupa (the stage of development between fly and maggot stages) that live in the soil over the winter. Do this by keeping weeds cleaned out around trees and by running poultry in the orchard.

Blackened limbs. Caused by attacks of certain bacteria and fungi.

Prune off and destroy affected limbs.

Black rot. A fungus disease of grapes, causing half-grown fruit to shrivel.

Destroy affected fruit, to break the cycle.

Use horsetail spray frequently as a preventive (see Mildew) in early summer.

Blight. (See Chestnut blight.)

Borers. Worms that tunnel into the base of tree trunks and into limbs. A gum forms at the hole where they enter.

Destroy worm by cutting out with a knife.

Repel worms by painting trunks with a thin paste of wood ashes and water.

Prevent entry of worms by wrapping trunk base with masking tape from 3″ below ground to 4″ above, replacing dug-out soil afterward.

Brown rot. A fungus disease of peaches, causing fruits to decay.

Spray with garlic solution (using garlic press, squeeze juice from one garlic clove into one gallon of water).

Gather affected fallen fruit and shrunken fruit on branches, and destroy.

Spray with wettable sulfur, when blossoms show pink; when shucks fall; 2 weeks later; and a month before fruit ripens.

Cane borers. Half-inch-long worms that burrow through entire length of currant and gooseberry canes, dwarfing plants.

Remove affected wood at ground level, and burn.

Cankers. Open wounds on trees caused by bacteria.

Prune off and destroy affected limbs.

Prevent infection by treating cuts with protective paint.

Chestnut blight. A fatal fungus disease of chestnuts. Leaves shrivel but cling persistently.

Plant resistant varieties.

Chestnut borers. The larvae burrow under the bark, especially of unthrifty trees.

Practice good orchard sanitation; keep trees in good health.

Codling moth. Brownish-gray moth ½″ long with copper-colored wing tips. The pest is its larva, a pinkish worm ¼″ long, that bores into fruits of apple and pear.

Use 3 percent miscible oil dormant spray in early spring before buds open.

Scrape loose bark off trunk in early spring and scrub trunk with soapy water.

Trap worms on trunk under bands of burlap, or under wads of burlap in crotches of limbs, and destroy.

Release trichogramma wasps.

Keep windfalls cleaned up.

Hang in the center of the tree top a quart jar with 2 table-spoons of molasses and 1 cup of water in it. Cover jar top with ¼″ hardware cloth. When jar has filled with trapped moths, empty it and renew the solution.

Spray with ryania, at blossom fall and twice more at 2-week intervals.

Crown rot. A fungus disease caused by dampness. Attacks walnut trees in damp locations.

Remove a 4″-deep ring of soil around the tree and replace it with gravel.

Curculio beetles. Larvae of this insect cause wormy cherries, plums, nectarines, and sometimes peaches.

Loosen beetles by shaking trees, and catch on sheets spread on the ground.

Run chickens under trees and shake beetles loose.

Band tree trunks with Tanglefoot.

Currant worms. Inch-long green worms that eat edges of currant and gooseberry leaves.

Hand-pick or dust with pyrethrum.

Fire blight. Disease by bacteria producing black, burned-looking limbs.

Promptly remove and destroy affected wood.

Mulch trees with horse manure.

Flea beetles. Tiny jumping insects. A species and its grub-like larvae feed on grape leaves.

Dust leaves on both sides with rotenone and pyrethrum.

Keep weeds down near vines.

Dust with mixture of fine ashes and tobacco dust.

Fungi. (See Mildew.)

Leaf blight. A disease of hickories, showing up as brown spots on leaves, which then die.

Gather and destroy affected leaves.

Leaf-curl. A fungus disease of peach and nectarine trees. It appears in early spring, causing leaves to discolor and distort, then fall.

Remove and burn leaves if only a few are affected.

If most leaves are affected, give the tree an extra feeding of nitrogen—1 pound of blood meal for each inch of trunk width—after removing and burning affected leaves.

Leaf hoppers. Wedge-shaped insects, very active. A red-and-yellow species sucks the juice from grape leaves.

Spray or dust with nicotine.

Spray with rotenone or pyrethrum.

Leaf rollers. Small caterpillars that attack apple and pear leaves, folding themselves inside the leaves for protection.

Use a 3 percent miscible oil dormant spray in early spring before buds open.

Spray with wormwood solution (steep 1 cup of crushed leaves 30 minutes in a gallon of warm water).

Mildew and various fungi. A variety of diseases affecting leaves of fruit trees and grape vines, showing up as powdery patches and as discolored spots.

Prevent by painting trunks and spraying foliage with horse-tail solution (*Equisetum arvense*) (steep 2 cups of the crushed stems 30 minutes in a gallon of water).

Spray with a solution of 1 pint skim milk and ½ cup of blood in a gallon of water.

Mites. Tiny bugs of various colors, related to spiders; they suck plant juices.

Use 3 percent miscible oil dormant spray in early spring before buds open.

Spray at other times with solution of 1 cup flour and 2 tablespoons buttermilk in enough water to make a thin paste, stirred into 1 gallon of water.

Nut casebearer. Small insect that hides itself in a small cell it constructs, from where it attacks young shoots and nuts of pecans.

Release trichogramma wasps.

Nut weevils. Snout beetles that invade nuts of hickory, hazelnuts, and chestnuts.

Destroy infected nuts to break cycle.

Oriental fruit moth. The larvae, small pink worms, bore into peach twigs in spring, and later bore into fruit.

Use 3 percent miscible oil dormant spray in early spring before buds open.

Powdery mildew. A fungus disease that attacks leaves of chestnut trees, spotting them with floury blotches.

Spray or dust with sulfur.

Scale. Various kinds, consisting of colonies, usually, of small sucking insects under protective scalelike coverings.

Use 3 percent miscible oil dormant spray in early spring before buds open.

Release ladybugs or lacewing flies.

Shuckworm. Attacks pecan trees.

Keep fallen hulls cleaned up and burned.

Release trichogramma wasps.

Twig blight. A die-back of twigs on walnuts and butternuts, caused by a fungus.

Remove and burn affected wood. Give trees extra nitrogen.

Walnut caterpillars. Appear in late summer, feeding in groups. The caterpillars are about 1½" long.

Hand-pick or knock off trees with poles or jet of water.

Web caterpillars. These insects occur in colonies encased in webs that are gathered around bunches of leaves.

Burn out colonies with pole torch.

Prune off and burn twigs holding webs.

Remove and burn any leaves showing clusters of small white eggs on undersides.

White grubs. These insects live in the soil and are larvae of beetles, often of June bugs. They are light-colored, curved, with dark heads. They attack roots of strawberries.

Spade the earth and kill grubs.

Avoid planting strawberries in newly turned sod for 3 years. Treat soil with milky disease spores for grubs of Japanese beetles.

Yellow-leaf. A fungus disease of plums. The leaves turn yellowish and drop off, weakening the tree.

Break cycle by keeping fallen leaves cleaned up and burned.

BENEFICIAL INSECTS

Aleochara beetles. Shiny black, ⅙″ long, slender and flexible, with brown legs. They live in the soil.

DO NOT KILL. The larvae are parasites of maggots.

Ant lions. Also called doodlebugs. Brown, up to ½″ long, with forceps-shaped jaws. Found at bottom of small conical depressions they make in sand, as traps for ants. Widely distributed, especially in the South.

DO NOT KILL. Ant lions eat ants and other injurious insects.

Aphid lions. Larvae of lacewing flies. Cigar-shaped, ⅓″ long, yellowish or mottled red and brown, with projecting hairs and large forceps-shaped jaws. Widely distributed.

DO NOT KILL. Aphid lions eat aphids, mealy bugs, scales, thrips, mites, whiteflies, leaf hoppers, moth and butterfly eggs, caterpillars, and other injurious insects. This is probably the most widely useful garden insect.

Aleochara beetles. Shiny black, ⅙″ long, slender and flexwith slender bodies and long legs. They move awkwardly on plants, catch other insects with their forelegs, often held as if praying, like praying mantids. Widely distributed.

DO NOT KILL. Assassin bugs destroy injurious insects in young stages.

Centipedes. Flattened bodies, brown, many-legged. Bodies are segmented. Usually found under wood or stones. They move quickly when discovered.

DO NOT KILL. Centipedes eat snails, slugs, and other pests. (For comparison, see Garden centipedes, and Millipedes, both of which are injurious.)

Damsel bugs. Winged, long-legged, pale gray, about ⅜″

long. They resemble assassin bugs in general form. Widely distributed.

Do Not Kill. Damsel bugs capture other insects with their forelegs, like assassin bugs, preying on aphids and larvae of injurious insects.

Dragonflies. Large, colorful insects with slender bodies up to 2″ long, two pairs of equal-sized net-veined wings held out straight from each side and up to 3½″ in spread. Very agile flyers. The prominent eyes are extremely efficient. Dragonflies catch other insects in the air, seizing them with legs and devouring them in flight.

Do Not Kill. Among the harmful insects dragonflies prey on are mosquitoes. "Mosquito hawk" is another name for the dragonfly.

Ground beetles. Many kinds, found under stones, boards, etc. Black or brown, small heads, ovalish bodies. They run quickly when disturbed.

Do Not Kill. Though some beetles may do a little damage, both adults and larvae feed on injurious insects.

Hornets and yellow jackets. Large predators, some of them up to ¾″ long or more. These are wasps, and their sting is painful but they are not ordinarily pugnacious toward humans if they are not disturbed.

Do Not Kill. These insects feed on flies and caterpillars, stocking their nests with the cut-up bodies.

Lacewing flies. Delicate looking, about ½″ long or more, having prominent golden eyes. The oval wings are brown or green, and are transparent. Widely distributed.

Do Not Kill. Larvae of lacewings are aphid lions, valuable predators.

Ladybugs. Also called lady beetles and ladybird beetles. Adults are shiny red or tan, sometimes with black dots. Looking like tiny tortoises, they are about ⅛″ long. Larvae are wedge-shaped, blue, orange, or gray, slightly larger than adults. Widely distributed.

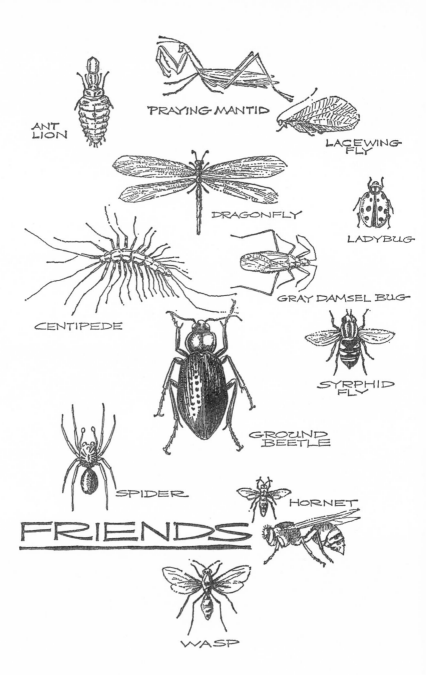

ANT LION

PRAYING MANTID

LACEWING FLY

DRAGONFLY

LADYBUG

CENTIPEDE

GRAY DAMSEL BUG

SYRPHID FLY

GROUND BEETLE

SPIDER

HORNET

FRIENDS

WASP

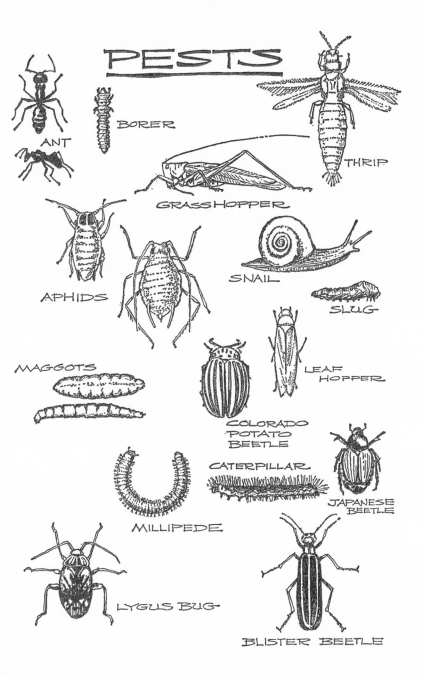

PESTS

ANT

BORER

THRIP

GRASSHOPPER

APHIDS

SNAIL

SLUG

MAGGOTS

LEAF HOPPER

COLORADO POTATO BEETLE

CATERPILLAR

JAPANESE BEETLE

MILLIPEDE

LYGUS BUG

BLISTER BEETLE

Do Not Kill. Both adults and larvae are highly beneficial, feeding on aphids, spider mites, scales, and mealy bugs.

Pirate bugs. Several kinds, most of them black with white spots or streaks. They look like very small oval beetles, about ¹⁄₁₆″ long. The nymphs resemble the adults but are brownish. Widely distributed.

Do Not Kill. Both forms feed on mites and other small pests under bark and on flowers.

Praying mantids. Large greenish, leggy creatures up to 5″ long, with prominent abdomens and wedge-shaped heads that can turn, which is unusual in insects. The powerful forelegs are held together as if in prayer, and are used to catch other insects. Widely distributed.

Do Not Kill. Mantids destroy many injurious insects.

Spiders. Not insects, but arachnids, and always 8-legged. Many kinds and sizes. With the exception of red spiders, which are mites, nearly all spiders are welcome in the garden.

Do Not Kill. Spiders feed on injurious insects.

Syrphid flies. Several kinds, the adults looking something like yellow jackets, brightly colored, yellow and black, up to ⅓″ long. Easily identified by their habit of hovering over plants. Widely distributed.

Do Not Kill. Syrphid flies are harmless, and their larvae, looking something like slugs, eat aphids and other injurious insects.

Trichogramma wasps. Tiny insects that lay their eggs in the bodies of injurious insects.

Do Not Kill. The larvae destroy their host insect when they hatch. Among their victims are apple worms, the larvae of the codling moth.

Wasps. Many kinds and sizes, from the tiny trichogrammas to the largest hornets. Widely distributed.

Do Not Kill. Wasps prey on injurious insects, among them aphids, leaf hoppers, and caterpillars.

10

How to Grow Your Own Organic Vegetables

"PEAK OF PERFECTION" is something you often hear in connection with fresh vegetables. It is a good way to describe an organically well-grown vegetable, harvested at full ripeness—but until you have tasted such a vegetable *freshly taken from your own garden,* you aren't likely to know true peak of perfection. What can match the sweet, crisp goodness of a pea shelled and eaten the moment it is picked from its vine? Or a tender sprig of parsley nibbled as you walk the garden path—always a favorite with children, we've been interested to note, when we show them our garden. Perhaps it is instinct, for a tablespoon of chopped parsley is rich in iron and has 290 units of vitamin A.

Harvesting is indeed the glory of gardening. It is the end toward which all the other efforts are directed, and in this chapter we take up the culture, from seeding to harvest, of the more than 50 vegetables and herbs most popular with home gardeners.

Artichokes, globe. Even if you didn't eat it, a globe artichoke would be worth growing just to look at. The large, sharp-lobed leaves are an agreeable gray-green, and the buds, which are the part you eat, will open into spectacular purplish flowers if allowed to.

Globe artichokes are native to the mild coastal Mediterranean climate, and their ideal climate resembles that one—almost frost-free winters, with some fog during the temperate summers. We are presently living in such a climate, in coastal central California, and globe artichokes thrive here. They are perennials, and a single plant spreads to 4' wide or more, and grows 3' to 4' tall.

If you don't have the climate for globe artichokes but want to try growing them, plant them in the spring after frosts are over, give them frequent fine-spray waterings all summer, and protect them in winter by cutting them off a few inches above ground level and covering this stub with a flower pot, next a bushel of straw, and finally 2' of earth.

In artichoke country, fall or winter planting is customary. Suckers that come from the base of old plants are pulled up with some roots, cut to stubs about 5" long, and planted 4' apart with crowns just above ground. Good garden soil enriched with compost suits them, with some fertilizer such as cottonseed meal worked in around them at the rate of 1 cup per plant once or twice during the season. A weekly watering is essential, and an open, sunny location will encourage production.

Once a planting is started it is self-perpetuating through the suckers, and old plants are ordinarily removed after about 3 years of cropping. Suckers to start a planting can be purchased (they cost from 50¢ to about $1.50 each) or seed can be planted about 6 weeks ahead of transplanting time. Seed will not grow plants exactly true to the variety producing the seed, however. Green Globe is the variety usually offered in either seed or suckers.

One plant can produce about a dozen buds per season. They form at the tops of the stalks and should be harvested while still tightly closed, and with 1″ of stalk attached. At the end of cropping, when the leaves turn yellow, cut the stalk off near ground level. In California artichoke country this is done in July and winter growth is then stimulated by fertilizing.

By the way, with this plant it is especially important to consult your recipe just before harvesting. If you plan on serving stuffed artichokes, one per person, you'll want a large bud; but small and tender ones are required if to be chilled after boiling and served whole or quartered, with a sauce or in a salad.

Aside from occasional aphids, globe artichokes have almost no pests in most home plantings.

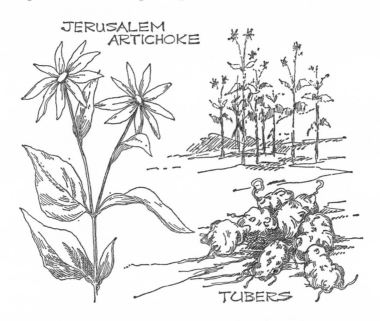

Artichokes, Jerusalem. A native American despite its name, and growing wild in places, the Jerusalem artichoke is a relative of the sunflower, and provides a root, or tuber, that rivals the famed water chestnut in texture and taste. It can be cooked or used raw. We have grown Jerusalem artichokes successfully in widely different climates except the deep South, and consider them a staple of our garden. However, they are not at all well known or the seed tubers easily found, and we are always having to explain to friends what they are eating at our table that tastes so unusual and delicious. You can order tubers from Burgess or Nichols.

Planting is done in the spring or fall, placing tubers 3" or 4" deep and about 2' apart. Nearly any soil seems to suit Jerusalem artichokes. We give them the benefit of compost well spaded in, and since the crop is perennial we then give the planting a top dressing of compost each spring, about a 3" layer.

The stalks grow from 6' to 12' tall, looking much like sunflowers and bearing small yellow flowers. Put the planting on the north or west side of the garden to avoid shading other things. The stalks die to the ground in the late fall, when they should be cut down. This is the best time to start digging tubers as you need them, though you can dig some from an established planting at any time of year. Use a spading fork and start probing for tubers a foot or more from the base of the stalks. One plant can produce a pound or so in a season, and the simplest way to perpetuate the planting is to leave a few of the tubers in the ground. In fact, you can hardly help doing so. A winter mulch will keep the earth diggable; we find it convenient to dig a pound of tubers at a time and store them in a plastic bag in the refrigerator.

Leaf hoppers occasionally bother Jerusalem artichokes, but on the whole this is a pest-free plant.

Asparagus. This vegetable takes long-time planning, like an investment in a growth stock that won't pay dividends for the first two years. There *is* a quick dividend in appearance, though, as the beautiful ferny growth of asparagus is so ornamental that we always try to locate a bed of it where it will serve as an attractive garden border.

Asparagus prefers some winter rest, and is not usually a good cropping plant in the South from Florida to Texas.

The Washington varieties are old, standard, and good, but some promising new ones have appeared, such as California 500 (Field), Faribo Hybrid (Farmer), and Brock Imperial Hybrid (Gurney).

To start an asparagus planting you can use seed, but you'll gain a year by planting roots your supplier has grown from seed. One-year roots are the best and cheapest. Roots are usually sold in lots of 25 and cost from 10¢ to 25¢ each. A 1-year asparagus root consists of a crown and several slender roots with a spread of up to twice the length of your hand, but in time it spreads greatly and also tends to work its way nearer ground level by growing new rhizomes above the old ones.

Spring planting is usual, and full sun in a well-drained site is required. The traditional way is to dig a trench 1' wide and 1' deep. You then add 2" of rotted manure or good compost to the trench bottom, mixing it with the earth. If your soil is acid, stir in one pound of hydrated lime for each 10' of trench, preferably doing this 2 to 4 weeks before you put the manure or compost into the trench. The final step in planting is to water the trench lightly and set the asparagus roots in it, crowns upward, spreading the roots well and spacing them 18" apart, measuring from the middle of one crown to the middle of the next. Fill the trench gradually during the season as the plants grow, starting by raking 2" of earth back in to cover the roots.

Two rows spaced 3' apart, each 20' long, will furnish a family with a good supply from the two dozen plants this space will accommodate. If you like asparagus as much as we do, you'll want a larger planting and a surplus to can or freeze.

We find that an asparagus bed responds best to feedings of well-ripened compost or rotted manure. Give two such feedings, one 4" thick in the fall before freezing weather arrives, and a 2″ one in late spring after the season's asparagus harvest is over.

The ferny top growth should be allowed to remain through the winter, and should then be cut back near ground level in the spring. Some shallow cultivating is also helpful at this time.

Do not harvest any spears the year you plant the bed, and do only a very little sample harvesting the second year. The third year you can harvest from mid-April till the end of May. But—from the fourth year on, and for twenty years or more, you can harvest from mid-April to the end of June, a good 10 weeks of abundance. When spears begin to get skinny, stop harvesting for that season.

An average yield is 1 pound per plant per season, but returns of up to 10 pounds have been reported.

As to the technique of harvesting, controversy waxes hot. Some gardeners snap spears off near ground level with their fingers, others use a V-notch asparagus knife, and still others use any knife. We cut spears near ground level with a knife, or snap them off if we have no knife. On our Missouri farm we harvested twice a day, early morning and late afternoon, to keep up. That's how fast a well-started and well-fed asparagus bed grows.

Only a few insects bother asparagus and seldom cause concern in home gardens. A rust is a troublesome disease, but planting resistant varieties takes care of this.

Beans, lima. Bush limas are more convenient in a small garden, but if you have room for a trellis of pole limas, they will reward you with a larger crop, and some consider their quality higher. There is also a choice of types in both kinds, the large so-called potato limas and the small-seeded ones. All are rich in proteins and in vitamins B_1 and B_2, and are good sources of vitamins A and C.

You'll need a long hot summer to grow limas, 3 to 4 months for pole limas and up to 3 months for bush limas.

If your summers are hot enough, including warm nights, but shorter than this, you can get a jump on the season by starting limas in peat pots indoors a month ahead of warm weather.

All seed houses handle lima beans, and Burpee's is famous for its Fordhook variety, introduced in 1907. Henderson is a still older variety, and still excellent.

Plant limas in full sun, dig in compost, and 6 weeks later work ½ pound of cottonseed meal into about each 30′ of row if plants need a boost. Too much nitrogen, however, will cause them to grow more leaves and fewer beans. Space bush beans about 8″ apart, in rows 3′ apart. If you grow pole limas up a trellis, space plants 3″ apart, thinning to 6″ after they are up and growing strongly. To grow them up a pole, plant 3 beans around the pole and space the poles 2′ apart, in rows 4′ apart. In each case, plant beans 1″ deep with "eyes" facing down—the eye being the dark spot, where the root will sprout. Before planting, treat seeds with a nitrogen-fixing inoculant such as Legume Aid, for surer growth. A light mulch over the planting is good insurance to keep soil from crusting.

You can harvest limas when they are barely filling out their pods, just large enough to cook quickly in melted butter. In our house one of us prefers them this size and the other prefers large mealy beans. Fortunately, a planting is bountiful enough to supply all tastes in most families.

As noted in Chapter 9, beans have a good many pests though none may give you much trouble. We find that healthy plants grow fast enough to mature crops despite some pests—and we always heed the old warning to avoid touching the plants when they are wet, as this may spread bacterial and fungus diseases.

Beans, snap. We like any snap bean but still think Kentucky Wonder the best. It is a pole type, and bush types called Kentucky Wonders are something else. Blue Lake is a fairly new and good bush snap bean. Wade is also good and is resistant to mosaic and powdery mildew, and a purple-podded bean called Royalty fools bean beetles into mistaking it for something they don't care for.

Snap beans don't need as much warm weather as limas, and in fact, we have regularly grown bush snap beans in the cool coastal climate of California. The bush types mature in 7 or 8 weeks, and the pole beans need about 10 weeks. No fertilizing after the initial compost feeding when planting the seed is needed. In other respects, snap beans are cared for the same as limas.

Some gardeners harvest snap beans when they aren't much larger than match sticks, but we think they gain flavor when allowed to grow more. Try this: Harvest some that are half-grown, along with some others mature enough for you to shell out the beans before cooking. Put both into a pan with some vegetable stock and a strip of bacon. Simmer for 2 hours, then add small, just-dug potatoes, well scrubbed, and continue cooking till the potatoes are tender. Serve with a large platter of buttered roasting ears and a huge plate of ripe red tomatoes—an epicurean meal from your garden.

Beets. Beets have a reputation for disliking acid soil, though we haven't found them consistent about this. Possibly the compost makes the difference. Some beets grow surprisingly fast, and 8 weeks is about average. Crosby's Egyptian, and Detroit are good varieties, and Cylindra is sausage-shaped and easily sliced. Beets also come in yellow and white varieties, and in varieties that grow especially lush leaves. This leafy bonus is well worthwhile—½ cup of the cooked leaves contains a whopping 19,000 units of vitamin A, being one of the best sources of this important nutrient. Two good leafy varieties are Long Season and Lutz Greenleaf; both take about 12 weeks to mature roots. We have found Lutz an exceptional keeper when left in the ground where grown and, in fact, have used some that were there for a year.

Plant beet seeds in rich soil, well-spaded, and with compost worked in at the rate of a bucketful to 5′ of row. Most beet seeds are capsules containing more than one seed. Plant them 2″ apart and ½″ deep, thinning later to 6″ apart. We thin them by transplanting the extras. Beets need moist soil to grow well, and be especially sure to keep the soil moist while the seeds germinate. When plants are half-grown, mulch them with compost to supply feeding and retain soil moisture. The first planting can be in early spring, with succession plantings every 2 or 3 weeks.

You can store beets in a cool room during the winter, leaving 1″ of the stems still attached. Beets form the essential ingredient of that perfect snowy-night meal, Red Flannel Hash. We make it this way:

To serve 4 persons, cook 2 strips of bacon in a skillet, remove, dice, and reserve them. In the rendered fat, cook 1 chopped onion lightly, then add 1 pound of chopped beef and cook over medium heat, stirring, till the color leaves the beef. Gently stir in 1 steamed and cubed large potato, and 3 steamed and cubed medium-sized beets. Add salt and pepper and the diced bacon, and heat through. Serve topped with a sauce made by heating 4 tablespoons of butter to bubbling, then stirring in 2 tablespoons of cream and 1 tablespoon of cognac at the last moment.

Home-garden beets are not usually much bothered by pests, though cutworms can be a nuisance.

Belgian endive. To get Belgian (or French) endive, you first grow witloof chicory and then grow sprouts from its roots during the winter. These elegantly pointed, solid little sprouted heads, blanched to a pearly white and delicate yellow like the tender heart of a bibb lettuce, are usually found in expensive markets as an import. Flown in from Europe, they cost more than $2 a pound. A few years ago we found we were growing better ones at home for 10¢ a pound.

Witloof chicory seed is carried by most seed houses. Plant it in late spring; in the Midwest we seeded it about May 15.

Seeding too early, say in March, can cause the plant to bolt to seed, spoiling the root for sprouting. Spade in 4″ of compost spread over the bed, then plant seed ¼″ deep in rows 18″ apart, and space plants 6″ apart when they are a few inches high. They develop into rank-growing stemless plants about 18″ tall. Give them about 4 months of growing time, and work wood ashes in between rows 2 months after seeding, about a bucket of ashes to 15 square feet, to supply extra potash.

Witloof chicory leaves are a bitter but good cooking green. We use a few for this purpose but not enough to deprive the roots of nourishment.

Chicory has no troubles of any consequence.

When the first frost is expected, trim the tops to 1″ above ground level, dig the roots, brush them clean, and store them where they won't freeze. A good root will be the size of a medium-large carrot and sometimes larger. They may fork or grow distorted in lumpy or rocky soil, but this will not hurt their sprouting ability.

To grow the Belgian endive, get a nail keg and bore six ½″ drainage holes in the bottom. Put in a 1″ layer of coarse gravel, then 10″ of garden soil. Trim off the *bottoms* of a dozen chicory roots, if necessary, so that they are all 7″ long. Then push them into the earth in the keg, spacing them evenly, until only the tops show. Wet the earth well, then put an 8″ layer of sawdust in the keg and wet the sawdust well. We used to use sand, but sawdust works as well and is more easily rinsed off the sprouts afterward.

Now cover the top of the keg with several thicknesses of newspaper and give the sprouts a month to start breaking the surface of the sawdust. Harvest them by pulling some sawdust aside and cutting the sprout loose at its base with a sharp knife. If you avoid cutting into the root, a cluster of small new sprouts will grow and give you a second harvest.

In mild-winter climates you can do as we are currently

doing in coastal California—sprout your Belgian endive right where the chicory grew in the garden. Merely trim the tops to 1″ above ground level in late fall or early winter, enclose the bed with boards 10″ or 12″ wide, spread 2″ of earth over the bed and then 8″ of sawdust, wetting it down and seeing that it stays moist under the top inch or so of the sawdust.

Aside from gophers or raccoons, no pests bother Belgian endive.

If you'd like to make chicory coffee, peel one of the roots, chop it, and dry it in a 225° F. oven until it is brown. Grind it (you can do so with a mortar and pestle if necessary) and make coffee by mixing 1 part of chicory and 2 parts of coffee. One part chicory to 10 of coffee makes a light brew, and 1 to 1 makes a dark, strong brew. The chicory adds color, body, aroma, and a pleasant bitterness to the coffee, and is popular in the South.

Broccoli. (See Cabbage group.)

Brussels sprouts. (See Cabbage group.)

Cabbage group. Being related and taking the same general care, we take up here these seven crops in this order: broccoli, Brussels sprouts, cabbage, cauliflower, collards, kale, and kohlrabi.

Broccoli. Did you know that the plants of the cabbage group are famous health foods? They are popular because of their taste, but in this case the palate is the friend of the body. High in vitamins B and C, and in minerals such as calcium, these are basic foods in a good diet.

Though cauliflower has long had the name of being the aristocrat of this group, broccoli has enjoyed such a meteoric rise in favor during the past thirty-five years that it may be said to now hold first place as the cabbage-type of distinction.

Broccoli is often still identified as Italian Green Sprouting. Like the other members of its group, its very earliest ancestor was probably a wild cabbage that grew along parts of the European coast.

We always include broccoli in our garden, even if we don't have any of its relatives, as it is a plant that keeps on giving a good return for the space it takes. For a long time we depended on the De Cicco variety, and still do, but in recent years we have also planted Green Comet Hybrid. It is not as fast for us as some seed houses say it is, but we were delighted with its immense central head, as large as a cauliflower, and the good side sprouts. It is also low-growing and sturdy, needing no staking. Incidentally, a very deep mulch is a good way to support a broccoli plant.

Like the other cabbage-group plants, broccoli wants a cool season, though broccoli is not as insistent about it. Seed it in early spring for an early summer crop, and in mid-summer for a fall crop. It is best to start the spring crop indoors in flats or pots. De Cicco matures its central head in about 2 months, and you can harvest side shoots, rising from the leaf axils, for at least another month. Green Comet's timing with us is about the same. Calabrese is a good variety but takes nearly 3 months to mature. Spartan Early is a bit faster and good, and Waltham 29 is a good variety from Massachusetts.

All the cabbage group are heavy feeders, and we find they respond well to a dug-in 4" layer of compost before seeding or transplanting. They want full sun but should not be planted any place where some of them were growing the season before.

Sow broccoli seed ¼" deep. Plants should stand 18" apart in rows that are 30" apart. We have crowded them when we were short of space, but it isn't the best way.

Harvest broccoli by cutting the sprouts with 4" to 6" of stalk, and while the buds that form the sprout are quite tight. Later they open into small yellow flowers. This is another vegetable that is superb when harvested only minutes before cooking. One cup of cooked broccoli contains 5 grams of

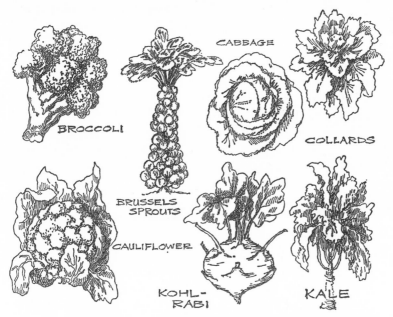

protein, 5,100 units of vitamin A, and appreciable amounts of calcium, thiamin, riboflavin, niacin, and vitamin C. And *only* 45 calories. Both stem and sprout are edible, and so are the very nutritious leaves.

Though the cabbage group has a lot of potential pests, broccoli is not usually attacked by many. The main culprits are the cabbage worms, aphids, cutworms, and maggots.

Brussels sprouts. This plant is a garden oddity in appearance, the sprouts looking like tiny cabbages the size of ping-pong balls, and clustered thickly up and down the clublike central stem, in the axils of the leaves. The flavor is much milder than that of cabbage. The plant will go through a mild winter, light freezes helping the flavor. In the South it is a winter crop.

There are both dwarf and tall types, the dwarfs being most popular in home gardens. Jade Cross Hybrid is a good variety and so is the well-known Long Island Improved. Both grow about 2' tall. Plan on a minimum of 3 months from seeding to harvest. You can start plants indoors, but we have found that direct seeding in the garden grows good plants with less trouble. Follow the broccoli directions for culture of Brussels sprouts.

The lowest sprouts on the central stem ripen first. Pick them with a slight twist to loosen them, starting as soon as the plant's lowest leaves begin to yellow. When you remove a sprout, also remove the leaf from whose axil it grew. This is to make the plant grow more leaves above, and thus grow more sprouts. The sprouts ripen gradually, so you work your way up the stem over a period of several weeks. A good plant can produce about 100 sprouts.

Like broccoli, Brussels sprouts are subject to pests that attack cabbage, but usually are not bothered by all of them.

Cabbage. We plant cabbage only occasionally, preferring to give the garden space to its relatives. Red cabbage and the curled-leaf savoy are interesting variations in a garden, however, and there are new midget cabbages that can make attractive bed borders while they grow into nutritious and delicious little heads. Two of these are Little Leaguer and Morden Dwarf. Among the standard sizes, Golden Acre is resistant to the troublesome yellows disease, and so are Stonehead Hybrid and Marion Market. Good red cabbages are Red Acre and Red Danish, and a good savoy is Savoy King.

The midgets mature in about 2 months; figure on 3 months or a little more for the others, to be safe, though some early cabbages such as Earliana and Emerald Cross Hybrid are close to the midgets in speed.

Cabbage is grown in the South the year around except in the summer. Where winters do not get much below 10° F., plants set out in the fall will grow slowly through the winter, usually without protection, and produce an early spring crop.

Cabbage is grown as a spring and fall crop in the North, the fall one being grown for storage and use over the winter.

Plant cabbage seed ½″ deep, and thin plants to stand 18″ apart in rows 30″ apart. If planting indoors for setting plants out in early spring, give them at least a month from seeding to transplanting. In the garden, a side dressing of cottonseed meal when plants are half-grown is helpful, at a rate of about 1 pound for each 4 or 5 plants. Give midgets half as much, or use compost tea to feed them, 1 cupful per plant, 2 or 3 times during growth.

Harvest cabbage by cutting the stalk just below the bottom of the head. If the heads show cracks, it means the cabbage is growing too fast, but this doesn't hurt the quality if you use the cabbage promptly. To store cabbages easily in winter, pull them up with roots attached and simply put them in a box in a cool place such as a basement.

Cabbage is often attacked by insects, including cutworms, maggots, cabbage worms, harlequin bugs, weevils, and aphids, and by several diseases, as listed in Chapter 9. Using disease-resistant varieties is simply common sense. Also be sure not to plant cabbage or any of its relatives 2 seasons in succession in the same spot. Better yet, let 3 or 4 years elapse between plantings on the same ground.

Cauliflower. A bit more particular about growing conditions than cabbage, cauliflower won't take as much cold weather and it won't head properly in weather too warm. Consequently, it is a spring and fall crop except in the South, where it also grows in winter. Sow seed indoors 4 or 5 weeks ahead for the spring crop, and set plants 2′ apart in rows that are 30″ apart. The fall crop can be seeded in the garden, and must be timed so that it will be starting to head as cool weather arrives, so check maturity time of the variety you plant. In the Midwest, a fast variety such as Snow King Hybrid, heading in about 7 weeks from setting out plants, could be seeded about 12 weeks before the average first fall frost date—say July 15.

The culture of cauliflower is practically the same as for broccoli. Early Snowball and Super Snowball are good varieties, maturing in about 8 weeks under right conditions. Purple Head, a purplish green, takes a good 12 weeks. To keep white cauliflower white, tie the leaves over the head in a loose covering when the head starts to form.

Harvest cauliflower promptly when the head reaches the right size or it will open up and lose quality. A late crop can be stored in the way we mentioned for cabbage, but won't keep for much more than one month.

The usual cabbage insects also bother cauliflower. Give the plants plenty of water in dry spells to keep them growing strongly, and also mulch them, and you'll avoid some troubles.

Collards. All of the cabbage-group plants are good for you, but the collard is far and away the most nutritious. It is also a delicious and robustly flavored vegetable. The plants grow 2′ or 3′ tall and produce a good crop of leaves, which is what you cook. We strip them off as we need them but you can cook a young plant whole. The top rosette of leaves is the choicest part.

Georgia is a good variety, widely listed. Though collards are often thought of as a plant of the South, they are quite adaptable if you grow them in the cool weather of spring or fall. They grow through the winter in the South. Give them the same culture as broccoli, but they will take closer spacing, about 15″ between plants in rows 30″ apart.

Cabbage insects attack collards but often are not serious pests, and the plants are usually free of diseases.

Kale. Everything said about collards applies to kale except that it grows more compact plants and is a good deal more ornamental. Blue Curled Scotch and Dwarf Siberian are excellent varieties. Space them about 12″ apart in rows 18″ apart, seeding directly in the open or starting plants in flats.

Kale takes freezing weather in stride—even gaining flavor from it.

Harvest kale's outside leaves, and the inside ones continue to grow. Old leaves become pretty tough. Also like collards, kale is very nutritious. The tenderest leaves can be used in salads, but though we used to do this, we finally decided we liked kale cooked.

Kohlrabi. Kohlrabi grows a bulb about the size of a small apple, and grows it above ground. Give kohlrabi the same culture as broccoli but space plants about 6" apart in rows 15" apart. Early White Vienna and Early Purple Vienna are the varieties usually offered.

Harvest the bulbs when they are 3" wide or a little less, which takes about 2 months. Peel the bulbs like potatoes before cooking. The flavor is mild and good.

Spring and fall are the growing seasons. Start the spring crop in flats 4 weeks ahead of early spring planting; a light frost won't kill the plants. Seed the fall crop in the open garden in time to mature before freezing weather comes.

Insects and diseases are seldom a problem with kohlrabi.

Carrots. A freshly dug young carrot is a taste sensation to anyone who has been acquainted only with the store product. The fresh carrot is crisp and its flavor so delicate and sprightly it could be a different vegetable from the other. We consider carrots so useful for seasoning alone that we would plant them for that even if we had no other need for them. They add necessary flavor to soups and stews, meat loaves, braised greens, and to some sauces.

Carotene, the substance the liver turns into vitamin A, is named for the carrot, which is high in it. This vitamin not only helps eyesight but is an aid in keeping you looking and feeling young, and is good for your skin.

We plant a 4' row of carrots every month, and a family of four might want to double this planting. You can start planting carrots in early spring. When we are living in a cold-winter climate we make a final large planting of carrots in late summer, supplying us with fresh carrots into the winter, as they can be mulched and let stay where they are growing, to be harvested as needed.

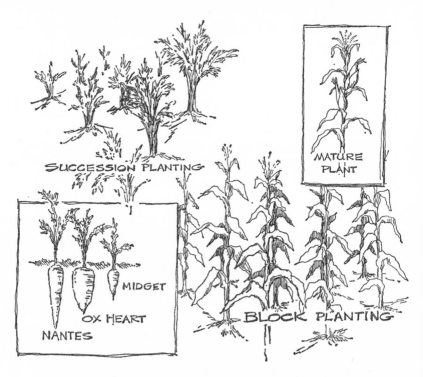

Carrots especially like well-spaded soil and will fork or bend if they meet obstacles. Dig in compost when preparing the seed bed and plant seeds ½″ deep. The usual spacing between plants is 2″ to 3″, but we find they are not temperamental about this and grow quite well without much thinning. However, the young carrots you pull when thinning the row are delicious merely scrubbed and eaten raw. You can also transplant very young thinnings.

Carrots aren't as demanding of full sun as the fruiting

plants and will get along in partial shade. Keep them well watered to keep them growing well.

Nantes and Chantenay are good medium-length carrots, and for heavy soil, Oxheart is a good bet, with a short and chunky root. Waltham Hicolor is 12″ long, and there are several midget carrots 2″ and 3″ long. The shape and length of the root is the main consideration in a variety choice as nearly all carrots take about the same time to mature— 2 months.

Though carrots are not free of pests, not many insects or diseases bother them in home gardens. The potentials are covered in Chapter 9.

Celery. The most important point to remember about growing celery is to plant it far enough ahead so it will mature. We seed it about 10 weeks ahead, starting it in a flat and barely covering the seeds because they need some light to help them germinate. We move the plants to the garden in early spring, though in a mild-winter climate we seed in the open garden in late winter, and have done so as early as January on the West Coast.

Though transplanting sets celery back slightly, it helps it grow a better root system—though we haven't noticed much difference in home-garden plantings between transplanted and non-transplanted celery. Maturity times date from when plants are set out, and since 4 months is average, figure on a good 6 months from seeding to maturity.

To grow the happiest celery, dig in a 4″ layer of compost when transplanting or seeding in the open garden. Two months later for transplants, and 3 months for open-seeded plants, mulch the bed with 2″ of compost. We have also tried our instant compost, as described in Chapter 3, with celery, and it loved it. Celery wants moist soil for steady growth, and any compost helps here, too.

Plants should stand 6″ apart in rows 2′ apart. Full sun is good, but plants will accept some shade part of the day.

Utah and Golden Plume are good varieties, as are the Pascals, and Burpee's Fordhook has done well in our gardens. Any home-garden celery will make store celery seem bland. Another advantage of growing your own is that you can strip off a few outside stalks—which is often all you need for some recipes—and keep the plant growing along, the same way you harvest chard. And you can start harvesting celery when the plants are only half-grown. You can also dig a plant up at the end of the season and bring it indoors to grow all winter in a pot for your seasoning needs.

Though many people think of celery as only a relish plant, to be eaten raw or in salads, it has a great many more uses in cooked dishes and is a necessity in many Oriental ones. Combine it with tomatoes, shallots, and basil for a full-bodied dinner dish, or cut an entire bunch lengthwise into quarters, and simmer in a rich chicken stock. Dried celery leaves are a handy seasoning. Follow the drying directions given under herbs in this chapter.

We don't whiten celery, but if you want to, just tie a band of brown paper around the plant for 10 days.

Celery can be attacked by a fair number of insects, but they often are not present in home gardens. Good air circulation will help prevent diseases from getting a foothold.

Celeriac. This is a kind of celery that is grown for the big root it forms, not for the top. The root tastes like celery flavored with English walnuts. We like it and sometimes use it in Oriental dishes and in casseroles. Peel it, slice, and parboil first. It is also very good breaded and fried in butter.

Two fine varieties are Alabaster and Giant Prague. You grow celeriac the same way you do celery, and it takes about as long to mature. However, the roots can be used from the time they are 2″ wide, though they grow to 4″ or more. To store, dig them when cold weather is due, cut off all but 1″ of the top, and put them in a box in a cool place. They will keep for months.

The same pests that may attack celery will also attack celeriac.

Corn. Corn takes more space than some home gardens have since it is tall and must be planted in blocks for good pollination. Midget varieties offer a compromise and are well worth growing, too. All corn needs from 10 to 12 weeks of warm summer weather after the earth has warmed up in late spring.

Our favorite corn is Golden Bantam, and there are some very good hybrids that are also resistant to some corn diseases. Illini Xtra-Sweet is an unusually sweet hybrid that keeps its sugar longer after harvesting; don't plant it near other varieties, or the cross-pollination that will result will lower the Illini's sugar content.

For a long harvest season, plant varieties that ripen successively; check maturity times in seed catalogues on this point. For example, four good yellow corns that ripen over a 4-week span are Early Sunglow, Spancross, Golden Bantam, and Burbank Hybrid.

Corn needs at least 6 hours of sun a day on a well-drained site. Dig in 4″ of compost to start with and mulch with compost when plants are about 2′ tall. Plant seed 1″ deep and about 4″ apart in rows 30″ apart, thinning later so that plants are about 12″ apart. Four such rows will form a satisfactory block planting. The point is that corn pollen is carried on the tassels at the tops of the stalks and shakes down onto the silks of the ears when the wind blows. If you planted just a single row of corn, most of the pollen would fail to land on the silks, and you would get poorly filled-out ears. Just to make sure, we clip off a few tassels and shake them over the silks ourselves.

You can expect from one to three ears from each corn plant. The sign of maturity is well-dried silks, but you can start using the first ears a few days before maturity, and ears hold their quality for a few days after maturing.

Picked minutes—and we mean minutes—before cooking, corn is one of the really delicious products a garden can produce. We pull off the outside shucks, loosen the inside husks and remove the silks. Then we twist the inside husks securely around the corn and put it into a 375° F. oven for 15 minutes. The ears come out with the husks crisp and the kernels partly steamed, partly roasted, ready to be rolled in melted butter in a hot platter. If we are cooking over coals, we remove all shucks and husks and then broil the ears for about 10 minutes, turning them frequently. When you taste such corn you will be savoring that famous peak of perfection.

Corn has several pests, but the one most apt to bother home-garden plantings is the earworm. Control measures are given in Chapter 9.

Cress. There was an item in a San Francisco newspaper not long ago commenting admiringly on the keenness of an English gardener who had identified garden cress for a restaurant owner who wanted to add this item to his menu. Garden, or upland, cress is indeed a nice addition to a meal, but it is certainly no problem to find, or at least to find seeds. Practically every seed catalogue lists it, often in both the flat-leaf and the curled-leaf types. Also called pepper grass, it is botanically *Lepidium sativum.* We usually grow the curled type and find it a good substitute for water cress, a beautiful and edible garnish and a piquant addition to salads.

Cress is a cool-weather crop, growing so quickly from seed that you can start using it in 3 weeks. Seed it shallowly in very early spring and make succession plantings every 2 or 3 weeks until late spring. Cress is not winter-hardy in the garden, but it will grow indoors in a pot all winter.

You'll get stronger plants by thinning them to 3" apart in any planting, but we find that thinning isn't a necessity. We frequently use cress for a fast-growing border planting.

Except for a few voracious leaf eaters such as slugs, cress is free of pests.

Cucumbers. Long-time favorites of the garden, cucumbers are available today in many interesting varieties, including very good hybrids that overcame once fatal cucumber diseases. Cucumbers are relatives of squashes, pumpkins, melons, and gourds, all being in the same family, Cucurbitaceae. All need a fairly warm summer, lots of sun and air, and fertile soil.

Most cucumbers take about 2 months to mature, though you can use them before they are fully ripe. In short-summer climates, plants can be started indoors about 3 weeks ahead of warm weather. We have done as well by seeding under Hotkaps in the open garden.

To plant in hills, a good way with this family of plants, dig a bushel of compost into the planting spot and sow 6 or more seeds, spacing them evenly in a circle the size of a dinner plate. When seedlings are a few inches tall, remove all but the best three. One good hill will supply a family with fresh cucumbers; if you want more, space hills 6' apart. Another planting method is to seed in a row along a fence; space plants 2' apart and let them climb the fence.

To keep them growing well and tasting right, give cucumbers a good deep watering each week, equal to at least a 1" rain.

Burpless is a variety recently widely advertised as agreeing with people who can't eat other cucumbers. Black Diamond and Fortune are two good older varieties. Burpee Hybrid has done splendidly for us, and the little pale yellow cucumber called Lemon is nicely sweet and mild. If you want cucumbers for pickling, West India Gherkin, Ohio, MR 17, and Chicago Pickling are all good, the last two being especially resistant to some diseases.

We find that an excellent way to take care of a cucumber surplus is this: Slice the cucumbers thinly, wrap enough slices in foil for an individual serving, and put into the freezer. To

serve, pour cream mixed with a few drops of lemon juice over the still frozen slices.

Like the other cucurbits, cucumbers can have a goodly share of troubles, including two insects honored with the plant's own name—striped cucumber beetles and spotted cucumber beetles. Sanitation is most important, and so is rotation planting. Other control measures are covered in Chapter 9.

Eggplant. We grow eggplants whenever we are gardening in a climate with a long and really warm summer, seeding in flats or pots 2 months before the weather will be thoroughly warmed up for outdoor planting. Eggplants are attractive plants, about 2' tall, with lobed, grayish-green leaves, and the pendant purple fruits look almost self-consciously ornamental. There are also other colors of eggplants—red, white, green, and striped—and some of the purple kind are shaped like cucumbers. An eggplant is right at home in a flower bed, and was grown almost entirely for this purpose years ago. Today there are also some good midget eggplants, Morden Midget bearing medium-sized fruits on small plants. Among the standard types, Black Beauty is famous, and Burpee Hybrid is known for high resistance to disease.

You can expect to harvest 6 or more fruits per plant. Ten weeks is average ripening time, from setting out plants, but you can start harvesting sooner, as young fruits are delicious. Pick fruits when they have become glossy and well-colored. Luckily, they ripen one at a time.

Give eggplants rich soil in a full-sun spot where they or peppers and tomatoes were not grown the previous season. Space plants 4' apart, with midgets 2' apart. Plants need no support, as the stems are sturdy. A peculiarity of this plant, though, is that a *woody* stem indicates a plant that will never amount to much.

Eggplants need mulching to retain soil moisture, and compost is an excellent mulch for them.

Though several pests attack eggplants, we have often had pest-free plantings. Resistant varieties are a good choice, and control measures for other pests are given in Chapter 9.

Florence fennel. You may have to acquire a taste for this vegetable, but you'll like its looks on sight—emerald-green and ferny, much like asparagus. It is related to the herb fennel, and the part of Florence fennel that you eat is the flattened bulb at the base of the stalk. Finocchio is another name for Florence fennel.

Fennel's flavor is somewhat like tarragon or anise (and it is sometimes called anise, though incorrectly). Fennel can be used raw in salads, but we cook it. To do so, trim off the stalks, wash the bulb and cut into quarters. Cook it in vegetable stock until it is tender. You can finish it in butter or olive oil, with a little lemon juice and salt.

Sow fennel seeds in the spring, ¼" deep, and later thin plants to 6" apart in rows that are 30" apart. Plants grow 2' tall, or a little more, and mature in about 3 months, though you can start harvesting sooner.

Fennel has no serious pests.

Herbs. Among the many culinary herbs, the ones we consistently grow are basil, chives, marjoram or oregano, Italian parsley, rosemary, tarragon, and thyme. Occasionally we grow chervil, dill, sage, and spearmint. (Use a sprig of spearmint as a brush to put a marinade on lamb as it broils; it imports a subtle flavor.)

Tarragon from seed is not the tarragon usually employed in cooking, but the other herbs named can be so grown. Most perennial herbs are multiplied by cuttings or divisions, though. With chives, thyme, sage, and spearmint, dig up the plant in early fall, pull it gently apart into two or more clumps, complete with roots and top, and plant each clump.

You can also make cuttings of thyme, sage, and spearmint, and of marjoram, oregano, and rosemary. To do so, strip off firm but not woody-brittle side stems any time during the summer and plant them up to their middles in sandy soil (or add a handful of sand to the soil). Keep the soil damp while roots form, which usually takes at least a month. For more assurance of success, dip the cut ends into a root-promoting substance such as Rootone before planting.

Tarragon can also be grown from cuttings, but seems to do better from root divisions. Dig the roots in early spring, pull them gently apart into two or more bunches, and plant each.

If your winters are cold, give perennial herbs protection with a 1'-deep mulch of straw or leaves. In the coldest regions, moving the plants to a coldframe is good practice.

To Dry Herbs

Taking the top third of each stem, cut about a quart of sprigs as plants are starting to bloom. Early morning is the best time of day for this. Rinse the sprigs and spread them on foil in a 225°F. oven and let them stay until crisp but still greenish, which takes from 30 minutes to more than 2 hours, depending on the succulence of the particular herb.

We get rid of stems by rubbing the dried herbs through a colander, and put the stems in the compost pile.

Compared with fresh herbs, we use only one-sixth as much of a well-dried home-garden herb in cooking, rather than the one-fourth usually suggested.

Here is how we rate some herbs for drying:

Basil: Holds flavor if not overdried. Air-dry it till it is almost but not quite crisp. Then finish drying it quickly in the 225°F. oven.

Chives: They can be grown indoors in winter, so there is no point in drying.

Marjoram/Oregano: These are related, and both dry well.

Parsley: Loses flavor. Better to grow a pot indoors in winter.

Rosemary: Dries well, lasts long.

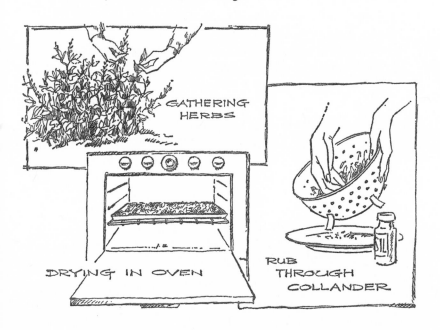

GATHERING HERBS

DRYING IN OVEN

RUB THROUGH COLLANDER

Tarragon: Like basil, good if not overdried.
Thyme: Excellent drier, good keeper, in all varieties.
Chervil: Only fairly good drier with us.
Dill: Good drier and an unusually good keeper.
Sage: Dries well, keeps well.
Spearmint: Dries acceptably.

Horse-radish. Growing your own horse-radish is the only way to taste this pungent seasoning at its masterful best, as fresh roots freshly grated are what yield top flavor. (If you must dig them ahead of time, you can hold good home-garden roots for a week in your refrigerator's vegetable keeper with the minimum loss possible for pre-dug roots.) A horse-radish plant grows about 2′ high, is vigorous, and tends to sprawl.

You plant roots, usually the small side roots that grow out from the large root you harvest. The small ones are the thickness of a pencil, more or less. Plant them by digging a hole with a slanting side, deep enough so that the top of a 6″ piece of root will be 3″ or 4″ below ground level. Lay the root on the slanting side of the hole, thicker end up, and fill the hole with soil. The thicker end will be the one nearest the main root from which the small root grew. Space plants 18″ apart. For most families, three or four plants will be enough, but if you plant more than one row, space the rows 3′ apart. And after a first planting, you'll have more side roots for planting than you know what to do with.

Horse-radish doesn't demand rich soil, but spading compost into it before planting will encourage larger roots, and they grow straighter in well-dug soil.

Horse-radish does best in climates with cold winters, though we have grown it satisfactorily under milder conditions. It is a perennial, of course, but not one that should stay in the same spot year after year. Dig it up and move it every second or third spring, making a new planting with side shoots. This is to keep from growing woody old roots that won't grate well.

And grating, or grinding, is the way to process horse-radish. Dig carrot-sized or larger roots, wash and peel them like potatoes, then grate or grind finely. Add white vinegar or lemon juice, to make a sauce of the right consistency. For a milder sauce, grate in some turnip. Store sauce in the refrigerator in a capped jar, and grate only as much as you'll use in two or three weeks, for best flavor, though it will keep much longer.

Fresh horse-radish is famous as an accompaniment to corned beef. Try adding a little to mayonnaise for sandwiches, and include a tablespoon of horse-radish in a cup of white sauce to be served over some bland vegetable.

Though we have had gophers eat out a bed of horse-radish, the plant has no serious insect pests or diseases.

Leafy greens. This group of plants are all eaten, usually cooked, for the sake of their highly nutritious and tasty leaves and, sometimes, stems. Some other greens are described under the botanical groups they belong to—under cabbages, in the case of collards and kale; beet tops under beets, turnip greens under turnips.

Chard is one of the longest-lasting greens. We've had plants continue to produce for more than a year in a mild climate. You plant and care for chard, also called Swiss chard, as you do beets; they are closely related. Space plants 12″ apart in rows 30″ apart.

Harvest chard a leaf at a time, removing the outer stalks at their bases with a twist. The inner leaves continue to grow. Lucullus is a splendid variety; there is also an attractive red-leaf kind, though not to our taste on flavor.

Chard and beets have the same pests. Cutworms may menace the young plants, but home-garden plantings often have no serious troubles.

Mustard. This plant belongs to the same family as the

cabbages. It should be seeded early in spring, then again in September if you want a late crop. Give it the same culture as lettuce and space plants 8″ apart in rows 15″ apart.

Harvest mustard a leaf at a time for longer cropping. Green Wave is a good variety, as is Southern Giant Curled.

Maggots, aphids, cabbage worms, and some of the other pests that attack turnips also may attack mustard. However, mustard escapes some troubles by growing quickly, maturing in 5 or 6 weeks, and it can be picked sooner.

Spinach. A cool-weather lover, spinach will even go through a moderate northern winter with some mulch protection. Spade compost into the bed to get spinach off to a fast start, and seed early in spring. Plants can stand as close as 1″ apart, in rows 12″ apart. Bloomsdale Long Standing is a good variety, maturing in 7 weeks. Hybrid No. 7 is a week earlier. A number of non-related plants are sometimes called types of spinach—Malabar spinach and tampala are two; both are good leafy greens, as is New Zealand spinach, another non-relative. All three stand hot weather better than true spinach.

Aphids, cutworms, and slugs may bother spinach. Resistant varieties are helpful in avoiding some diseases.

Lettuce. We consider lettuce the salad plant supreme and grow a lot of it in several varieties; also, we are presently in a climate where lettuce grows the year around. When the crop gets ahead of us we cook some of it as a delicate leafy-green dish, with a little olive oil, lemon juice, and a dash of nutmeg.

For most of the country, lettuce is a spring and fall crop, wanting a fairly rich soil and lots of moisture. A peculiarity of the plant is that it insists on an abundance of organic matter in its soil, so dig in at least a 4″ layer of compost when making the seedbed. Lettuce is also touchy about the soil's pH, wanting it a little on the acid side. A soil testing pH 6.0 would be quite suitable, though, and this acidity suits other vegetables, too.

There are four types of lettuce: loose-leaf, such as Grand Rapids and Simpson; butterhead, such as Bibb and Butter King; crisp-head, such as Pennlake and Imperial; and cos, also called romaine, and available in closely related varieties such as Paris White, Valmaine, and Parris Island. There is also a very good midget cos that goes by various names. Farmer lists it as Sweet Midget Cos.

Loose-leaf lettuce will take more summer heat than the others and is more tolerant of soil conditions. The others won't die in hot weather, but they won't head and they'll probably bolt to seed. We grew leaf lettuce in summer in the Midwest by planting it in a partly shaded place—and all lettuce will accept some shade.

For a quick start with all but leaf lettuce, seed the spring crop in flats indoors or in a protected coldframe (cover it with burlap at night). Damping-off is sometimes a problem with seedlings, but by using equal parts of compost, garden soil, and builders' sand for the planting mix, we have avoided this. Sow seeds no more than ¼″ deep, and transfer plants to the garden as soon as the soil is workable. Also seed loose-leaf varieties in the garden at this time. Spacing plants 12″ apart, in rows 16″ apart, is fairly standard practice, but they will accept closer planting.

Leaf lettuces mature in about 6 weeks. Butterheads are next, at about 10 weeks. Cos and the crisp-heads need close to 3 months.

If you are short of lettuce, harvest only the outer leaves of leaf lettuce, leaving the rest of the plant for later. Also, by cutting any lettuce plant off just above ground level instead of pulling it up when harvesting, you will get a bonus of little sprouts from the stump.

Aphids, cutworms, and slugs may bother lettuce. Diseases are not usually serious in home gardens. An occasional plant lost to bottom rot is no cause for alarm, and tipburn is an organic trouble related to temperature and, again, nothing to worry about in a home planting.

Melons

Cantaloupes. If you have a space 5′ to 6′ square available in the garden, a hill of cantaloupes there will be a delightful experience—a luscious fruit you can grow in a single season. And if you don't have that much space, there are some nice new midget cantaloupes that will grow in only a 3′ square. As with cucumbers, you plant cantaloupes in compost-enriched soil, in hills, and care for them the same way.

A good midget, developed at the University of Minnesota, is Minnesota Midget Muskmelon. Farmer, Gurney, and Park list it. In 2 months it produces attractive little 4″ melons. Most of the standard-sized cantaloupes need 3 months. Netted Gem, which is the same as Rocky Ford, is a very good and long-established variety. Two others that do well in home gardens are Hearts of Gold and Delicious 51, the latter a Cornell University development and resistant to fusarium wilt. Some good hybrid cantaloupes are Mainerock Hybrid, Burpee Hybrid, and Sampson Hybrid; they mature, in the order given in 11, 12, and 13 weeks.

Besides cantaloupes, other melons for home gardens are casabas, honeydews, and crenshaws. The first two do best in warm weather. Four months is about the average maturity time for all, though a honeydew called Honey Mist is as fast as a slow cantaloupe.

Judging when a cantaloupe is ready to pick is something you learn by doing. We can usually judge by smell, a ripe melon having a fine, full fragrance. A rule of thumb, literally, is to touch the melon's stem with your thumb, and if the melon comes loose easily, it is ripe. You can pick a honeydew green and let it ripen indoors, but cantaloupes ripen perfectly only on the vine.

Cantaloupes can have nearly as many pests as cucumbers have, and in addition are intolerant of long rainy spells and of humid weather. Sanitation and crop rotation are important control measures; others are given in Chapter 9. Incidentally, though light-textured soils with some sand in them are usually specified for cantaloupes, we have raised them to perfection in heavy clay soil.

Watermelons. Standard-sized watermelons take as much or more space as cantaloupes, but here again there are midgets that are about as compact as midget cantaloupes. You plant and care for watermelons the same way you do cantaloupes and cucumbers, except that watermelons prefer a more acid soil, pH 5.5 to 6.5 A general rule here is to dig a bucketful of sphagnum peat into the hill before seeding.

Two midget watermelons that you can find listed by many seed houses are New Hampshire Midget and Golden Midget. They mature in about 10 weeks compared to most of the standards' 12 or 14 weeks. This earliness is also shared by some new hybrids, and may enable you to grow watermelons if you live in one of the northern zones where the first fall frost has always come a little too soon for the older varieties of watermelons to ripen. Three of these hybrids are Faribo 5–11 (Farmer), You Sweet Thing (Park), and Fordhook Hybrid (Burpee). Some hybrids are seedless, but you have to plant a standard variety near them to get fruits.

Sizes of watermelon fruits range from the 5-pound midgets up to some standards of more than 100 pounds, such as Black Diamond (Park).

When is a watermelon ripe? When it makes a deep hollow sound as you thump it, when the tendril where the fruit stem joins the vine is dry, when the melon comes loose easily if you hold its stem and shake it gently, and when the part of the melon resting on the ground is deep yellow. The little Golden Midget has a foolprof ripeness sign—it turns from green to yellow when ripe.

Watermelons have some of the same pests as cantaloupes, but not as many. Control measures are given in Chapter 9.

Okra. If your climate offers it warm weather, okra will grow an attractive plant that bears many beautiful hibiscus-like flowers that produce the pods you harvest. It starts bearing in about 8 weeks. Keep the pods picked, and the harvest will extend to at least a month. We aren't living in a warm enough climate at this time to grow okra, and we miss it. The only way to make a good chicken or crab gumbo is to have your own okra.

Most garden soils will suit okra. Plant seed ½" deep, after the soil is thoroughly warm in late spring, spacing plants 8" apart, in rows 3' apart. Dig some compost into the soil before seeding, and give okra the usual weekly 1" garden watering. In general it takes the same care as tomatoes.

Okra plants average 4' tall except for some dwarfs such as Dwarf Green Pod, which top off at about 2' but bear normal size pods. Clemson Spineless is a well-known standard-sized variety, and Spineless Green Velvet is a new one.

Aphids and corn earworms may bother okra, but it is usually quite pest-free.

Onion group. One or more of the onion plants that follow should be in any home garden because they are good for you, and in many cases they are grown for their reputed insect-discouraging qualities. They aren't overly fussy about soil types, they take but little space, and they are attractive plants, ideal for border plantings if space is scarce. In general, they are cool-weather crops and are often sensitive to day-lengths. Spring planting is the rule, although fall planting in mild climates is also practiced.

Chives. To get fresh chives you must raise them. Dried or frozen chives are lamentably poor substitutes for fresh ones. To get a start, buy a pot of chives or sow chive seed.

Chives are perennial, and they multiply well. Dig the clump

in early spring, pull it apart into small clumps of 10 to 20 bulbs each, and plant them 12" apart.

The tops die in late fall, even in mild climates, but if you transplant some clumps to pots before this happens, you can grow chives indoors all winter.

You harvest only the leaves, narrow tubular stems. Cut them near the base of the plant, and new ones will quickly sprout.

Chives have no pests to speak of.

Garlic. It is often hard to find good garlic in markets, and so it is convenient to have it growing along in the garden, where you can also give it organic care and take advantage of any insect-repelling it can do for you.

The pinkish garlic keeps better than the white kind. Divide a bulb of either into its segments, called cloves, and plant them in early spring, about 2" deep, pointed ends up, and 6" apart. The tops make their best growth in the cool spring weather, and after that, the bulbs grow, taking about 4 months from planting, though we have found they take longer in some mild climates. You can scrape away some earth and feel the bulb for size, if in doubt. If the soil is rich, you may have to bend the leaves over to halt further growth so you can prepare to harvest, but ordinarily the plant itself decides this by gradually dying at the top. Earlier harvesting is also possible though the bulb will be smaller. And if you need a little garlic flavoring still earlier, snip off a bit of leaf and use it.

When you do dig the bulbs, dry them outdoors for a few days, then store them in a dry, airy place. A garlic clove will give you about a 10-fold return, and sometimes much more.

Root maggots sometimes invade garlic, but in our experience they have to be desperate for food to do so.

Leeks. They do take their time about growing, but leeks are good vegetables for home gardens and are seldom seen there. Broad London is a good variety, Unique is noted for long stems, and Elephant is a little faster than others. Most leeks need 4 months to mature, but you can harvest them younger. We have taken them at 8 weeks or so.

You grow leeks from seed. Plant them ¼″ deep and space plants later to 6″ apart in rows 18″ apart. You can transplant thinnings.

A leek forms a thick stem up to 2″ wide when mature. The white lower part of this stem is what you cook, and it will be 4″ to 6″ long. You can include a little of the green part of a young and tender leek. Banking a leek with earth will blanch the stem, but we don't do this because it makes the leek harder to wash. Anyway, a fine crisp home-garden leek doesn't need pampering. After harvesting a leek, the best way we know of to wash it is to quarter it lengthwise and hold the quarters under running water to flush away any particles of earth that have sifted in between the outer leaves.

We found leeks so little affected by cold that we left them in the garden all winter in the Midwest and East, mulched with straw.

A favorite way with us to use leeks is in Vichyssoise, that perfect soup for a cold winter night. We also serve it cold occasionally on hot summer days, with thin Melba toast, but prefer it hot. Here is our recipe: Melt 4 tablespoons of butter in a heavy saucepan. Slice 4 medium-sized leeks thinly, using part of the tender green section. Chop 1 dry onion or 4 scallions, and stir onions and leeks into the butter. Peel and chop 4 medium-sized potatoes, add them to the pan, and stir. Add 2 cups of vegetable stock, cover the pan, and cook over medium heat until the vegetables are quite soft, about 15 minutes. Mash them well with a potato masher—much faster than using a sieve or a blender, and an easier clean-up. When well blended, add 2 cups of rich homemade chicken stock. Bring the soup to a boil, reduce heat, and *slowly* stir in the contents of 1 large can of evaporated milk. Continue stirring until the soup begins to simmer. Remove from heat, let stand for 2 or 3 minutes, then serve in warm mugs with generous

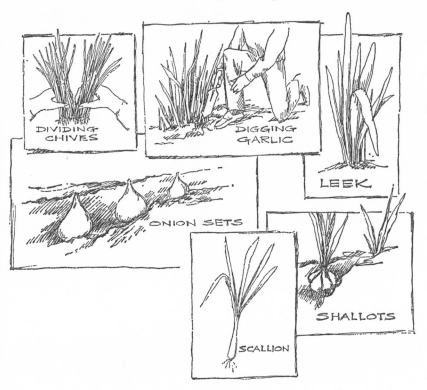

wedges of Southern cornbread, preferably in front of a roaring fire.

Except for occasional maggots, few pests bother leeks in home gardens.

Onions. Here we mean globe onions. Raising them from seed will give you a wide choice of varieties, but we must add that onions from seed don't always germinate well and grow well. Alternatives are to plant sets—little onions raised from seed the year before—or plants. Onions grow best where the summer temperatures don't go over 75° F.

In any case, make a finely worked seedbed, digging in extra compost. The plants prefer a slightly acid soil, pH 6.0 to 6.5.

Sow seed shallowly. Space plants from 3″ to 6″ apart, depending on the size the variety grows. When putting in sets or started plants, they can be spaced 1″ apart if you plan to use thinnings as scallions. Sets should be planted with the necks just at ground level. Onions from seed take about 4 months to mature; plants and sets take about 3 months. Midway in their growth, onions benefit from a side dressing of fertilizer, so work 1 pound of cottonseed meal into each 20′ of row, alongside plants.

The Bermuda and the Sweet Spanish are still excellent onions, and today there are also many good hybrids. A Sweet Spanish hybrid has done well for us in coastal California where nothing else succeeded, and Early Harvest is a good hybrid in the North. In the South, Yellow Bermuda is good. In the Northeast and Midwest, the Southport onions are recommended, and Hybrid Abundance. For the middle latitudes, the hybrid El Capitan is good, and Sweet Spanish is favored, too. When deciding on what onions to grow, pay special attention to seed catalogue recommendations for your particular climate.

By the way, you cannot tell the strength of an onion from its color. Red onions are not strongest and white mildest, as some people think. Pungency depends entirely on the variety.

Onions are ready to harvest when the tops die back. Dig them, spread them on the ground to dry for a few days, and when the tops are dry as straw, cut off all but 1″ of them and store the bulbs in a cool, dry place where they won't freeze. Net bags are good containers.

Maggots can be troublesome to onions, but the plants usually have few pests.

Scallions. Variously called spring onions, multiplier onions, bunching onions, Egyptian onions, and green onions, as well as scallions, these are the slender onions so much used in Oriental cooking and also eaten raw from relish trays. They are a fair substitute for shallots in cooking and are occasionally sold under that name since green shallots look almost exactly like them.

There are perennial types of scallions, such as Beltsville Bunching, though we find it better to treat them as annuals. No true scallion forms an underground bulb, though some enlarge slightly, and most grow well from seed, though they may germinate slowly. Evergreen Long White and White Spanish are good varieties. Some perennial scallions, the Egyptian or tree onions, multiply underground and also form small bulbs on the tips of the main stems; these bulbs can be planted like sets. In fact, the fastest way to get a scallion *is* to plant an onion set, and then harvest it before it forms a bulb. We have been able to gather these substitute scallions as quickly as 2 weeks after planting sets, under ideal growing conditions. From seed, 4 months is normal maturity time.

Scallions take the same care as globe onions but are less demanding as to temperature and day-length. Scallions can live through a good deal of winter cold. In Missouri we harvested them through the winter by giving them a straw mulch. Since they can also be harvested at any stage of their growth, this made for quite a long period of freshly harvested scallions.

Onion pests, principally maggots, sometimes attack scallions.

Shallots. Southern Louisiana is where most shallots in the United States are grown, and a good many more are imported, this plant having a great name with food lovers. Unless you live in New Orleans or thereabouts, you won't see shallots offered in the green stage, looking like scallions, but may run across them as dry bulbs about the size of garlic cloves and with papery gray or brown skins.

These bulbs are what you plant. Shallot seed is rarely found and, in our experience, doesn't germinate well. If you can't find shallots in local markets—and you probably can't—two sources are Nichols and Le Jardin. Buy enough to plant a dozen or more, and from then on you can plant some of the surplus bulbs if you have success. Shallots can be temperamental growers, but we have had returns of 25 or 30 bulbs for one. Plant bulbs 1″ deep in the spring, blunt ends down, and otherwise handle them the same as garlic but don't give them as much watering.

You can harvest some of the tops of shallots while they are growing, using them like the tops of scallions. You can also take shallots green, as they do in the South, gently detaching an outside plant from its clump. For dried shallots, harvest and store them, as you do garlic, when the tops die down. They store quite well. They are milder than onions and are deservedly famous with connoisseurs of good food.

If shallots have pests, they will be those that bother onions.

Parsnips. Parsnips simply aren't widely popular, but a parsnip lover is a parsnip lover forever. The vegetable can be French fried when young, and if parsnips have always left you indifferent, before you give up try some from your own organic garden, with a pork roast or with ham.

Parsnip seeds germinate best in late spring, when the soil is warm. Dig the bed well, adding compost, and sow seed ½″ deep. Thin the plants to 3″ apart in rows 18″ apart. They will need about 4 months to mature roots, but you can harvest some earlier and can also let the last ones stay in the ground, to be used during the winter, with only a little protective mulch. Some freezing improves the flavor, in fact.

Good varieties are All American, Hollow Crown, Harris' Model, and Guernsey.

Few if any pests bother parsnips in home gardens, but weeds slow them down, so cultivate or mulch the planting.

Peas. You have to grow your own peas to experience the delight of peas as good as peas can be. They are very nutritious, too, rating up to 7 percent of protein, and being rich in vitamins, including the anti-sterility vitamin E.

Spring is the ideal time to plant peas, and the way to spread the harvest is to plant, all at the same time, several varieties that mature at different times. In the South and on the West Coast, fall planting is also possible, and resolute home gardeners in other areas are sometimes able to squeeze in a late crop by seeding in late summer. Early varieties mature in 8 weeks, late ones in about 11 weeks, and midseason ones are somewhere in between.

Plant peas 1″ deep and 3″ apart in double rows only 3″ or 4″ apart. A supporting trellis in between the rows is needed for tall varieties. For lower-growing kinds, push branchy pieces of brush into the soil for the peas to climb. Most garden soils will suit peas as long as they have enough watering.

There are two main groups of peas: the sugar or snow peas, with edible pods; and English peas, which are shelled out for cooking. English peas come in smooth and in wrinkled types, the wrinkled ones being sweeter.

Mammoth Melting Sugar and Dwarf Gray Sugar are the edible-podded varieties usually offered, both being excellent. Good varieties of English peas are Sparkle, an early pea; Wando, a late one; and Burpee's Blue Bantam, midseason. There is a new dwarf English pea, Mighty Midget (Park) that grows only 6″ high.

Harvest English peas when the pods are plump but still succulent. Edible-podded peas should be harvested just as soon as you see a slight swelling of the peas showing on the sides of the pods. Try some of these dainties stir-fried in butter with sliced mushrooms. And English peas are wonderful in that delicious dish, *arroz con pollo*.

Peas have fewer pests than beans do, the more likely ones being aphids and root rot.

Peppers. Although we have managed, barely, to grow peppers in a cool-summer climate, we must admit it was hardly worth the effort. The pepper is unhappy if cool and wants to be set in the garden only after the weather is thoroughly warm. Thus, it is best to start the seeds indoors a good 2 months before outside planting time. We have also started seeds in flats protected by coldframes.

Plant pepper seeds ½″ deep, and since damping-off can be a problem, use the soil mixture recommended for lettuce. In the garden, pepper plants can be spaced about 18″ apart in rows 30″ apart. Give peppers the same care as you give tomatoes.

There are two big groups of peppers, the sweet peppers and hot peppers. Both form such attractive plants, they are an ornament to the garden, and both grow various-shaped fruits. Most in both groups turn red when ripe, though there are some yellow ones and some novelty white ones and chocolate-colored ones (listed by Farmer). Hot peppers are allowed to ripen, but sweet peppers can be used at any stage of development.

Sweet peppers come in four shapes: blocky (Pennwonder, Bell Boy Hybrid, California Wonder); heart-shaped (often called pimento, as Burpee's Early Pimento, and always mild); tomato-shaped (Sunnybrook); and long (Sweet Banana). There are also some small sweet peppers, not commonly listed, such as the 1½″-wide Cherry Sweet (Field).

Hot peppers come in various sizes of cherry shapes and in long shapes that are slender or plumpish.

You can expect to start harvesting sweet peppers about 10 weeks after setting plants out, and the fruits conveniently ripen in succession until frost kills the plants. A good yield is 8 to 10 large peppers per plant, though the long-fruited types may triple this.

Sweet peppers are good both raw and cooked, and can make the main dish of a vegetable meal when stuffed with corn and chopped tomatoes, and roasted. Or they can be quickly sautéed in olive oil with sliced mushrooms. We seldom bother to remove the skin of green peppers, but when we do so with ripe ones, we put them into a 375° F. oven for about 8 minutes and then plunge them into ice water. This loosens the skin, which can be slipped off. Try slicing these peppers into a bowl after seeding them, then marinate them in French dressing in the refrigerator for a few hours. You'll find them a delicious dish—and good for you, as a medium-sized raw red pepper contains a surprising 2,670 units of vitamin A, and 122 milligrams of vitamin C.

Though peppers are not pest-free, they are not apt to be much troubled in home-garden plantings, in our and others' experience. However, we cover the several possible ⁻roubles in Chapter 9.

Potatoes, sweet. Though often thought of as a southern crop, like peanuts, sweet potatoes can succeed for you if you have 5 months of growing weather, counting frost-free days of late spring and early fall, and a warm summer. This usually means you must start the plants indoors. You can do so by planting some sweet potatoes in a box of sand and keeping them moist and warm, 75° F. or higher. Each sweet potato will grow several sprouts. Some sweet potatoes sold for eating are treated to prevent sprouting, and you can order sprouts from a few seed houses. Burgess, Field, and Olds' handle them. Porto Rico is a well-known variety; All Gold is early, and it and Gold Rush are good keepers.

Plant the sprouts when the weather turns warm. First spade the soil well, adding compost only if the soil is poor. Then make ridges with your rake, 4″ high and 30″ apart. If you are growing your sprouts from a sweet potato, pull them gently off, along with the roots they will have formed, and plant them on the ridges, 18″ apart. As they grow, they will form a dense shade mulch with their leaves, and will need less watering than most garden vegetables.

The most important part of the harvesting is proper curing. Do this: Dig the sweet potatoes before frost, clipping off the vines beforehand. Handle the potatoes carefully, spreading them out to dry after you have separated each from its root. Let them dry for 2 or 3 hours in the sun, then pack them one or two layers deep in cardboard cartons and put them in a warm, airy room for 2 weeks. Then store them, ideally at 55° F. If any are bruised or cut, use them as soon as the 2-week curing is over, or sooner.

A sweet potato well grown and correctly cured, baked in its jacket until the sweet syrup oozes, then split and served with a pat of creamery butter, is a luscious vegetable and ideal winter food, a single medium-sized sweet potato containing about 10,000 units of vitamin A.

Sweet potatoes have only a few enemies, and often none in the home garden.

Potatoes, white. There is an old saying that planting potatoes is good for the soil. Even though the potato takes a good deal of nourishment from the soil, it improves the tilth very much the way earthworms do. Another admirable quality about potatoes is a social one—children are enchanted with digging them. We have never seen it fail, and we try to keep a few potatoes growing right along to entertain visiting children. This isn't hard—since potatoes are such persistent growers, they'll often sprout from peelings accidentally dropped or from small tubers that were overlooked when digging a potato crop.

Potatoes prefer cool weather, so plant in very early spring, and again in mid-spring for a later crop. At 85° F. or higher, they won't even form tubers, though the tops will look wonderful. In our cool coastal climate we plant them the year around, but even here they do best in spring.

Though they do well in slightly acid soil, potatoes don't insist on it. A bucket of peatmoss to 10′ of row will suffice in most garden soils that are not fairly acid to begin with. The main point here is to discourage the disease called scab; however, it merely disfigures the potato skin. Certified seed potatoes are treated against scab, but you can plant potatoes you buy for food, and this is a good use for those starting to sprout. Sprouting or not, cut the potato into 3 or 4 chunky pieces, each with at least one eye. The eyes are buds from which tops and roots grow. A potato has to be 3 or 4 months old to sprout, so don't plant new potatoes.

Let the cut chunks dry for 2 or 3 days, then plant them 2″ deep in heavy soil and up to about 4″ deep in light soil. Dig compost in beforehand, and plant with the eyes or the sprouts pointing upward. We usually plant 3 or 4 chunks in hills spaced 2′ apart, but you can plant chunks at 10″ intervals in rows about 2′ apart.

Sprouts will show above ground in 3 or 4 weeks, and it takes another 2 months for early varieties to form crops—though you can steal a few young potatoes a month early by digging gently and feeling for them. They are a rare treat. If the plant produces flower buds, this is a time signal, as all tubers are set at this period, though they then develop at different rates, which is why you get various sizes of potatoes from the same plant when you harvest them.

The time to harvest is when the leaves turn yellowish. A good yield is 1½ to 2 pounds for each foot of row, but the great merit of the home-garden potato is its crisp delicacy of flavor. Some gardeners eat them raw like apples. Store your potato crop in a dark place to keep them from turning greenish.

Potato bugs (Colorado potato beetles) are the worst potato pest, and leaf hoppers and aphids can be troublesome. There are several other insects and diseases, covered in Chapter 9, that may bother a planting, especially if tomatoes are growing nearby, but a home planting is often free of serious troubles.

Pumpkins. Considering its husky looks, the pumpkin is surprisingly touchy about heat and cold. The chill of spring is too cold for them to start growing, and they refuse to thrive in a southern midsummer. Planting the seed under Hotkaps in spring is a way around the chill. Plant the seeds 1″ deep in hills, about 6 seeds to the hill, and thin later to the best three plants. This plant needs space, so make the hills 10′ apart, except for midget varieties, which can be spaced 5' or 6' between hills. A way to save space is to plant pumpkins along with corn, since pumpkins will grow in partial shade. Compost dug into the soil before seeding is a good idea, about a half-bushel per hill.

Standard-sized pumpkins need about 4 months to mature. Small Sugar is a splendid pie pumpkin, a standard that is only about 7" wide; Big Max, another standard, is huge, 100 pounds or more. Young's Beauty is a good in-between size. Two good midgets are Cinderella and Tricky Jack, the latter offering the bonus of hull-less seeds that can be eaten like nuts after drying in the oven.

Well before frost, harvest pumpkins with stems attached, let them dry in the sun for a week, then store in a cool place.

Though subject to the same troubles squash is, pumpkins are considerably more trouble-free as a rule.

Radishes. Radishes are noted for speed, producing edible roots in 3 weeks, which makes them a good choice for impatient gardeners and for children. Also, radishes will grow in most garden soils, doing best in spring and fall, and they have very few pests. The cabbage maggot is the worst, but only in certain areas. Our present area happens to be one of these, but when we are living in a more favored region we often grow a dozen varieties of radishes, including winter ones.

Spade the radish bed well, dig in about 2" of compost, and plant seed ⅛" deep in depressions made with your finger tip. Give them plenty of moisture as they grow, and a feeding of compost tea the second week of growth.

Cherry Belle and Crimson Giant are excellent red varieties, and Burpee White has long been our favorite white. A new white is All Seasons, so called because it keeps its crispness for weeks in the garden after maturing in 6 weeks. Most radishes mature in 4 or 5 weeks and should be used soon after.

Winter radishes need 8 to 10 weeks, and are seeded in summer for fall and winter use. Chinese Rose, Celestial, and Black

Spanish are the varieties usually offered. They are large compared to most other radishes, like large parsnips, and there is a round Black Spanish the size of a turnip. There are also some Oriental radishes such as the Sakurijima that are grown for winter use and that form immense roots, 15 pounds and sometimes a great deal more. You can slice winter radishes thinly into salads, or cook the roots very much as you do carrots or turnips.

As already noted, maggots are the most serious pest of radishes. For a small bed, a screen-wire cover is a control measure, to keep the maggot fly from laying the eggs that hatch into the maggots.

Rhubarb. Like horse-radish, rhubarb is a permanent resident of the garden, a perennial vegetable, so plant it to one side where it won't be in the way of seasonal work. It is supposed to prefer cool and moist summers, but it has done well for us in hot-summer climates, too. It also prefers cold winters, but again, this isn't vital. Many such imperatives are aimed at commercial plantings and can be ignored in home gardens, where a yield of less than peak performance doesn't mean financial disaster.

Nearly any good garden soil suits rhubarb, and if you prepare the bed as you would for asparagus, rhubarb will thrive. Instead of planting a row like asparagus, though, plant rhubarb in hills, about 4' apart.

You can start rhubarb from seed, but starting with roots will save you a season's time and offer a better selection. Plants from seed also vary a little from parent plants. In early spring, set the roots 4" deep, and don't harvest any stalks the first season. In the fall, and each fall thereafter, spread 2 or 3 buckets of compost over each hill, and spread a mulch of any kind in the spring. If any seed stalks form, remove them.

Every 6 to 8 years dig the planting up, cut each root into several pieces, each with a bud, and plant them as in the original planting, making a new bed in the same spot or else-where. This is because roots will crowd each other badly if allowed to stay in the same place, and production falls.

MacDonald is a good old standard variety. Others are Can-ada Red and Victoria.

Early spring is the harvest season for rhubarb, though we have harvested into June without hurting the planting. Re-move stalks at their base, with a slight twist. One caution: *Don't eat the rhubarb leaves;* they contain oxalic acid. It is all right to put them in the compost pile, though.

Rhubarb is one of those happy crops with few or no pests.

Rutabaga. This fine yellow vegetable, related to the turnip, is one of the crops to end the growing season on, and then to use during the winter right out of the garden. In the South, rutabagas are also planted in the spring, but in most other U.S. climates fall cropping is best. For this, plant the seed in July or August to allow the roots to mature before hard frost. They will need about 3 months.

Sow seeds ¼″ deep, spacing plants 3″ apart in rows 18″ apart. Work 4″ of compost into the soil beforehand. In gen-eral, you grow rutabagas the way you grow beets.

American Purple Top is the variety most often found. Lau-rentian is also good and is popular in Canada, where rutabagas are much grown, and there are some white-fleshed rutabagas, such as Macomber and White Swede.

By mulching the planting at the onset of cold weather, you can dig rutabagas all winter as you need them. Or dig them in the fall and store them like potatoes, in a cool place where they won't freeze.

Rutabagas are sometimes bothered by such cabbage pests as aphids and maggots.

Salsify. This root crop, looking like slender parsnips, has a most agreeable flavor, tasting so like oysters that it is com-monly called the oyster plant. Although it is a beautiful plant, it is not much grown, and more home gardeners ought to try it. Salsify is one of the older plants, known for about 2,000 years, and native to the Mediterranean area.

Culture of salsify is the same as for parsnips, and it needs as long to grow—about 4 months. You can also let salsify roots stay in the garden all winter where they grew, with just a little protective mulch, digging them as needed.

Sandwich Island Mammoth is the one variety of salsify we find offered. The plants called black salsify and Spanish salsify are not related to the oyster plant salsify.

No pests to speak of will bother salsify.

Squash, summer. A summer squash is a marvelously attractive plant with its spreading leaves and such magnificent golden flowers that one day an artist friend brought her easel to our garden and painted our zucchini's portrait. We first tasted zucchini during a potato famine in New York City years ago, when a frantic French restaurant chef served it as a substitute, and we have liked it ever since. It grows splendidly in our present cool-weather climate, but in the hot Midwest it was surpassed by cocozelle, which is also a good squash, a kind of less-refined zucchini. Yellow crookneck has always been our favorite, however, and it too prefers a warm summer. Other popular summer squashes are yellow straightneck and scallop, also called patty pan. A new patty pan is a little greenish fellow called St. Pat. Our favorite zucchini is Burpee Hybrid, a compact bush type, but there are various other good ones. Most summer squashes start bearing in 7 or 8 weeks, and go on producing all the rest of the season till frost flattens them.

You plant and care for summer squash the same way you do cucumbers.

You are usually advised to harvest summer squash when it is young. Though this is good advice, we find that if you keep the plant growing smartly along, even large fruits are buttery and good, and without objectionably firm seeds. Once in a while a zucchini hiding under a leaf grows to a whopping 2 pounds or more, and is still tender.

A single ambitious zucchini plant may produce about 3 dozen fruits, so if you find yourself swamped by the harvest you might try drying some. We did, intending to use them in soups and casseroles later on, and then found them nice for snacks, like potato chips. Here is the recipe we worked out:

Cut the zucchinis into slices ⅛″ thick. Lay the slices separately on a cooky sheet you have covered with paper towels and then waxed paper. Put into a 150° F. oven and dry for 2–3 hours. Turn slices, reduce heat to 140° F. and continue drying for about 3 more hours, till slices are as crisp as potato chips. Store in a closed container such as a coffee can.

Summer squash is subject to several of the same pests that trouble cucumbers. See Chapter 9 for control measures.

Squash, winter. Though winter squash is kissing cousin to summer squash, they are like different vegetables, and you can even make a pie out of a winter squash that tastes like pumpkin pie would if it could. All winter squashes have hard shells and store well.

We have always liked Hubbard squash, and we grow it when we have a large garden in a warm climate; hills must be spaced about 8′ apart. The smaller fruited Butternut and Buttercup, weighing up to 5 pounds compared with the Hubbard's 15 pounds or so, are excellent for a smaller garden; so are Acorn and Table Queen, though we prefer the others. If you have only a little space for winter squash, say a spot 3′ by 3′, try one of the midgets. Kindred and Gold Nugget are widely listed and were All-America Award winners.

Winter squash take the same care as cucumbers and summer spaced about 8′ apart. The smaller fruited Butternut and Butfruits standards needing nearly 3 months, and the large-fruited ones 4 months or a little less. So figure backward from your first fall average frost date when you seed winter squash, as they should be harvested before frost, and must be fully matured.

Harvest winter squash with a stub of stem attached, dry them in the sun for a few days, then store them in a cool, dry place where they won't freeze. Despite their hard shells, they must be handled with care so they won't be bruised, and they will then keep all winter. A single cupful of cooked winter squash has 6,500 units of vitamin A, just what a winter diet needs.

Winter squash, like summer squash, is subject to many of the pests that attack cucumbers. Chapter 9 covers control measures.

Swiss chard. (See Leafy greens.)

Tomatoes. Seedsmen say that the tomato is the most popular home-garden vegetable, and it certainly is adaptable about climate. We even manage to grow tomatoes in the cool coastal climate of central California, though it takes some doing (the sunniest spot, reflected heat from a wall, and patience). There are a great many types of tomatoes, varying in size, shape, taste, color, and in plant size. Every seed house carries a selection of tomatoes, and some carry dozens of varieties.

Hybrid tomatoes have made big strides in the past several years, and many home gardeners plant no others. However, a non-hybrid (open-pollinated) variety may be a better choice for some. We've had hybrids outclassed by Marglobe, Rutgers, and some other good old kinds, and we recommend our own practice, which is to try some new varieties, hybrids and others, every year or so, along with proven varieties. Different climates have different effects on the same variety, too, and we have found we had to drop certain favorites when we tried them in other climates.

Start seeds of tomatoes indoors, 6 to 10 weeks before your weather is due to warm up in spring—and by seeding your own tomatoes, you get a great choice of varieties. We have often rushed the season by moving little plants to the garden, protected by Hotkaps, 3 or 4 weeks after seeding indoors. When transplanting tomatoes, set the plants deeply, up to the lowest leaves. Space plants 2′ to 4′ apart, depending on the growth habit of the variety, and such smaller midgets as Tiny Tim can be spaced only 12″ apart. Choose a sunny, well-drained spot for tomatoes and dig in half a bucket of compost for each plant. This, along with a compost mulch, will usually take care of fertilizing needs in good garden soil.

If you stake tomatoes, which we do for neater looks and clean fruit, set the stakes at the time of transplanting. You can use old nylon stockings for tying plants to the stakes.

Tomatoes are noted for wanting warm nights in order to set fruits, though we have found they vary by variety on this score.

To keep a strong-growing plant from doing more growing than fruiting, pinch out the tips of side shoots that sprout in the axils of the branches. These sprouts are called suckers, and

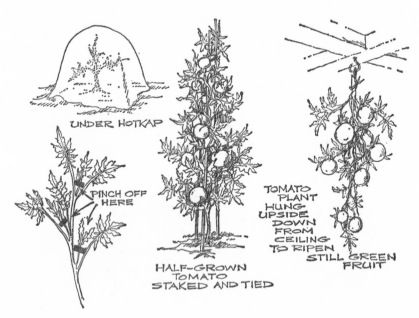

UNDER HOTKAP

PINCH OFF HERE

HALF-GROWN TOMATO STAKED AND TIED

TOMATO PLANT HUNG UPSIDE DOWN FROM CEILING TO RIPEN STILL GREEN FRUIT pinching their tips off lets them stay alive but keeps them from growing as large as they otherwise would. Their leaves are helpful to the plant and also protect fruits from the sun. The only exception here is in cool-summer regions, where sunlight on fruit hurries ripening.

When the first fall frost is expected, gather the sizable green tomatoes still on the vines, and bring them indoors to ripen. A dark place at about 65° F. is ideal. An old stone-walled cellar in our farmhouse turned out to be almost exactly right for this, and all through the late fall almost to Christmas we had wide board shelves studded with scores of greenish-yellow tomatoes placidly turning red. Another way is to pull up whole plants and hang them upside down, tomatoes attached.

You can also cook green tomatoes for that country treat, green fried tomatoes: Slice them, dust with flour, and fry in butter or bacon drippings.

Resistant plants are the best protection against tomato diseases, mainly wilts. A number of insects attack tomatoes, and control measures are given in Chapter 9.

Turnips. Turnips are a virtual essential to the flavor of a stew, and the tops are nutritious, high in vitamin A. Young turnips, right out of the garden after being quickly grown, are so delicate and distinctive you can hardly recognize them as the same vegetable you usually see offered in the markets.

Though turnips do best in the fall, they are also grown in spring, and in winter, too, in the South. Make the spring sowing as early as the soil can be worked, and sow the fall crop in midsummer, 3 months before frost is due.

You grow turnips practically the same way as you grow beets.

Tokyo Cross and Just Right are new and fast varieties, said to grow usable roots in about 6 weeks. They haven't been that speedy for us, but may well be in some other parts of the country. A good old standard variety is Purple-top White Globe, and a good one for growing lots of leaves is Shogoin.

There are also some yellow-fleshed turnips, the only one usually listed being Golden Ball, also called Orange Jelly. Nichols lists a black-skinned turnip from France, Longue de Caluire, and also recommends a huge one, grown for livestock fodder, as good enough for the table. It is Gros Longue d'Alsace.

Maggots sometimes bother turnips, and they may have some other troubles of the cabbage group, to which they are related.

Witloof chicory. (See Belgian endive.)

11

How to Grow Your Own Organic Fruits and Nuts

ONE OF THE FIRST THINGS we did when we settled on our farm in Missouri was to plant fruit trees on an acre sloping gently to a little lake. We studded the acre with apple, peach, pear, and plum trees. In the vegetable garden we planted raspberries and strawberries. And the farm already had an apple tree, two cherry trees, three Damson plum trees, two native plum trees, six or eight seedling peach and nectarine trees, and acres of blackberries. Seems like a lot of fruit for two persons, doesn't it? Well, it was. So we didn't really need to plant more fruit, but we did it anyway because there is something about fruit trees.

A fruit tree is such a generous tree, a shimmering bouquet of blossoms, a very bride of a tree each spring; then the bestower of peaceful shade in summer, and a haven for songbirds; and as if that isn't enough and more, this lovely sturdy plant then heaps you, lap and larder, with juicy delights in reckless abundance.

You have an excellent selection in sizes of plants, among the fruits you might grow. Tree fruits are borne on dwarf trees, semidwarf trees, and standard-size trees. Grapes grow on fencelike structures, arbors, or on buildings. The berry fruits are borne mostly on bushes up to about 6′ high, and the delectable strawberry forms a neat little mound up to 8″ high and 12″ wide.

With the exceptions of the far South, far North, and some parts of the West Coast, all the fruits mentioned in this chapter will grow in American home gardens, given a reasonably good site and reasonably good care. Fruit trees are not nearly as demanding as many people think, and a fruit garden takes much less attention than does a vegetable garden. And speaking of care, we suggest you seriously consider dwarf trees whenever they are available since they are much easier to look after than standards or even semidwarfs. Today's dwarf trees are also good bearers for the most part, and some carry astoundingly large crops—the spur-type apple trees, for instance, also called double-dwarfs, yielding up to 200 or 300 pounds of apples *per tree* each season. Such a tree may be only 8′ high, more or less, compared to 25′ or more for a standard apple tree. Many commercial fruit growers today are, in fact, switching to dwarfs, they are so easy on labor and so high-yielding.

Planting. In general, dwarf trees can be planted 10′ apart. This measurement is between trunks, so you could plant a little 6-tree orchard on a piece of ground 20′ by 30′, which is close to the space a 2-car garage would occupy. Planted to dwarf apples and pears, this mini-orchard could give you 500 pounds of fruit a year and possibly a great deal more. At today's prices—even if you could buy fruit as good and naturally grown—this can top $100 with no trouble at all.

Spring planting is most usual, though fall planting is feasible in mild-winter climates. Choose a site that gets 6 hours or more of sun a day. A gentle slope is an advantage, giving better drainage and air circulation.

Garden soil is good for fruit trees and other fruit plants, but as a substitute, if necessary, fill the planting hole with compost and soil mixed half and half. The hole should be deep enough and wide enough to let the roots spread out. Plant the tree at the same level it was growing (the part of the trunk that had been underground will be darker), and firm the earth well, adding a bucket of compost tea at the halfway mark in the filling. If your site is windy, tie the tree to a stake at this time. Also, protect the trunk from rodent bark-eaters with a hardware cloth cylinder 5″ in diameter and long enough to go 4″ underground and 12″ or more up the trunk.

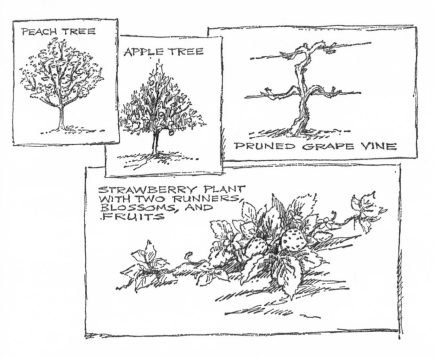

Pruning. Peach, nectarine, and apricot trees are usually grown in the vase shape, to open the top of the tree to sunlight, and the 3 or 4 main limbs curve upward from close to the same height on the trunk. At planting time, select these limbs-to-be, prune each to two buds, prune the top of the trunk back to 2″ above the highest of the other limbs you are keeping, and remove all other branches. After peaches and nectarines come into bearing, annual pruning consists of cutting back about half of the new wood on the end of each shoot, this being the wood that will bear that season's fruit. Apricots bear fruit on spurs that persist for about 3 years, so merely cut out any dead wood and keep the tree open to sunlight.

Apple, pear, cherry, and plum trees do well when grown in the pyramid shape of a Christmas tree. At planting time, select for keeping permanently from 3 to 5 limbs that are fairly evenly spaced from each other up and down the trunk and around it. Prune them to about 10″ long, prune the top of the trunk to 12″ above the highest of these, and remove other limbs. After these trees come into bearing, merely prune away any dead or poorly placed limbs; too little pruning is better than too much, and apple, pear, cherry, and plum trees all bear fruit on long-lived spurs—so that you can drastically reduce the crop by overpruning.

Grapes are pruned to two canes when planted, each with two buds. After growth starts, the weaker of the two canes is removed. The one left is the vine's future trunk, and is tied at this time to whatever support the vine is to grow on. As this trunk grows upward, canes sprout from it, to form the framework of the plant. Yearly pruning thereafter is done in very early spring or late winter. It consists of retaining only 4 to 6 canes of the previous season's growth, plus a 2-bud stub of a cane near each of these. The purpose of the stubs is to grow canes for the grapes to be borne the season after that, and the purpose of the 4 to 6 canes is to bear the current season's grapes. For, like peach trees, grapes bear their fruit on wood that grew the previous year.

Feeding. If you mulch your fruit trees, the mulch will usually supply any nutrients they need in addition to what they forage for in the soil and receive from snow and rain. If you want to feed them anyway, nitrogen is the only element they'll be interested in. You could give a young tree 1 pound of blood meal, putting it into half a dozen holes poked into the ground with a crowbar around the tree a little farther from the trunk than the branches reach. A mature tree could take 20 pounds. But unless it is looking unthrifty, you may be pleasing yourself more than the tree by feeding it.

Grapes and berry fruits are also light feeders (or good foragers, to put it another way), and mulching them with compost is usually sufficient feeding. Strawberries, however, respond to a feeding after their fruiting period is over. Give them 1 pound of cottonseed meal per 5' of row. Do this in August for June-bearing strawberries and after the early crop is harvested, in the case of everbearers.

Pollination. The fruits that usually need another variety nearby in order to have their blossoms pollinated so they can set fruit, are apples, pears, sweet cherries, and plums. There are a few exceptions but you'll be well advised to plan on planting two different varieties of any of these four fruits, unless a nearby neighbor is already growing another variety. Nursery catalogues usually mention pollination needs under each listing. We note pollination needs below, under each fruit.

Pests. If you don't live near a commercial fruit-growing area, you may have few pests and no serious ones. The chances are, you'll have some, though, and for handling these, see the lists of pests and controls, at the end of Chapter 9.

APPLES

The apple, most popular and versatile fruit, is available in a great number of varieties, some of them centuries old and others so new they were unheard of until they appeared a few years ago as a seedling (a tree grown from a seed), or a bud sport (a mutation that shows up on a tree as a branch bearing noticeably different-looking or different-tasting fruit from that on the other branches).

Jonathan is a splendid early fall or late summer apple, and there are several new hybrids with Jonathan blood in them, the Jonalicious being one reminiscent of England's Cox's Orange Pippin. The most widely grown apple in the U.S. is Red Delicious, but our own preference is for a more tart apple such as the superb white-fleshed McIntosh, the Winesap, or the Golden Delicious—which is also one of the few apples that will set fruit without the help of another variety.

Most apple trees need some cold weather to break their dormant period, though fog serves this purpose in some areas. If your winters don't get as cold as 10° F., ask your county agent which, if any, varieties of apples you might plant.

PEARS

Duchess is a good pear and one of the very few that is self-pollinating. It will also pollinate most others. Comice and Seckel are famous pears, Bartlett is probably the best-known one, and two quite new and blight-resistant varieties from the U. S. Department of Agriculture are Moonglow and Magness. Kieffer is a rugged old pear that connoisseurs belittle, but it grows in areas other pears die in—and when properly ripened it is a pretty good pear, too. We grew a Kieffer-type pear on the Mississippi Gulf Coast where no other pear would grow, and were happy to have it.

Proper ripening, by the way, is a must with almost all pears. Few pears ripen well on the tree. Here is how you ripen them: Tilt a pear upward when it is still hard to the touch, and if it comes off easily in your hand, the crop is ready to pick. Wrap each pear in a paper towel and put them in a cool room to ripen. This takes from a day or two to several weeks, depending on the variety. Once ripe, you can keep them longer by storing in the refrigerator in plastic bags.

Peaches and Nectarines

Botanically, peaches and nectarines are so alike (in fact, the same species, *Prunus persica*) that if you plant a seed of one, it may grow into a tree bearing the other. This had happened on our farm, a previous owner having planted a lot of peach seeds that grew into trees bearing small but sweet and luscious fruit—either nectarines or peaches.

Elberta is the most famous peach; Bonanza is new and so dwarfed it will grow in a tub; Belle of Georgia is a good old late variety. Most peaches and nectarines are self-pollinating, so that a tree planted alone will set fruit.

Apricots

You can use an apricot tree as an ornamental, it is so pretty, and also get fruit with only one tree as most apricots are self-pollinating. Moorpark is a good variety that originated in England, and Hungarian Rose is one of the best.

Apricots take about the same care as peaches and have fewer pests, but the fruit needs to be thinned drastically in order to develop good size, and also so as not to exhaust the tree and cause it to bear only every other year instead of annually.

Cherries

Sour cherries are smaller trees than sweet cherries, and are easier to grow, less particular as to climate, and are all self-pollinated. Also, though called sour, they actually are merely tart, and some such as Montmorency are sweet enough to eat fresh, and of course are famous for use in pies, preserves, and ice cream toppings. A good new dwarf sour cherry is North Star.

Sweet cherries are not happy in very hot summers. They also prefer milder winter climates than sour cherries will grow in. Nearly all sweet cherries need not only cross-pollination, but some particular variety or varieties to pollinate them, so check this point carefully when ordering nursery stock. Van is a good sweet cherry, and it is also a good pollinator for the excellent Lambert and Bing.

PLUMS

Although some European plums are self-pollinating (Damson, for instance, and also Green Gage and Stanley), plums in general are very choosy on this point, so check it when ordering nursery stock. Prunes, by the way, are also plums—plums sweet enough to be dried if wished.

There are a number of native American plums bearing small red or yellow fruits, often found growing wild, but some being quite worth cultivating. The third great class of plums is the Japanese, which cannot take very cold winters. Two good ones are Santa Rosa and Redheart, and they also pollinate each other.

STRAWBERRIES

New strawberry varieties come on the market every year, giving you a chance to sample around. This has another advantage: A strawberry plant should be retired after from 1 to 3 fruiting seasons, giving you room for new ones. The reason for not keeping plants is that older ones bear fewer berries and are prey to diseases.

The replacements can be new plants from nurseries, or runners that old plants have set. A runner is a stem that grows out along the ground and takes root, forming a new plant. These new plants can be allowed to grow where they root, or can be transplanted. We seldom let a plant set more than 1 or 2 runners, however, as setting runners reduces a plant's crop of berries. You control this by chopping off surplus runners as they appear.

A June-bearing strawberry has its crop during a short period, about 2 weeks—usually during June. An everbearing strawberry spreads the crop from spring to fall. Both yield about the same amount of berries. The best berries are those from June-bearers, though there are some good everbearers, Ozark Beauty and Geneva being two. Among the June-bearers, Surecrop is new and dependable under even poor growing conditions, Dunlap is a good old one, and two excellent varieties are Suwannee and Fairfax.

Nearly all strawberries are self-pollinating.

When planting, be sure that the crown—the solid part between roots and top—is neither buried nor sticking up into the air. Set the crown's "waist" just at ground level.

White grubs and leaf rollers may attack strawberries, though a planting will often have no insect problems at all. Aphids transmit a virus disease, but the best control here is to buy plants sold as virus-free. Fungus diseases are best controlled by discarding plants after 2 to 3 years of bearing.

RASPBERRIES

The raspberry is a delicious small fruit, easy to care for and with a fairly long life, about 10 years. Since each plant will grow new plants every season, once you plant raspberries you have them from then on.

The best-known raspberries are the red ones and the black ones, but there are also purple (hybrids of red and black), and yellow kinds (mutations of reds). There are both summer-bearers and everbearers in each color. Good red raspberries are Canby and Latham, and Indian Summer has been an excellent everbearing red with us. Black Hawk is a good black one, Sodus a good purple, and Fall Gold an everbearing yellow.

Raspberries do well over a wide area of the central and northeast U.S. Though not as happy where summers are hot and dry or where winters are severe, they cheerfully accepted temperatures over 100° F. in summer and down to 12 below zero in winter in Missouri for us.

Red and yellow raspberries usually have strong, fairly erect canes with few side branches (laterals). Black and purple raspberries are more arching, and their many laterals are the fruit-bearing wood.

Spring planting is usual. Choose a fairly sunny, well-drained site where tomatoes, peppers, potatoes, or eggplants have not been recently grown, to prevent transmission of any verticillium wilt. Space plants about 5' apart, working a bucketful of compost into each planting spot and spading the earth well. After planting, cut off all but 2" of the plants' tops.

Mulch the plants in summer, and each summer thereafter, with compost—for both fertilizing and for moisture retention. They like at least as much water as the vegetable garden, 1" of rain or the equivalent each week.

Raspberries are self-pollinating.

Canes are often tied to posts or to wires run between posts, but no supports are needed if plants are kept low by pruning to the heights we specify below for spring pruning. Prune raspberries this way:

Black and purple summer-bearers. In early spring remove weak canes at ground level. Those canes that you retain should be spaced 4" to 6" apart. Cut the laterals on these to 10" in length.

All summer, pinch off the tips of new shoots of blacks

when the shoots are 24″ tall, and pinch off the tips of new shoots of purples when the shoots are 30″ to 36″ tall. This pinching makes plants growthy and sturdy.

After harvesting the crop, cut off at ground level all the canes that have borne berries; these are the 2-year-old canes, and they are now through. Dispose of them by burning, a sanitary measure against raspberry diseases.

Red and yellow summer-bearers. In early spring, remove weak canes at ground level. Those canes that you retain should be spaced 4″ to 6″ apart. Prune these retained canes to a height of 36″ to 48″.

During the summer, *do not prune at all.*

After harvesting the crop, cut off at ground level all the canes that have borne berries and burn them.

All everbearers. Prune everbearing raspberries exactly as you prune summer-bearers of the same color—except after the *fall* harvest. This is because the fall harvest of an everbearing raspberry is borne on the outer end of the cane in each case, and there will be a crop the next summer on the rest of this same cane. Therefore, do not remove these canes after the fall harvest. Wait until they have borne their *summer* crop the following year, then remove them at ground level and burn them.

Raspberries have few insect pests. They are subject to some diseases, the controls for which are the sanitation measures we have suggested, plus using resistant varieties from reliable nurseries, keeping weeds down, and promptly removing and burning any sickly canes or plants.

BLACKBERRIES

The blackberry—a really luscious fruit when picked at its full-ripe perfection—takes the same care as do black raspberries, with these minor exceptions:

During spring pruning, leave longer laterals—about 15″.

In summer, pinch tips of new shoots when the shoots are about 36″ tall. Blackberries are strong growers, so keep new shoots to a spacing not much closer than 6″ apart.

Good blackberry varieties are El Dorado and Darrow. Thornless and Smoothstem are fairly recent U. S. Department of Agriculture developments without thorns.

All blackberries are self-pollinating. The crop ripens in midsummer, the time depending on variety and climate. Our Missouri blackberries ripened in July.

Pest problems and controls with blackberries are the same as with raspberries.

ELDERBERRIES

Elderberries are the fruits of the tall (to 10′ or higher) and attractive white-flowered shrub known as the elder, botanically of the *Sambucus* genus. The berries are small, deep purple and juicy, have small seeds, and are more used for making jam and wine than for eating fresh. They ripen in late summer.

Wild elderberries grow on vacant land and in hedgerows in most states and in Canada, favoring rich soil and moist spots, even partly shaded ones. Cultivated species prefer the same conditions—both are hardy and able to take a good deal of cold weather. Both kinds can be propagated by planting the freely produced suckers, or from cuttings.

The varieties usually offered by nurseries are Adams, Johns, and York. Plant any two varieties for proper pollination.

The elderberry has no serious pests.

FIGS

Our fig trees in the South topped off at 12′ to 15′ and were ornamental and productive, ripening two or more crops during the summer. Most commercial production is in southern California and along the Texas Gulf Coast, but figs do pretty well in many home plantings elsewhere.

A good standard-sized variety for eating fresh is Turkey. We preferred it to Celeste, though both are good. Several mail-order nurseries offer dwarf varieties that may grow no taller than 2'. You can plant these in tubs and move them indoors before frost, to encourage the fruit to ripen. The fig plant itself is fairly winter-hardy, taking cold spells down to about 0° F. with a protective wrapping of straw or sacking. If frozen, cut it back to ground level and a new top is quite apt to sprout. New plants can be grown from 8" stem cuttings taken in the fall and planted deeply, with only the tip showing.

Most home-garden figs are self-pollinating.

All figs are heavy feeders if given the chance, and will welcome compost as a mulch.

Figs are subject to several diseases, though they are often never attacked. If they are, the practical control is to prune off and burn any affected parts—leaves, wood, or fruit. Borers, mites, and scales may cause occasional trouble. See the list at the end of Chapter 9.

GOOSEBERRIES

Those who like gooseberries are often mad about them, and in parts of England it amounts to a mania. The English climate also suits the plant, and the most successful U.S. growing regions are the Great Lakes area and both Northeastern and Northwestern coastal sections. However, we've known them to grow well for home gardeners in hot-summer climates, too.

Plant gooseberries in the spring, in a shady, moist place, spacing the bushes about 8' apart. If your soil isn't rich, work a bushel of good compost into the planting spot and mulch with more compost after growth gets well under way.

Gooseberries are self-pollinating.

Pruning during the first few years should be light, and should be done in early spring. Remove canes after they are three years old, when they will have finished productive fruiting, and also cut out any weak young canes. Prune the bush as a whole to an open-top, vase shape, with about a dozen branches, divided evenly among 1-year, 2-year, and 3-year wood.

Plants last 15 or 20 years, grow to 4' or 5' high, and produce large crops under good conditions. The berries are ripe in June or July, when they change from green in color to yellowish, lavender, red, or pinkish, depending on variety and growing conditions. The varieties most offered for home-garden planting are Welcome, a University of Minnesota development, and Pixwell, said to be less thorny than most others.

Insects are seldom serious pests in home plantings. See the list of pest controls at the end of Chapter 9. Check diseases by promptly removing and burning any affected wood. Because gooseberries harbor a fungus—blister rust—that attacks white pines, they should not be planted where white pines grow.

CURRANTS

Currants are an attractive fruit and take the same general culture as gooseberries, which they also resemble in plant habit. They are prized for jellies, preserves, and pies. The dried fruits called currants and looking like little raisins, really *are* raisins, by the way, not currants at all.

There are white, black, and red currants, the reds being

the ones most nurseries offer. Wilder, Perfection, and Red Lake are the varieties usually available.

If you plant a currant bush in the fall, you may get some fruit the following summer, as they bear on 1-year canes as well as on those 2 and 3 years old.

Currants have much the same pests as gooseberries. Also like gooseberries, currants are host to the blister rust that attacks white pines, so should not be planted where white pines grow.

GRAPES

Most home-garden grapes have been of the American species, *Vitis labrusca*, with the exception of the South, where muscadine grapes, *Vitis rotundifolia*, are grown, and the West Coast, where European grapes, *Vitis vinifera*, thrive. Today, however, a number of good European-American hybrid grapes are available, and will flourish where most American species do—in some cases will even do well in the South.

Some good American varieties are Beta, a blue grape that can take cold winters; the more tender Catawba, a high-quality red grape; and the enormously popular Concord, blue, all-purpose, and hardy. Two well-known and good muscadines are Scuppernong, a white grape; and the blue-black James. Good European-American hybrids are the large-bunched and all-purpose Golden Muscat; and Himrod, a seedless yellow grape that thrives in most of the South and also does well where most American grapes grow.

Grapes will grow up an arbor, a porch, a shed, or almost any convenient structure, but for best production grow them on two wires stretched between posts 10′ apart, the bottom wire being 2½′ above ground level, and the top wire 5′ above the ground.

One of the nice things about a grapevine is its long life, lasting over several decades. It also needs little feeding; a compost mulch often sufficing. Normal harvest from a healthy vine is 30 to 50 bunches a season, and an old one can have hundreds. Most varieties of grapes are self-pollinating.

Birds may be a nuisance, insisting on harvesting the grape crop before you can. For a small planting, encasing each bunch of grapes in a paper bag which is then tied loosely around the stem of the bunch is a defense. For a larger planting, a better tactic is the use of netting spread over the entire planting. A plastic netting for this purpose is carried by some garden supply stores and some seed houses and nurseries.

Pests often don't bother grapes at all. Possible troubles and controls for them are covered in the lists at the end of Chapter 9.

Growing Nuts

If you live in the country, or at any rate not in a city, you may be able to supply yourself with nuts from native trees. This was the way we got hickory nuts and black walnuts in Missouri, and hazelnuts grew wild there, too. But if you must plant your own nut trees, you have a good chance to choose among English and black walnuts, pecans, hazelnuts, almonds, butternuts, hickory nuts, and chestnuts. And we include peanuts, too.

You can get varieties of all these nuts that will grow in most parts of the country. A good deal of work on climate tolerance has been done in recent years, particularly with English walnuts, almonds, and pecans.

In our eyes, one of the most important things to know about a nut tree, once you know it will grow well in your climate, is: How big is it going to grow? This is especially true in the case of pecans, black walnuts, hickory nuts, and butternuts. All grow to about 100' or taller. This can be awkward if you plant one on a lawn where anything growing taller than 30' will cut the sun off from other plants. And since the leaves of nut trees are very staining to walks and painted surfaces, a nut tree near the house can become a problem. We once lived with a cluster of black walnut trees too near the house, and another problem was the dropping of the nuts, encased in husks, on lawn furniture and occasionally on us.

But, once you have planted any of these tall nut trees, or other ones, where you and they can be comfortable, you have got yourself a lifetime bounty of some of the best food on earth, and some of the most nutritious, too, rich in energy, perfect companions at table with fruits, which are high in vitamins. As to harvests, a mature paper-shell pecan tree can supply you with 50 to 100 pounds of nuts each season, a hickory tree or an English walnut tree can provide 200 pounds or more, and a black walnut can go much higher, well over 1,000 pounds, with the other species varying between perhaps 25 to 100 pounds.

Nut trees take but little care, and are still agreeable about bearing an annual crop. They don't even insist on as good a site as a fruit tree wants—though it seems only fair to give these willing providers as good a break on sunlight and on air circulation as you can manage.

Planting. Nut trees are planted exactly as fruit trees are. The main differences in the nursery stock are two: A young nut tree is usually a single, unbranched stem, called a whip; and there is often a long tap root. Be sure to dig the hole deep enough to accommodate the tap root without kinking.

Pruning. At planting time, remove the top third of the young tree. This is to encourage branching.

The pyramid form, as with apples, is standard for all nut trees except hazelnuts, which are grown in the vase shape, like peaches. Pruning directions are given in the previous part of this chapter dealing with fruits.

After tall-growing nut trees have been growing for 2 or 3 years, prune off any lower limbs that are not at least 6' above ground level. This is to make harvesting the nuts easier in future years.

Feeding. Fertilize nut trees the same way you do fruit trees. In other words, very little fertilizing is needed under most growing conditions.

Pollination. Nut trees are seldom a pollination problem. Where exceptions occur, we note them under the kinds of trees involved.

Pests. Though nut trees are not always free of diseases, it is a rare home-garden nut tree that needs, or gets, any attention. In fact, the most practical treatment consists of good sanitation, and good growth resulting from a favorable location. This is fortunate since the size of many nut trees makes it impossible for a home gardener to combat disease effectively. For those problems that can be coped with if they occur, see the list of pests and controls at the end of Chapter 9.

Almonds

If you live where peaches do well, you may be able to grow almonds, using one of the new hardy varieties such as Hall's, listed by Burpee and Gurney. Almond trees grow to 20' or so, are lovely in flower—and vulnerable to late-spring frosts. Pollination is critical, and you'll probably need two or more almond trees, so check this point with the supplier when ordering.

Harvest almonds when the husks start to split, shaking the limbs to bring the nuts down, then husking them by hand.

BUTTERNUTS

Often called the white walnut, the butternut grows like a black walnut into a big spreading tree, bears early and lives long. You hardly ever see these nuts on the market, but they are good both fresh and for cooking. They are rich, spicy, and high in oil content.

CHESTNUTS

These are Chinese chestnuts, resistant to the blight that wiped out the magnificent native chestnuts years ago. Chinese chestnuts grow to the size of fairly large standard apple trees. Avoid planting them on poorly drained sites.

HAZELNUTS

You'll need two hazelnut trees for pollination, sometimes of different varieties, so check this with your supplier. The plant is more bush than tree, growing from 5' to 8' tall, so they accommodate themselves to small space. Hazelnuts are also called filberts.

HICKORY NUTS

Though an excellent nut, the hickory nut is not widely grown, and nursery stock may be hard to find. Field, Gurney, and Stark's handle them. Pamper the young trees a little, staking and mulching them, and they will grow into 100' giants.

PEANUTS

Peanuts are the fastest nut crop you can grow. The plant is a garden annual, a small bush a foot high and about as wide. You'll need 4 months of warm weather, and though commercial production is largely in the South, peanuts are grown in home gardens even in Canada by using sandy soil (quick to warm up in the spring), and planting along the south side of a solid fence or a wall. Nearly every seed house handles peanuts.

Harvest the crop just before the first fall frost by digging plants up whole, shaking earth from the peanuts, which grow underground, and hanging the plants for 3 weeks in an airy but protected place. Then pull the peanuts off and let them cure for another 2 or 3 weeks indoors in a cardboard carton.

Roast only as many as you need at one time, in a shallow uncovered baking pan, for 20 to 25 minutes in a 300° F. to 325° F. oven. They are done when the shell is brittle and the inner skin flakes off, when they are an epicurean triumph.

PECANS

You can now get paper-shell pecan trees that will grow a crop in the North because they mature faster than Southern varieties. One of these new varieties is Colby, and you'll find others listed by nurseries. You will get a larger crop from each by planting two trees, though it isn't a pollination necessity.

WALNUTS

Both black and English walnuts are offered as nursery stock, and there are several good varieties of each. The news in

English walnuts is something called the Carpathian, a variety that was found growing in the cold mountain country of Poland a few years ago. It will thrive in cold-winter areas here, too, so that today a great many people who never could hope to raise English walnuts before, now can. The Carpathians are also agreeably smaller than the usual English walnut tree, topping off at 40′ to 50′. The Lake is a widely sold strain of Carpathian.

12

How to Have Your Own Fresh Vegetables in Winter

WE HAVE DONE a good deal of our gardening in the Midwest and the East, where the outdoor growing season closed down for about six months, from some time in October till some time the next April. If we wanted our own fresh vegetables during this stretch, we had to do some unorthodox gardening. Most gardeners are springtime or summertime gardeners, but if you'd like to try winter gardening, you will find it isn't a fraction of summertime gardening's work, and carries a fine flourish of accomplishment all its own. Also, it is *freshly picked* organic vegetables that are richest in the vitamins needed to contend with winter's health hazards.

We went about getting fresh wintertime vegetables (1) by protecting vegetables growing outdoors; and (2) by growing new vegetables in the winter.

PROTECTING VEGETABLES GROWING OUTDOORS

We did this in two ways. Some vegetables were allowed to stay in the open where they were growing. Others were enclosed in coldframes.

In the open garden. Vegetables that were left where they were growing, we protected with a blanket of straw or leaves. In effect, this was a mulch. Where wind is a problem, some earth on top of such a covering will anchor it. We put this protection on the less hardy plants before the first freeze. Part of the reason for this protection was to keep tender vegetables from exposure to sunlight, as they could have frozen a little despite the protection, and sunlight would have thawed them too quickly.

All these plants that were left in the garden had to be seeded long enough beforehand to be past their youth when the cold weather came. This was both for their good and ours; we got plants big enough to amount to something, and they had arrived at an age when they could take more cold than young plants could. In the following list of vegetables that can be protected outdoors we suggest planting dates that should bring them to a good stage of growth by mid-October; this dating is based on the general weather pattern of the country's midsection. In colder areas allow from 2 to 4 more weeks. In all cases, keep these crops growing along smartly.

Parsnips, salsify, and root parsley. All are hardy and need only light covering, mainly to keep the earth from freezing so hard you can't dig them. Sow each in early May.

Turnips and rutabagas. Both will take a good deal of cold, especially rutabagas. Sow both from mid-July to mid-August and thin to 6″ apart.

Beets and carrots. Both are hardy and need only light covering. Sow seed in mid-July to mid-August.

Celeriac. It stands cold better than its cousin celery, but give it a long time to grow, seeding in mid-May and transplanting to 12″ apart.

Jerusalem artichokes and horse-radish. Both these perennials form roots that can be dug all winter. Both would survive without protection, but giving them some will keep the earth from freezing so iron-hard that you can't dig any roots. Horse-radish roots must be freshly dug to be their best, so dig them during the winter as needed.

Winter radish. This is an interesting vegetable for a change in winter. It can be sliced thinly into salads raw or cooked like a carrot. Sow seed early in August and thin to 6" apart. Give the plants moderate covering for winter.

Leeks. An ideal winter vegetable that needs little or no protection. Leeks are slow growers, so seed them in June in rich soil and thin to 6" apart.

Kale, collards, and Brussels sprouts. These are the best bets among the cabbage group for the winter garden. Even without any protection they can take short spells of as low as 10 degrees below zero. Kale, in fact, gains in flavor from this. Brussels sprouts are the slowest growers of the three, so seed them early in June and give them room—about 3' apart. Seed kale and collards in late July and thin to 12" apart, or 8" for dwarf kale.

Spinach. Sown in late August and given winter protection, spinach is a willing keeper in the garden. In colder areas give it a foot-deep straw mulch.

Chard. Though a little awkward to protect when tall, chard will reward you for the care. Seed it in July 8" apart.

In the coldframe. This was a two-way punch, as we ran two winter coldframes in different ways.

One was a growing-frame. The idea here was to be able to go into winter with a little lettuce bed that would keep on growing for a good while after winter had come in earnest. We seeded leaf lettuce in a 3' by 6' bed about the middle of September, thinning very lightly. This produced a thick growth, as we used plenty of compost in the bed and kept it moist. When the first frost felt imminent (October 15 was the average date) we simply dropped a flat-topped 3' by 6' coldframe over this bed. The sash was two old windows, and the frame was made of 2" by 12" planks. With this protection, later reinforced by earth piled against the outside of the frame walls, bales of straw to the north behind the frame, and a cover of straw or burlap for the sashes, we kept the young lettuces growing while we were using up what we had in the other frame, which was handled as follows:

This frame was exactly like the first one, but in it we transplanted as many nearly mature plants as we could crowd together. This was more a heeling-in or live storage than it was a transplanting. Most of these plants were lettuces, but we also included Batavian and curled endive, celery, and Chinese cabbage. They stood jammed together, their roots in the moist earth, and they kept us in fresh salads and some leafy greens until about Christmas. By then the lettuces in the other frame had made enough further growth to be worth while, and we cut it over the next two or three months.

Some years a severe cold spell killed plants in these frames, but we were never entirely wiped out.

Growing New Vegetables in Winter

Growing Plants. We'll assume you don't have a greenhouse. Consequently, you'll be restricted to seeding in pots or a planter for growing most food plants indoors. Parsley and chives take kindly to indoor pots. Transplant some of both from the garden to pots before the first fall frost. The parsley may throw up a seed stalk before winter is over, but will still produce a nice lot of tender leaves. Garden cress can be grown in a pot from seed. A few garlic cloves planted in a pot will send up leaves you can clip and use for flavoring just as you use a garlic clove itself. Shallot bulbs will do the same; their flavor is mild and much like chives, though the raw bulb is fairly strong.

Put pots at a south window if possible, not so near the glass that plants may get chilled on cold nights. Turn the pots now and then to keep plants growing evenly. Too little watering is better than too much.

If you are willing to settle for just a little salad occasionally during winter, you can keep a planter of lettuce growing. This is what the townspeople of old Quebec were described as doing, in Willa Cather's novel, *Shadows on the Rock* (Alfred A. Knopf, 1931). Late in October farmers brought to town boxes of earth with young lettuce plants growing in them. The Quebec people kept the boxes in their cellars and thus managed to have fresh salads for about two months. Leaf lettuce such as Simpson or Oak Leaf, or cos lettuce, are good choices for this purpose. And rather than taking entire plants, harvest a few leaves from each when picking a salad. This will give you a longer season. Start the plants in the garden, seeding at least a month ahead of moving inside, and about two months for cos.

Sprouting Roots. The most notable crop sprouted from roots during winter is Belgian endive. The roots here are those of witloof chicory, and the entire culture is covered in Chapter 10 under "Belgian endive."

Among other roots you can sprout in winter are beets and turnips. Put the beets or turnips in boxes of earth or sand in the basement. Cover them 1″ deep. Space them 1″ to 2″ apart. Keep the earth or sand damp and provide drainage through holes in the box bottom. If you have no basement, you can sprout the roots in the house.

It is also possible to sprout asparagus and rhubarb roots in winter, but most gardeners are reluctant to sacrifice these long-lived and expensive roots for a one-shot crop. A way around this problem is to sow *seed* of both plants outdoors in the spring, expressly to raise roots for forcing the following winter or in any future winter.

In the fall, dig the largest rhubarb roots and expose them to freezing weather. Store them for about two months in the basement. Then plant them in a mixture of half garden soil

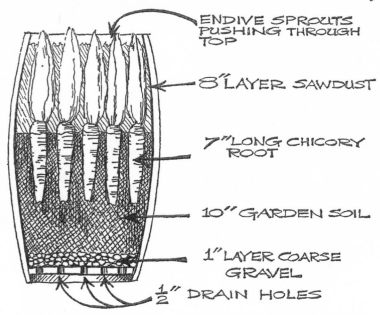

ENDIVE SPROUTS PUSHING THROUGH TOP

8" LAYER SAWDUST

7" LONG CHICORY ROOT

10" GARDEN SOIL

1" LAYER COARSE GRAVEL

½" DRAIN HOLES

and half compost. Keep them watered and dark, and edible stalks will be ready in two months or less. *Don't eat rhubarb leaves*—they contain oxalic acid, a poison.

Dig asparagus roots after the top growth dies down in the fall. You can store them like rhubarb until you are ready to sprout them. Plant asparagus roots the same way you plant rhubarb, but keep them in a light place or hang a light bulb over them. Edible sprouts should be ready in about a month.

13

The Healing Herbs

A GOOD WHILE before the dawn of wonder drugs, and when going to a hospital was a desperate last resort, every family still depended heavily on home remedies to keep healthy or to fight diseases and other troubles when they came. Formulas for such remedies were a part of old-time handbooks for housewives, often as part of a cookbook, and were the legitimate descendants of the herbal lore taught by medieval religious orders to the mistresses of households —who did most of the doctoring that was done in those times. These lore-wise ladies were also their own beauticians, and many a receipt for lotions and cosmetics was sandwiched among the healing formulas.

A large share of the venerable dosings dated back to antiquity—as in Egypt, where five-sixths of all the hundreds of official remedies were of plant origin. The old term for such a plant was "a simple," sometimes understood to mean a plant with one specific medical function. But most were used to treat more than one ailment.

Wild exaggeration and even some witchcraft got into some of the remedies, but more often than not the plants used had some of the powers attributed to them, as science ultimately proved. One of the more famous examples was the old use of the foxglove to treat dropsy. Dropsy is associated with heart trouble—and foxglove became the source of digitalis, the heart stimulant.

It took skill and experience to use the old herbal remedies safely and effectively, particularly when taken internally. Foxglove, for example, can paralyze the heart, and other otherwise helpful herbs may also be poisonous in overdoses.

Knowing when and how to gather herbs was likewise an art. A general rule for those that flower was: Gather them only after they were in bloom, when secretions of waste products would be present in only small quantities in the plant tissues. This was also sound botany. The gathering was done in fair weather, when the plants were not sodden from rain, and only healthy plant parts were saved. If roots were being gathered for future use, they were brushed free of earth and put aside to dry. The upper parts of plants, if they were not to be used at once or set to steep, were usually dried in the shade, turned several times during drying, then were stored loosely in cloth bags.

Here are some of the ways people used their garden plants and others—uses that are still employed to some extent today:

Tea made from *borage* leaves once had a great name for cheering the drinker and generally improving his health and even his memory. A usual recipe for a herb tea was a pint of boiling water poured over a handful of fresh leaves or one ounce of dried ones, steeped for 20 minutes in a covered teapot. This was made fresh each day. One teacup of it was an average dose for one day; less for the very old and the young.

A tea of *marjoram* leaves was also used as a pick-up, and to be where one could frequently smell wild marjoram— meaning oregano—was thought in medieval days a sure way to good health. We smell it daily in our own garden and, whatever the reason, do enjoy good health.

In much more recent times *oregano* tea was being used as a relief for headaches, as a nerve tonic, and for indigestion and rheumatism. The oil from oregano has been used in liniments. *Catnip* tea has its advocates today as a headache cure, and one day in our garden a visitor who happened to have a headache was idly nibbling a sprig of fresh catnip when, after ten minutes, she suddenly exclaimed, "Why, my headache's gone."

Once upon a time it was considered an omen of a return to health if a sick person dreamed of *cucumbers*. Though not everyone thought well of cucumbers, the sixteenth-century herbalist John Gerard calling them poisonous, they figured in various beauty preparations for the skin. The juice of wild *strawberries* was also used for the complexion. In parts of the Mediterranean regions of Greece and France there still exists the tradition of perfuming rinses for the hair with the fragrant blossoming *rosemary*, and oil of rosemary is an ingredient in eau de cologne.

Reducing diets are not a modern problem, and as recently as a century ago, *dill* weed cooked in a broth produced, some believed, a preventive to gaining weight. In the seventeenth century *fennel* prepared in the same way was believed to reduce weight. On the other hand, *wormwood* was supposed to promote appetite.

For bruises, leaves of *chervil* were applied, or dried *marjoram* mixed with honey. For bee stings, leaves of *summer savory* or of *plantain* were applied to the skin.

Parsley was once used as a dressing for wounds, as were the petals of *calendulas*, and in recent times *parsley root* has been used internally in infusions for a number of ailments including dropsy and neuralgia.

The ancient Saxons thought that *lettuce* induced sleep, and there was something to this as lettuce is a mild sedative. A

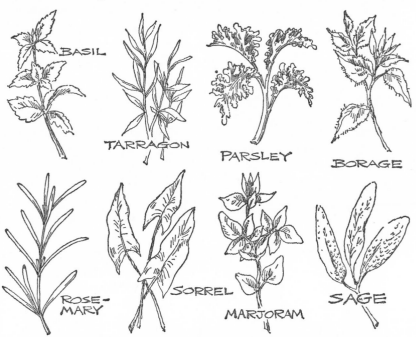

materia medica that we consulted stated of lettuce: "Highly valued as salad, and as such acts as a feeble hypnotic." In ancient Arabia it was thought that *tarragon* aided sleep.

The Saxons, among others, also esteemed *rosemary*, pounding the leaves and mixing them with oil to make an all-purpose ointment. From our own experience we can say that this was not merely wishful thinking. By bruising a cupful of fresh rosemary leaves in a mortar with a little vegetable oil, stirring this into a pound of melted petroleum jelly and an ounce of paraffin, then straining the mixture through cloth, we have made a hand cream that is agreeable to use and remarkably effective in quickly healing cuts. Out of curiosity we also tried some of this ointment on a sudden outbreak of athlete's foot, though nowhere have we seen rosemary called a fungicide. Nonetheless, the fungus attack subsided at once and disappeared completely within forty-eight hours. Prior to that, it had always taken a standard fungicide such as Whitfield's Ointment to handle it. A leading expert on infections, Dr. W. A. Altemeier of the University of Cincinnati Medical School, stated to the American College of Surgeons at its fifty-seventh annual clinical conference in 1971 that twenty-five years of experience with antibiotics has seen no decrease in infections, and their number and complexity may even have increased. This brings to mind the familiar—to natural gardeners—history of some chemical pesticide failures over the same period, due to growing insect resistance. Yet no such resistance to natural insecticides has shown up. Inevitably, one wonders if the old herbal remedies had virtues of the same kind—virtues that ought to be rediscovered.

In the sixteenth century, *rosemary* tea was taken for relief of coughs, and *peppermint* tea was used for the same purpose in recent times. Rosemary was also highly regarded as a kind of external tonic, used in the bath. For this, a quantity of the foliage was boiled in water then used to bathe in, the object being to gain vigor, good spirits, and even youth. *Strawberry* and *thyme* leaves were also used in this way, and a tea of thyme leaves was taken for relief from bad dreams.

Garlic, considered a health-giver by many today, was also favored by the old herbalists as a body builder, and was used in fairly recent times by doctors as a poultice and as a diuretic.

In the Middle Ages, *cabbage*—an old vegetable, popular with the ancient Romans—was used not only for food but was eaten raw before drinking wine, to prevent drunkenness. In case the drinker forgot to have cabbage, he could counteract tipsiness by eating plenty of *lettuce* or *parsley*.

Stomach-aches are as old as mankind, and three old remedies were *fennel, peppermint,* and *spearmint*—carried over to modern times in the forms of preparations from the oils these plants yield. A tea of *summer* or *winter savory* was another old remedy for stomach-ache, and also for fevers. The fresh leaves of *thyme* used as a seasoning are still in some favor for their reputed benefits to digestion, and the same is true of *parsley*, *sage*, and *majoram*. The roots of *dandelion* and of *witloof chicory* yielded a dosage for indigestion when steeped in boiling water. Their milky juice contains the medical principle; it is also known as a tonic and laxative, and has been used in treating liver troubles. A tea of *dandelion leaves* or of *strawberry leaves* was considered a blood purifier in the old days.

A toothache relief recommended by Gerard was *majoram*. The leaves were chewed, perhaps with some effect as the oil of marjoram's relative, *oregano*, was used for this purpose in recent times and was listed in *materia medicas*. It happened that this week a twenty-year-old neighbor of ours, suffering from a wisdom tooth she was cutting, soothed it with an application of bruised fresh oregano leaves. *Catnip* has also been used for toothache in fairly modern times, as has the oil distilled from the leaves and flowers of *thyme*.

Another ancient problem, rheumatism, was once treated by eating *celery*, and oil extracted from celery was still being used in the early years of this century to treat contusions and some inflammations. *Wormwood* was another plant used for rheumatism, its leaves and tops containing an anesthetic oil also useful for neuralgia; in each case it was rubbed on the skin.

One of the most favored healing herbs in both old and later times was *sage*. It was thought to blunt the unwelcome effects of old age, strengthening the memory and improving mental health and general well-being. In fact, sage's botanical name, salvia, comes from the Latin "to save." Smelling sage leaves or the steam from sage tea was believed to help clear the head. This suggests it was used for colds and sinus troubles in the historical past, an idea reinforced by the use of sage tea only a few decades ago as both a gargle and medicament for sore throats and coughs. For nasal catarrh, leaves of the common weed *mullein* were dried and smoked in pipes or made into cigarettes.

One of us had a grandmother who made a sage and honey cough syrup, both products coming from the garden. In the seventeenth century they went at it more gaily, steeping sage blossoms in white wine and then drinking the wine.

14

Money from Your Organic Garden

A HOME GARDENER in our vicinity has kept a small high-quality grocery store supplied with winter squash each fall. "We buy all we can get from him," the owner told us. Another store manager used almost the same words and said they never had enough specialty garden items, such as fresh herbs, rhubarb, turnip-rooted parsley, and horse-radish roots. Often all that is needed to sell such produce to stores is a phone call from a home gardener, telling them what he has. The usual arrangement is cash on delivery.

Many home gardeners can make part of their harvest cash crops. In our community a health-foods store is without a dependable source of fresh herbs or organically grown garlic. And an organic gardener has a big sales advantage where there is a demand for produce grown without chemical aids.

Even better than talking to store managers about surplus produce from your garden is to show them samples. Best of all, talk to them *before* you plant and see what they'll be interested in buying from you. This could start a profitable sideline for you that may put your garden on a self-supporting basis and even show a snug annual profit, perhaps enough to pay the property taxes on your home, or a good deal more.

Sometimes a little showmanship will go a long way in getting your name known favorably as a supplier of good home-grown specialties. Besides clean products, fresh and well grown, here are three other ways to distinguish what you sell:

1. Package your products to add value and recognition. Plastic bags make good containers for most vegetables and help retain freshness. In the Midwest, a convent with a fine asparagus bed fastened gift bunches with purple tape ties in neat tailored bows.

2. Label packages with hand-lettered tags stapled to the package, like this:

SUGAR PEAS, Dwarf Gray
1 lb. (the store will fill in the price)
SMITH'S HOME GARDENS
2318 Greenway Road

3. Include a little bonus such as a sprig of herbs appropriate for the vegetable packaged, or a recipe if it is an unusual vegetable.

DIRECT SALES

Not every home gardener will want to tie himself down to supplying a store, and an alternate way is to sell direct to the consumers—in your neighborhood, community, or countryside.

To get started often takes some publicity. Afterward your customers will take care of it by telling others. Here are ways to attract attention at first:

1. Talk to your local newspaper editor. A weekly paper is your best bet for a story about your garden. Supply a photograph, especially of something unusual you've grown—a giant sunflower or watermelon, a nicely designed herb bed or a

herbal oddity, a fine zucchini squash plant bearing its golden flowers and fruits in a living bouquet.

2. Invest in a small classified ad. Even a brief one: "GARDEN-FRESH vegetables, phone 765-8570," can work wonders. A friend of ours with a few walnut trees gets orders each fall from people who saw a three-line ad she ran five years ago.

3. If you don't mind interruptions, a neat sign where those in passing cars can see it is a splendid sales device, especially in the country.

4. Offer to supply a bouquet from your garden for a community, school, club, or church affair. It will attract favorable attention and may be mentioned in a program or bulletin, too.

SEASONAL SALES OPPORTUNITIES

SPRING SALES

Flat garden. Fill a flat with a mixture of one part screened compost, one part good garden soil, one part sand. If the flat is 18″ long, it will hold nine rows of seedlings, the rows 2″ apart, ready for your customer to transplant to his garden. Some things you can put in a springtime flat are celery, head lettuce, globe onions, curled and Batavian endive, broccoli, chard, thyme, and sage. Label each row. For a late spring flat, eggplants, tomatoes, peppers, basil, and marigolds would be appropriate.

We have given friends such filled flats—nicely varied instant gardens all ready to start lusty growth. A flat accommodates from 60 to 90 little plants, depending on their size. Price your flats to compete with what local garden suppliers are charging for plants like yours.

CUT FLOWERS

SHOW-WINDOW GROUPING

GOURD BIRD-HOUSE

WINDOWSILL HERB GARDEN

Cut flowers. We include this sales opportunity as a spring-time one because its season starts in spring, but sales can continue until late fall if you plant flowers that bloom in succession. Marigolds and zinnias are two annuals that are easy to grow and last long in arrangements. Seed companies offer new varieties every year, with blooms spectacular in size, colors, and forms. Sweet peas, all-time favorites, will, if properly planted and kept mulched and watered, have an early and long blooming period in a great variety of colors. Gloriosa daisies thrive under adverse weather conditions and make handsome bouquets. And shrubs and flowering trees can give you a wealth of flower-arrangement material if you time their pruning to suit your needs. With a framework of lilac and flowering quince, five jonquil blossoms or three tulips can make an outstanding arrangement.

When gathering cut flowers, pick them in late afternoon, cut with a sharp knife on a slant, and plunge stems at once into a full bucket of room-temperature water. Be sure to remove all foliage that would be under water when an arrangement is completed. Doing so keeps the water sweeter and helps the stems absorb more of it. Keep the flowers in the bucket overnight after picking, in a cool, draft-free place, and arrange them the next morning. One of the commercial preparations to keep flowers fresh will be a help. Varieties of flowers that ooze a milky juice should have cut ends singed first. This is conveniently done with a lighted candle.

Some of the best prospects for fresh-flower sales are banks, real estate offices, beauty parlors, bakeries, quality markets, travel agencies, hotels, insurance offices, restaurants, dress shops, jewelry stores, interior decorating shops, home furnishing stores and dentists, doctors, lawyers, and other professional men with waiting rooms for their clients.

Plan to deliver the flowers already arranged in a suitable container once a week. Remove the previous week's arrangement at this time. During the week, your customer should see that enough water is kept in the container to maintain freshness. Inexpensive glass or pottery containers are usually best, and we have found that a wad of chicken wire stuffed loosely but securely into such a container makes an excellent holder for flower stems.

For another sales possibility, get in touch with the altar societies of your local churches. They are apt to prefer flowers in bunches, as they arrange them according to custom. Also, some housewives without gardens of their own like to have a supply of cut flowers for arranging in their own containers, particularly if the price is right.

SUMMER SALES

Fresh herbs. Fresh herbs are very scarce, very few, and expensive when found. The only fresh ones we have seen recently in stores were some chives in plastic pots, and some bunches of dill. The chives cost 49¢ and the dill, 40¢. A single planting of chives would in one season multiply to enough for two or three pots, and one good dill plant would yield two or three of the 40-cent bunches. Small wonder that one seed house with a large herb list advertises: "Lifetime security on one acre."

Among prospective customers for fresh herbs are supermarkets, specialty food stores, health-food stores, ethnic-group food stores (Italian markets for basil, parsley, and oregano, for instance), and restaurants. If you become known for raising herbs, other sales avenues can open, such as farmers' markets (they are always short on herbs), and well-run roadside stands.

Some customers may want to buy their herbs on-site, in your garden. For others, herbs can be kept fresh after picking by rinsing and storing in a plastic bag with a damp paper towel. Keep them cool and shaded and deliver as soon as convenient.

Oriental vegetables. Another way to specialize is by cuisines, and a distinctive one is the Oriental. You don't have to live where there is a large Chinese or Japanese community to do this since Oriental foods are widely popular in the Western World. Some vegetables to try out under your climatic conditions are edible-podded peas (which take the same culture as other peas), edible soybeans, Oriental cucumbers, green onions, and Oriental radishes (you harvest them in fall and winter). Celtuce and tampala are two natives of the Orient now fairly well known here. An excellent substitute for water chestnuts is the Jerusalem artichoke, which is native American.

Corn. If you have the room to grow sweet corn it has possibilities as a summer specialty crop for a hand-picked group of customers—those who appreciate the difference between really fresh corn and the corn offered at any market. Such customers will gladly pay for all the sweet corn a gardener will sell them. And this can be a pick-it-yourself operation, because corn begins to lose sugar almost as soon as it is harvested.

By choosing varieties of different maturity times, you can plant several kinds of sweet corn that ripen in succession, spreading the harvest over weeks.

FALL SALES

Fall is a good time of year to offer decorating-vegetables such as ornamental corn, gourds, and pumpkins. Possible customers for them include gift shops, supermarkets, show-window dressers, caterers, commercial photographers, florists, garden centers, interior decorators, department stores, restaurants, and various shops interested in seasonal-display decorations.

Ornamental corn. Field corn with vari-colored kernels, and the little popcorn called Strawberry, with dark red kernels, are popular decorations. Sell the ears with the husks still on; they are part of the decoration.

Gourds. There are many sizes, shapes, and colors of gourds, all interesting and many of them useful, serving as birdhouses, for example, for which there is a demand, along with the demand for gourds as decorations. Gourds also make household containers—dippers, spoons, waste baskets, bins, and so on. All you need to do is to cut away any surplus part of the gourd, to shape it, and then dry it. Do the cutting with a sharp knife a week or two after harvesting the gourd, which you do at the end of the season, before frost and when the tendrils on the vines near the gourds start to shrivel.

There are two classes of gourds, the Lagenarias and the Cucurbitas. Both are decorative. The Cucurbitas can be used after a brief drying, or even at once as decorations if not cut into. They are attractive for about three months. Lagenarias are thinner-shelled, and though they may take several months to dry completely, they are good for years of service as containers afterward, as lightweight as plastic ones and more durable and appealing.

Pumpkins. Pumpkins are also available in several sizes, from the Small Sugar you can hold in one hand, to the 100-pound Big Max. Small and medium sizes are in most demand. Gourds can be trained on a fence, by the way, but pumpkins develop best when resting on the earth. Otherwise they take the same culture.

Everlasting flowers. Another possibility for fall sales, and for winter ones, too, are the flowers you can dry—the everlasting kinds such as Chinese lantern plant, statice, money plant, and strawflowers. You dry them by cutting them before they are completely mature, removing the leaves, then hanging them in loose bunches upside down in cool shade where there is gentle ventilation. They should be dried slowly.

WINTER SALES

Pot garden. An elderly friend of ours with no place to grow a garden nevertheless insists on some fresh herbs for cooking. She supplies herself by getting a few plants at nurseries each year and growing them in a pot on a windowsill. There are apartment dwellers and other people who would be glad to buy such pots of culinary herbs if they had any idea where to get them. And a pot of herbs in the house in wintertime is as attractive as it is useful.

Pot the herbs as small plants during the summer to have them growing along well for winter or fall sales. Chives are famous for growing happily in pots. Parsley will also do well, and the flat-leaf kind preferred by many cooks is seldom seen in stores. Other good herbs for pots are thyme, rosemary, marjoram, mint.

Dried herbs. If you grow enough herbs to dry them for

sale, this is a winter possibility. See Chapter 10 for directions on drying.

SELLING TO YOURSELF

Your own garden produce can *save* you more money than you may have realized. For example, you can save on gifts by making some of them from what your garden provides.

Get some plastic pill bottles from a drugstore, fill them with your own dried herbs, and make labels with a felt-tipped pen. We do this for our own use and for little gifts. It is one of the most welcome presents you can offer a good cook, and ideal for mailing because of being lightweight and practically unbreakable.

For a nearby friend you might make a gift of herb plants in pots, as already described. Herbed vinegar is also a nice gift. To make it, put ¼ cup of herb sprigs into 1 cup of luke-warm white wine vinegar. Basil, tarragon, thyme, and marjoram all make excellent herb vinegars.

Another interesting gift use for herbs is to make a little bouquet—a tussie-mussie—with a few herbs as they begin to flower. Basil is especially good because of its fragrance, as is rosemary. Oregano, sage, and mint all have refreshing aromas, too. Take one of these tiny bouquets along when visiting a sick friend; they are a welcome change from sometimes overly sweet-scented flowers.

Finally, never forget that the best return from your family garden is the produce you use on your table. Even if available in stores, this is expensive when high in quality, and especially so when organically grown. And a garden's convenience avoids many a last-minute shopping trip, saving you time and perhaps trip expense on top of food savings. For your own satisfaction, keep track of what your garden provides. A kitchen scale is a great help here, and a simple account book to credit the garden for value received. We can assure you the total at the end of a season will open your eyes. Like other well-managed investments, a garden can yield impressive dividends.

15

Is a Green Thumb Really Plant ESP?

As a gardener, you want your plants to grow well. As an organic gardener, you want them to grow well as naturally as possible. Now—if we should assume for the moment that plants have *feelings*, that they can react emotionally to what you do about them, that should make a difference in how well they grow, shouldn't it? Such a situation would, in fact, put a powerful extra gardening aid in your hands. Well, strange as it seems, plants apparently do have feelings —or something so remarkably like our own emotions that "feelings" comes closer to describing them than any other word.

Many gardeners have believed this. We have a friend who matter-of-factly talks to any of her plants that seem to need encouragement or to deserve praise, and Luther Burbank, one of the world's greatest gardeners, did the same thing.

But in just the past few years there has come along some evidence of plant reactions to people that is based not on what could, after all, be purely wishful thinking, but on scientific demonstration.

The tool used in the most striking such demonstrations has

been the one called the lie detector. There are several types, but in general they work by showing the fluctuations of an electric current on a subject's skin, the fluctuations being caused by such reactions to questions or objects as sweating, breathing, heart beat, and blood pressure. The technical name for the reaction is "psychogalvanic reflex." In the 1950s an American scientist working in England, Dr. L. Ron Hubbard, attached a lie detector to a tomato and then stuck a nail in the tomato. This produced a reaction that caused the detector to show what in a person could have been interpreted as pain or fear. Other experiments led Dr. Hubbard to speculate that plants, like animals, were more subject to disease if they lost the will to live.

Then, in the 1960s, another researcher used a lie detector on plants and revealed a much more startling plant-human communication. The experimenter here was Cleve Backster, director of a school of lie detection in New York City. As reported later in the magazine *National Wildlife*, and by the New York *Times* News Service, Mr. Backster attached a lie detector to a plant to see what would happen if he dipped one of the leaves into hot coffee. There was no reaction, although in a person, a finger dipped into a hot liquid would have produced a reaction. As reported, Mr. Backster then began thinking of what else he might do to produce some sort of response, and it occurred to him that a flame might do it. If he were to strike a match and burn the leaf—

And at this point, though he had done no more than just to *think* about burning the plant's leaf, it reacted strongly— the lie detector recording what in a person would have been fright. On the basis of this experiment as reported, and repeated many times, the only possible conclusion is: *plants can be affected by human thoughts about them.* Perhaps only some plants can so communicate, just as only certain persons can tune in on the thoughts of others through extra-sensory perception, ESP. Or it may be that what we call a green thumb is an ability to influence plant growth without necessarily knowing how you are doing it. This could explain how some enthusiastic but inexperienced gardeners sometimes succeed while going at everything backward.

A quite different series of plant experiments was made many years ago by an Indian scientist, Professor Jagadis Chunder Bose of Presidency College, Calcutta. He was a plant physiologist, and in his investigations of how plants responded to various stimuli, he showed that plants are startlingly like animals in nearly every physical respect. He even found that plants have the equivalent of a heart, and consequently have pulses. He found that plants grew tired when forced to perform a series of reactions without intervals of rest, just like animals. Plants could be numbed by cold, he discovered. But just as a person who dips a toe into ice water will jerk his foot back, so did a plant react when its tap root was dipped into icy water, retracting the root before the numbing effect of cold set in.

Sending an electric current through plants shocked them just as it shocks animals, Bose found, the plants showing what he called excitability through their leaf movements. In the case of one plant with delicate spiral tendrils, the electric current caused them ". . . instantly to uncurl—their free ends, as they did so, sweeping through large arcs. . . . These violent contortions were strongly suggestive of the writhing of a worm under torture."

Plants also have a kind of peripheral nervous system, this researcher found, "certain conducting channels" transmitting messages when the plant was stimulated. Furthermore, the speed of transmission was increased by warmth, reduced by cold, and blocked entirely by exposing the plant to an anesthetic—chloroform or ether.

So closely did plants resemble people in how drugs affected them, including what served them as hearts ("The rhythmic tissue of the plant maintains the ascent of the sap.

From such considerations it may appear not very far-fetched to regard a plant as possessed of a diffuse heart."), that it caused Bose to ponder on whether new medicines might be tested on plants first, to see how they would work on people. The quoted parts above are from Bose's book, *Plant Response*, a scholarly report on his experiments and conclusions, published in 1906 in London.

His findings make less surprising, perhaps, these more contemporary observations on how music affects plants: A New England violinist noted that seeds in a pot located in the room where she practiced, seemed to germinate better than did some not exposed to the music. And in Denver a series of scientifically controlled musical experiments on plants conducted by a housewife and mother who had gone back to college to get her degree in music, showed that plants leaned in the direction soft music was coming from, and grew beautifully, but leaned away from rock music and then went into a kind of nervous decline and died. The experimenter here was Mrs. Dorothy Retallack, and the work involved eleven experiments in controlled-environment chambers, a laboratory project in a biology course at Temple Buell College.

The plants used by Mrs. Retallack were kinds we are all familiar with—geraniums, radishes, squash, beans, petunias, marigolds, and so on. The loudness of the music was about that of an average adult-listening level—"3" on a 10-digit dial. Here is what happened in a 3-week summing-up experiment with four groups of plants:

Those in the first chamber were given three hours of acid rock music a day, those in the second chamber got contemporary modern music, those in the third chamber got calm devotional music, and the plants in the fourth chamber were grown in silence.

In four to six days the rock-music plants were showing distress. In three weeks they were dying. A squash had col-

lapsed, a morning glory had grown horizontally instead of up, heading away from the source of the music. All plants showed damage, and even their roots were stunted and were turned away from the music.

The contemporary-music plants were leaning slightly away from the music by three weeks, but were doing fairly well otherwise.

The religious-music plants leaned toward the music, grew sturdy tops and roots, and in 3 weeks were 20″ high—beating the silence-chamber plants by 2″.

At the conclusion of some earlier experiments, just to see what would happen Mrs. Retallack transplanted a few of the beans and squash outdoors. "The plants which had been subjected to the rock died anyway," she wrote us. "Those having East Indian, Bach, and jazz, grew beautifully."

None of these things would have surprised Luther Burbank, who, as we said, talked to his plants, and who must also have known of Professor Bose's discoveries. Burbank's object in talking to his plants was practical. He was always after results, and he felt he got them in this way. One time a young man, the son of family friends, asked Burbank how he could possibly keep track of the hundreds of experiments he had going on at the same time all the time. "I do it with love," he said. "I feel an affection for everything I am working with, and so I can keep in touch with everything that concerns them."

Years later, explaining to a swami friend his development of smooth cacti, Burbank was quoted as saying: "I often talked to the plants to create a vibration of love. 'You have nothing to fear,' I would tell them. 'You don't need your defensive thorns. I will protect you.'" Not long after that, Manly P. Hall, founder of the Philosophical Research Society, Inc., of Los Angeles, visited Burbank and subsequently wrote of how Burbank communicated with plants:

"He told me that when he wanted his plants to develop in some particular and peculiar way not common to their kind, he would get down on his knees and talk to them. Mr. Burbank also mentioned that man is proud of his five senses but that plants have over twenty sensory perceptions; but because they are different from ours, we cannot recognize them. He was not sure that the shrubs and flowers understood his words, but he was convinced that by some telepathy, they could comprehend his meaning." (This quotation and the preceding one by Burbank are from *Luther Burbank, The Wizard and the Man*, Ken and Pat Kraft.)

16

A Home in the Country —for You?

EVER DREAM about moving to the country, to a little farm of your own? Gardeners, especially natural gardeners, are very apt to cherish such a dream. More—it is one of the most popular of American desires. The director of science and education for the U. S. Department of Agriculture, Dr. Ned D. Bayley, told a 1970 scientific gathering at the University of Arizona that a 1968 poll asking Americans where they'd live if they could choose, turned up the surprising fact that a majority—56 percent—wanted a rural life.

Or maybe it isn't so surprising. Doesn't everyone need peace and privacy, freedom and beauty? Yes, and crystal-clear air, fragrances of hay curing and of sun-warmed evergreen boughs, the cathedral shadows of a woods and its shafts of sunlight in the clearings, the melody of a thousand bird and insect and animal voices as living creatures go their daily rounds.

A world of your own, *that's* what a farm is. It is the phrase that constantly comes to our minds about our own farm. We spoke of that farm in the first chapter of this book, and sometimes in other chapters. When we left it we did so only physically; we have continued to carry it in our minds and to plan its re-creation. To make you feel that way, a thing has to be very good.

We were not farm-bred. One of us had lived in the country but only as a child. We have an idea that most of the people who are hoping to move to the country have no more experience with it than we had. So what do you do to get ready for it?

In our case we read everything we could find on farm subjects and we got what practical experience we could while living in a suburban setting in wartime. The experience was that of trying out several new natural gardening techniques and of raising a back-yard flock of chickens. Government bulletins, though usually aimed at professional farmers, were useful. (For a list of subjects related to farming, write to Superintendent of Documents, Washington, D.C. 20402.)

We were also eager customers for any books on farming, especially on part-time experiences. We subscribed to magazines about farming and related activities and sent for literature from their advertisers.

So, when we started looking for a farm we knew what we wanted and what we were going to do, at least in theory. It worked out happily in almost every respect. After we had bought the farm and had been established for a year we were supplying nearly all the food we ate, and in less than two years we had changed a small and rather boxy farmhouse into a pleasant country home fronted by a Mount Vernon type veranda looking down a grassy slope to a pond we'd built and stocked with fish.

Our water came from a cistern (soft) and a spring (hard), piped into the house. Beef came from our Hereford and Black Angus steers, a laying flock supplied fresh eggs each day and another flock, fryers and broilers. A Jersey cow and a mostly-Guernsey provided more milk and cream than we could possibly use, and we made butter so sweet and delicate

—we had to store it in the freezer (an old soda fountain ice cream box) if we weren't going to use it up within a week. We kept guinea fowl and frequently had the gamelike meat smoked, for buffet parties. Apples, peaches, nectarines, plums, and cherries were borne on established trees, and by the second year we had raspberries and strawberries from plantings we made the first year. Blackberries, persimmons, and several kinds of nuts grew wild. Cordwood for the two stone fireplaces we built came from our woods, and so did Christmas trees and wreaths. For once we had a garden big enough to satisfy us.

We had a lot of guests (you do, on a farm) and the meals were Lucullan. We remember menus: spring luncheons of broiled chicken, asparagus, new potatoes, and strawberries with Devonshire cream; summer dinners of standing rib roasts, eggplant French fried in fine leaf lard we had rendered, lima beans, salads of tomatoes and cucumbers, and for dessert Peach Melba of homemade ice cream, tree-ripened peaches from our orchard and sauce from our Indian Summer red raspberries; winter dinners of hickory-smoked ham, baked Hubbard squash, a salad of Belgian endive sprouted in the stone cellar, and a pie made from one of our jars of stored fruit—apple, peach, cherry, blackberry.

And surely man knows few more solidly satisfying feelings than that of heading into winter with plenty of dry cordwood, a barnful of sweet hay and grain for the livestock, the cellar shelves gleaming with the jewel tones of fruits and vegetables in jar after jar, winter squash and apples laid down in the coolest corners, and the garden itself still plump with mulched root crops to be dug at intervals through the winter, and with banked coldframes chock-full of late leafy green plants.

Well and good, some people may think, but don't such results take a lot of work? Yes, they do. We would be doing you no service to pretend they do not. Once a friend told us, "I want the good country life just the way you had it, but I want it with push buttons." Not long after that he moved to a sixty-acre farm and discovered he had left most of his spare time behind him in suburbia. However, a dozen years have now passed and he is still on his farm. Like our farm and like those that most of you are probably thinking of, his is not an income farm. It is a home in the country. Used in this way, a farm can be one of the most delightful places on earth to live. To see if it might suit you, consider these pros and cons of life in the country.

Leisure. Would you be unhappy without a good deal of leisure time each day? Country life can provide stretches of luxurious leisure if you don't keep too many projects under way at once, but the leisure does not come in regular daily allowances. We learned to respond promptly—to an uproar in the chicken house, steers clambering over a sagging fence, a tornado warning. . . . When our leisure came, though, it was even more enjoyable.

Nature. You live close to nature in the country. The weather rules your life to a much greater extent than in town, and you are intimately and frequently concerned with trauma that accompanies the balance of nature. City lawns and hedges are replaced by rolling acres of fragrant meadows, and the quiet privacy of the woods. But the corner drugstore is miles away and so are the theater, library, restaurant, museum, dentist. Still, so are crowds and city noise, dirt, turmoil.

Can you make a living? A farm-bred person who has kept up to date on farming can retire to the country and probably make a living off the land, given some financing and a market. He may do well with some specialty crop particularly. But does this sound as if a city-bred person does *not* have a good chance at making a living off the land? That, in our opinion, is usually the case. There are exceptions, usually hard-won ones, but a moderate-sized farm can easily be a $50,000 investment, needing expert management and seasonal crop loans. Note, though, that we said "making a living." To make *part* of a living is something else again . . .

Can you supplement your income? If you are willing and able to adapt to market requirements, you can make some money from a country home's produce. We didn't plan to, but we made some anyway, as by selling surplus eggs to some city friends and their friends at retail market prices, and selling surplus cream to an ice cream plant. We can recommend this surplus-product cash-out since it makes few demands on the producer, and customers from the city will even save you the trouble of delivery by coming to you if you wish. Good sale items are eggs, garden vegetables (with naturally grown ones bringing a premium), strawberries, and herbs.

A pond stocked with fish may provide some income from fisherman, and selling surplus timber from your farm woods for lumber, cordwood, and fence posts, can put cash in your pocket.

Barter is another way to cash in on surplus from a country place. We occasionally did this with some merchants of the nearest town, such as trading two gross of fresh eggs, delivered two dozen at a time when we were in town, for a food mixer. Also, we sometimes paid for the cutting and baling of our hay with some of the hay itself, or traded a field of standing hay for some work on our fencing.

The work. So far, we have never known of anyone's living in the country without occasional hard physical work. So, any prospective country dweller should know his own limits. To be sure, most people who live in the country enjoy the work, or most of it.

Another reason, aside from livestock or crops, for physical work on a country place of any size is that certain help simply cannot be had as quickly as in town. On this account, and also for his pocketbook's sake, the prospective country dweller is better off if he can make a few plumbing and electrical repairs, do some basic carpentry, painting, and concrete work, and some tinkering with machinery. A garden tractor that can also haul a load is worth considering, as is a shredder to convert prunings to mulch and compost makings.

A part of the work will be that involved in being your own water and sanitary departments, but neither requires frequent attention. We installed a septic tank when we bought our farm and never had to give sewage disposal another thought. Living with an old system, as we did on two other country places, took occasional minor tank cleaning. Water usually has to be brought into country houses by electric pumps. They are long-lived and reliable, needing minimum maintenance. We have always found an outside hand pump an additional convenience and an assurance of water if the electricity goes off.

There is a temptation to spread yourself thin over many

projects in the country, often to gain time by starting everything growing at once. We tried to plant 500 young pines
and 2,500 multiflora roses for fencing during one weekend,
got less than half planted, and lost half of those through lack
of time to look after them.

Once you do the must jobs, the time you spend working is
largely a matter of choice. On winter days we sometimes spent
only one hour at it on our farm, feeding and watering livestock. During the rest of the year we averaged about eight
hours a day between us. But if we had not been interested or
had needed to hurry, we could have cut this in half or perhaps
less.

The money. The city man moving to a home in the country
may be shocked at the size of some bills. Feed for livestock
comes in wholesale-sized quantities, a fencing job you hire
done may involve not 50 feet but 1,000, and resurfacing a
fairly short lane may use up ten tons of gravel. A man we
know was advised to lime, fertilize, and seed a pasture. He had
been used to doing the same thing to his city lawn for about
$5. He hired it done to the pasture and the bill, a fair one,
was for $148.

Another example of farm outgo was our pond. We had it
dug by a commercial pond builder, where rain runoff from
about 20 acres would keep it filled. The pond was about one
acre in size, with a 15' maximum depth, and cost us just
about $1,000, counting the concrete stock tank it supplied via
filter and piping, a concrete spillway pipe we installed to
ease the load on the grassed spillway, seeding and fertilizing
the earth dam, and two piers. We felt the money one of our
best investments. We stocked the pond with sunfish and bass
(free from the state), fished, swam, boated, skated in winter,
and took comfort in the fire protection the million-gallon
reservoir provided. An up-to-date technical guide for building
ponds is available for 70¢ from the Government Printing

Office, Washington, D.C. 20402; ask for *Ponds*, Agricultural
Handbook No. 387.

Livestock. Do you like dealing with animals and poultry?
Most country homes of the type we're talking about have at
least a few laying hens, and many have cattle, pigs, and
other animals. If you don't really enjoy handling such living
creatures and having them dependent on you, it won't rule
out country living for you, but an acre or two on the outskirts
of a small town, instead of a farm, may give you everything
you're looking for and in more manageable size. Young creatures are very appealing, but they do need some close personal
attention. Both they and mature ones need housing, room to
exercise, a constant water supply and proper food—usually
including some pasture or range—protection from predators,
occasionally some rounding up, sometimes doctoring, grooming, and breeding. To anyone who likes animals, this is some
of the best of country living.

As mentioned, we had chickens for eggs and meat; cows
for milk; guineas and steers for meat. We also had hogs
once. We got a lot of worthwhile experience, pleasure, and
food from all these projects. Today on the same kind of
place we would have chickens and guineas, and would add
ducks, and perhaps milk goats in place of cows. The cows
gave more milk than we really needed, and both they and the
steers required more pasture and fencing expenses than we
might undertake again—though this is still a little iffy with
us, because we so enjoyed having the cattle.

Taking the steers as an example, here's the way costs and
returns ran: We had about 20 acres in pasture. We hired the
seeding, liming, mowing, and fence repairing done, at a cost of
about $300 a year on the average. We charged $150 of this to
the 3 steers we fed out each year. They usually had cost about
$100 each to buy, so that was $300 more, along with about
$100 for grain, supplements, butchering, and other expenses.
This brought the outlay for a year to $550. What did we get

for it? We got about 1,500 pounds of good grass-fed beef. Cost: 37¢ a pound. We could have sold one animal for about $250 at this point and still have had 1,000 pounds of beef from the 2 remaining, at a bargain 30¢ a pound.

However, there was another side to this coin. Much of the 1,500 pounds of beef was not in favored steaks and rib roasts, but in greater proportions of chuck, brisket, soup bones, and hamburger than we ordinarily bought at retail. This was even more the case with the hogs. We paid $12 each for 2 young pigs, raised them, had them butchered, and after observing the proportion of meat that we had little or no interest in, we did some arithmetic and found we could have bought 11 excellent 12-pound hams from a local smokehouse for what the whole enterprise had cost.

A dozen chickens (and you don't need a rooster to get eggs unless you prefer fertile eggs) should give you two to five dozen eggs a week, most in spring, least in winter. Figure on about a dollar a week for feed, to supplement foraging and garden and table waste.

A milk cow costs $200 to $300 or more, and will supply two to five gallons of milk a day for about 10 months; she rests, and calves, for about 2 months—so you must breed her each year. She must be milked twice a day; figure on twenty minutes, more or less, for each milking. In addition to pasture, feed will cost about $3 a week, averaged over a year.

A milk goat costs up to about $50, and gives 2 to 4 quarts of milk a day for up to 10 months; like the cow, she must be bred to renew production. Her feed, in addition to pasture, will cost up to 75¢ a week, averaged over the year.

What to Look for and How to Find It

We started looking in Maryland and Virginia for our farm while we were still in the District of Columbia area at the end of World War II. We found nothing there we wanted, but did find the right place later in our home state, Missouri.

Most of our looking was done with the help of real estate people. The licensed real estate broker handling farm properties is likely to have been in the business for years, and the person he sells a farm to will also become his neighbor, since a country community is closer-knit than a city one. We recommend you deal through one of these licensed brokers rather than directly with owners. It is also a good idea to hire a local lawyer to look after your interests when you make the purchase.

If you want to live in an area far from your present home, subscribe to a newspaper there, then get in touch with realtors advertising in the paper. When you can, visit the area. A national listing of farms that take guests is the *Farm and Ranch Vacation Guide*, 36 East 57th Street, New York, New York 10022, for $2.50. Some farm families that take guests advertise for them in newspapers (most often in a nearby big city). Chambers of commerce may have lists as may travel bureaus, auto clubs, and agricultural agencies in the locality. For a starter, you could write the county agricultural agent in the vicinity you'd like to investigate while spending a farm vacation; he will be at the county seat and can refer your request to the right persons.

During our own farm search, some important things we learned to notice or ask about were these:

Neighborhood trends. Note the general character of the country neighborhood as to maintenance of property. A shoddy country neighborhood has many of the drawbacks of a shoddy city one. Also note if any housing developments are reaching out from the nearest communities. Suburban sprawl has forced many country dwellers to sell out by restricting their activities and skyrocketing taxes.

Where is the value? Farm property prices are based largely on potential production. Don't buy something you won't use

—an expensive dairy barn, a mechanized broiler layout, rich bottomland. But a part-time farm's value, on the other hand, is usually based on the house.

Water. Good water and enough of it is so commonplace to many city dwellers, they take it for granted in the country. Don't. Country property lacking it is almost unsalable. And unlivable. Ask where the water comes from and if it has been recently tested.

Roads. A hard-surfaced road reduces dust and increases the price of a farm by 10 to 30 percent. A dirt or gravel road usually has less traffic and may serve your needs well enough. Also consider the amount of a farm's own roadway you will have to maintain.

Conservation. Has the land been well managed? Have there been animals to provide manure, and if so, was it well used, wasted, or perhaps even sold? Is the soil badly gullied? What conservation practices are being regularly followed, such as contouring and green manuring?

House. Could you live in the house as is, for a while at least? What would it cost in town? What might remodeling cost? Is the house too near animal quarters or the road? Is the view from inside it to your liking? Check roof, plumbing, and heating for age and condition.

Help. Are machinery, skills, and manpower available nearby? Hiring plowing or mowing on a large scale is often cheaper than buying machinery you'll seldom use. And a good neighborhood plumber, electrician, or carpenter is a boon.

Nuisances. Try to find what trespassing problems the place and the neighborhood have been having. This is common experience in the country and ranges from trifling to intolerable. The problems may include illegal hunting, camping, noise, theft, or vandalism.

Prices. City people, used to city or suburban prices and lot sizes, are apt to overvalue so much larger a piece of the earth as a farm. A friend used to $30,000 subdivision houses, on

50-foot lots could hardly wait to put earnest money on a 60-acre ranch he found priced at $18,000. The "ranch" was a remote parcel of barren land mainly in brush and second-growth timber, the house was cheaply built, the barn a mere shelter. We considered even $12,000 dear for the place and advised a check of other properties within a 25-mile radius. But the salesman, who was also the owner, hinted at another prospect just about to close on the property, and our friend grabbed it. Later it wasn't much comfort to learn of a snug 80-acre place across the ridge, with good native pasture, a sound five-room log house, and a quarter-mile of good river frontage, offered at $16,500.

Here are some other guidelines on what sets farm prices, authenticated by the U. S. Department of Agriculture with city buyers in mind:

A farm within about 30 miles, or commuting distance, of a city is apt to cost at least 50 percent more than one farther out.

A farm near a large city will cost more than one near a small city.

If you plan to buy land and build your house, financing it is easier if you pay cash for the land. Many local banks and savings-and-loan associations provide such financing for part-time farms. Also see the Farmers Home Administration, the Farm Credit Administration, and insurance companies.

In any case, get acquainted with a local banker and talk over property values, cost of money, taxes, closing costs, surveys, country zoning, utility services, and insurance.

After You Have Your Farm

The 40-acre farm we finally bought, in the Missouri foothills of the Ozark Mountains, had an old barn built partly of logs and partly of oak planks weathered silvery gray. It had eccentric gables and three or four different roof pitches and earth floors except in a feed room. One of the first things we were going to do was to build a clean, modern combination barn and poultry house with a concrete floor and the water piped in. A country friend who heard of our plans said, "Don't tear down anything on the place till you've lived there a full year." He didn't say why and we didn't bother to ask, because we didn't intend to take the advice.

As it turned out, we did take it, in a left-handed way, for the cost of some other projects kept us from doing anything about the barn that first year. And it was one of the luckiest things that happened to us. By the time we'd lived with the little old gray barn for a year we had discovered it was perfectly adequate for the use we made of it, and by then we had come to like its informal architecture and at-home look in its setting. All we did was to install electric lighting, and while we were doing it we also ran the line into the chicken house for lights and into a tiny shed to run an electric brooder for chicks.

So in the end we didn't tear down any of the old buildings. We discovered they were useful and we used them. Give your own farm a year or so to show you how it works. Even if you don't use the buildings for the purposes they once served, you may very well find they are good for other things.

We have known several people who bought their farms as weekend and vacation homes, with plans to move there permanently later on. In most cases it was working out well. Most had gardens, and some raised beef cattle, which don't demand daily attention. Neither do bees, and one family kept a flock of ducks that looked after themselves. Geese, guineas, and pond fish also get along with a minimum of care. But rabbits, hogs, and milk goats or cows are not for weekend farming.

Where such weekend farms had good pastures or cropland, owners sometimes rented it to neighboring farmers. This had some advantages, such as keeping places from looking deserted and realizing some income, but the usual reason is to obtain a tax shelter, reducing taxable income by charging farm expenses to it. To do this, the owner must be able to convince income tax authorities he has "a business motivation" before he can take any deductions for farm expenses.

A family that owned a second-home farm adjoining ours showed good judgment, we thought, in not modernizing it, though they planned to do so if they moved there permanently. They kept the big wood-burning range (a good idea for full-time living, too, when storms knock out electric lines), and by not piping in water, they had no worries about frozen pipes in winter. They pumped the water they needed from the cistern by hand. Their bathroom was the outhouse, also a good thing to retain on any farm, for convenience when working outside.

In conclusion, three basic suggestions:

First, don't spend your money on frills if your money is limited. Our veranda was a frill, we discovered. It did look wonderful but we used it very little, and the mud room we got when we built an attached garage was far more helpful. You live outdoors a good deal on a farm, and a mud room where you can shed boots and wet things as you come inside is a necessity.

Second, as with your farm itself, give yourself a year or two just to live with the neighborhood. Many city farmers are sure they know the answers to farm problems because they read them in a book. Generally speaking, organic methods will probably be considered strictly experimental by most of your farm neighbors—but you may be pleasantly surprised to find them as aware as you are of the value of organic matter, and perhaps quite a bit ahead of you in knowledge of terracing, contour plowing, cover crops, weather savvy, and a host of country skills.

Third, before a couple makes the move from city to country they both should be in favor of it. If one of them is opposed, the chances of disappointment are great. Even if one of them is willing but not really interested, the experiment is likely to fail. Life in the country is a partnership arrangement, and someone pining for the pleasures of the city cannot be a good country partner. Taking one of the farm vacations we mentioned is a way to sample farm life beforehand.

Appendix I:
General Information

SEED LIFE

If kept dry and cool, especially dry, most vegetable seeds will remain alive for years. This table is conservative.

Seed	*Average years of life*
Asparagus	3
Beans	3–5
Beet	5–8
Broccoli	5–8
Brussels sprouts	4
Cabbage	5–8
Cardoon	5–8
Carrot	3–6
Cauliflower	5–8
Celeriac	5–8
Celery	5–8
Chicory	5–8
Corn	2–4
Cucumber	5–8
Eggplant	5–8

Seed	*Average years of life*
Endive	5–8
Florence fennel	3–5
Kale	4
Kohlrabi	5–8
Leek	3–6
Lettuce	4–8
Melons	4–8
Mustard	3–6
Okra	3–6
Onions	1–4
Parsley	1–4
Parsnip	1–2
Peas	3–5
Peppers	2–4
Pumpkin	4–6
Radishes	4–6
Rutabaga	4–6
Salsify	1–4
Spinach	4–6
Squash	4–8
Tomatoes	3–6
Turnip	4–8

(Seeds of most herbs will remain alive for at least four years if reasonably well stored.)

AVERAGE ROOT PENETRATION OF VEGETABLES

Vegetable	*Depth in Feet*
Asparagus	10
Beans, lima	4
Beans, snap	3
Beet	3
Broccoli	2
Cabbage	2
Cantaloupe	4–6
Carrot	3
Cauliflower	2
Celery	2
Chard	3
Corn	3
Cucumber	3
Eggplant	3
Lettuce	1–2
Mustard	3
Onions	1
Parsnip	4
Peanuts	2
Peas	3–4
Peppers	3
Potatoes, sweet	4–6
Potatoes, white	3
Pumpkin	6
Radishes	1
Spinach	2
Squash	3
Tomatoes	6–10
Watermelon	6

Heat and Cold Tolerances of Vegetables

This table from the U. S. Department of Agriculture shows suitable times for seeding some popular vegetables in the garden, or for transplanting to the garden where this is usual practice.

Very hardy (seed or transplant 4–6 weeks before last spring frost)

Broccoli
Cabbage
Lettuce
Onions
Peas
Potatoes, white
Spinach
Turnip

Hardy (seed or transplant 2–4 weeks before last spring frost)

Beet
Carrot
Chard
Mustard
Parsnip
Radishes

Not cold-hardy (seed or transplant after last spring frost)

Beans, snap
Corn
New Zealand spinach
Okra
Soybeans
Squash
Tomatoes

Require hot weather (seed or transplant no sooner than 1 week after last spring frost)

Beans, lima
Eggplant
Peppers
Potatoes, sweet
Cucumber
Melons

Medium heat-tolerant (good for summer planting)

All beans
Chard
Corn
New Zealand spinach
Squash

Hardy (for late summer or fall planting except in North; seed or transplant 6–8 weeks before first fall freeze)

Beet
Collards
Kale
Lettuce
Mustard
Spinach
Turnip

Appendix II:
Where to Get It

(Suppliers of materials and information for gardeners.)

Bio-Dynamics

For information on this type of natural gardening, address: Bio-Dynamic Farming and Gardening Association, Route 1, Stroudsburg, Pennsylvania 18360.

Farm Vacations

For a list of farms that take guests, write for: *Farm & Ranch Vacation Guide*, 36 East 57th Street, New York, New York 10022. Cost: $2.50.

Magazines on Gardening

Flower & Garden Magazine, 4251 Pennsylvania Avenue, Kansas City, Missouri 64111. A monthly publication in three regional editions—Northern, Western, and Southern—covering both ornamentals and food crops. Subscription rates: U.S., $3.00; foreign, $5.00.

Family Handyman Incorporating Home Garden, 235 East 45th Street, New York, New York 10017. National circulation, covering all home gardening activities; 9 issues a year (bi-monthly July through December). Subscription rates: U.S., $5.40; foreign, $6.40.

Horticulture, 300 Massachusetts Avenue, Boston, Massachusetts 02115. Monthly publication of the Massachusetts Horticultural Society, but national in coverage. Main emphasis on ornamentals, articles by topflight horticulturists, primarily for the sophisticated gardener. Subscription rates: U.S. and Canada, $7.00; foreign, $8.00.

Organic Gardening & Farming, Organic Park, Emmaus, Pennsylvania 18049. The bible of the organic movement, this plump, pocket-sized, national monthly magazine covers a wider range of garden-related topics than any other in the field. Dedicated to conservation and to natural gardening methods, it features an editorial mix of career professional and amateur enthusiast, and is always interesting reading. Subscription rates: U.S. and Canada, $5.85; foreign, $6.85.

PEST CONTROLS—BIOLOGICAL

Bacillus thuringiensis

For this control of various caterpillars and worms, see your local garden suppliers first. If you cannot obtain the product locally, here are four manufacturers:

Thompson-Hayward Chemical Company, P. O. Box 2383, Kansas City, Kansas 66110 ("Biotrol").

Occidental Chemical Company, P. O. Box 198, Lathrop, California 95330.

International Minerals & Chemical Corporation, Liberty-ville, Illinois ("Thuricide").

Abbott Laboratories, Abbott Park, North Chicago, Illinois 60064 ("Dipel").

Milky spore disease

For control of Japanese beetles; two suppliers:
Fairfax Biological Laboratory, Clinton Corners, New York 12514 ("Doom").

Hydroponic Chemical Company, Copley, Ohio ("Japonex").

Ladybugs

Bio-Control Company, Route 2, Box 2397, Auburn, California 95603.

L. E. Schnoor, Rough & Ready, California 95975.

World Garden Products, 2 First Street E., Norwalk, Connecticut 06855.

Praying mantids

Eastern Biological Controls Company, Route 5, Box 379, Jackson, New Jersey 08527.

Gothard, Inc., P. O. Box 332, Canutillo, Texas 79835.

Lacewing flies

Rincon-Vitova Insectary, P. O. Box 475, Rialto, California 92376.

Trichogramma wasps

Rincon-Vitova Insectary, P. O. Box 475, Rialto, California 92376.

Pest Controls—Other

Botanical insecticidal materials

Desert Herb Tea Company, 736 Darling Street, Ogden, Utah.

Indiana Botanic Gardens, P. O. Box 5, Hammond, Indiana.

Ryania

Hopkins Agriculture Chemical Company, P. O. Box 584, Madison, Wisconsin.

S. B. Penick & Company, 100 Church Street, New York, New York 10014.

Sabadilla

Burgess Seed Company, Galesburg, Michigan. Dust.

Meer Corporation, 318 West 46th Street, New York, New York 10036. Seeds and dust.

Woolfolk Chemical Works, Ltd., Ft. Valley, Georgia. Dust.

Tree Tanglefoot

Obtainable in two forms, flypaper and spray-on, to trap crawling insects on their way up tree trunks, or any insect lighting on the sticky surface.

The Tanglefoot Company, 314 Straight Avenue, S.W., Grand Rapids, Michigan 49500.

Electric insect traps

Detjen Corporation, Pleasant Valley, New York.

Vita Green Farms, P. O. Box 878, Vista, California 92083.

Fruit tree spray

For the Bio-Dynamic formula spray of ryania, rotenone, and pyrethrum in a clay base, see:

> Peter A. Escher, Threefold Farms, Spring Valley, New York 10977.

POND FISH

For information on experiments in organic pond management for food fishing, write to: New Alchemy Institute-East, P. O. Box 432, Woods Hole, Massachusetts 02543.

SEEDS AND PLANTS

Burgess Seed and Plant Company, Galesburg, Michigan 49053. One of the few houses offering Jerusalem artichokes. Also handles fruit and nut trees, along with a line of hardy "Blizzard Belt" seeds.

W. Atlee Burpee Company, Philadelphia, Pennsylvania 19132; Clinton, Iowa 52732; Riverside, California 92502. This old and progressive house has one of the largest listings of seeds, and is famous for exclusive varieties. It maintains its own staff of horticultural scientists. Widely adaptable varieties are stressed, and fruits and nuts are also listed.

Cedarbrook Herb Farm, Route 1, Box 1047, Sequim, Washington 98382. A small, organic grower of herbs, some unusual; also shallots, elephant garlic, and geraniums in a dozen fragrances.

Farmer Seed and Nursery Company, Faribault, Minnesota 55021. Northern-adapted varieties are a specialty here, and this house works closely with the state experiment station—

as on the good listing of midget vegetables carried. A number
of fruits are listed. The catalogue, recently redesigned, is attractive and easy to read.

Farmer Mac's, P. O. Box 62412, Virginia Beach, Virginia
23462. Organically handled—except when indicated otherwise—vegetable seeds include some unusual varieties. Also
offered here are a "green-manure crop sampler" in home-garden size, and a collection of 18 farm-crop plants—wheat, hay,
soybeans, etc.—as a suggested educational project for children.

Henry Field Seed and Nursery Company, Shenandoah, Iowa
51601. Much information and unusual varieties are packed
into this plump catalogue. Nuts and fruits are also listed, and
bush cherries for the North.

Gurney Seed & Nursery Company, Yankton, South Dakota
57078. The interesting big catalogue, heavily illustrated, lists
a good selection of standard and of many unusual varieties,
for Northern and other growing areas. Fruits, including some
native ones, and nut trees, are also listed.

Joseph Harris Company, Rochester, New York 14624. This
reliable house is known for its frank and informative catalogue, which lists many varieties of vegetables, including
Harris's exclusives.

J. W. Jung Seed Company, Randolph, Wisconsin 53956. This
upper-Midwest house accents varieties adapted to Northern
growing conditions and has a representative selection of
others, along with fruit trees.

Le Jardin du Gourmet, P. O. Box 119, Ramsey, New Jersey
07446. Particularly featuring shallot bulbs, this house also
carries a line of vegetable seeds from Europe, and Jerusalem
artichoke tubers.

Henry Leuthardt Nurseries, East Moriches, Long Island, New
York 11940. Dwarf fruit trees are the specialty here, and
stock for use in espaliering is featured in the pocket-sized

handbook type of catalogue. Several varieties of wine grapes are carried.

Earl May Seed & Nursery Company, Shenandoah, Iowa 51601. The large-page, well-illustrated catalogue lists a number of interesting novelties along with better-known vegetables. Fruits and some nut trees are also handled.

Mellinger's, 2310 West South Range Road, North Lima, Ohio 44452. The plain and closely printed catalogue has a bit of everything in it, including many hard-to-find seeds and other plant material. Not many vegetables are listed, but there are all sorts of other seeds and plants, and some natural fertilizers.

New York State Fruit Testing Cooperative Association, Geneva, New York 14456. This nursery, part of the state experiment station at Geneva, tests through its members the new fruits it has developed. Anyone interested can join, the annual fee being $4.00. If you have a taste for experiment, you'll enjoy taking part. Many excellent varieties have been developed here over many years.

Nichols Garden Nursery, 1190 North Pacific Highway, Albany, Oregon 97321. In its unpretentious-looking catalogue, this house lists a high percentage of unusual varieties, including shallots, Jerusalem artichokes and more than 50 herbs. Nichols is outspokenly organic, stating they use no poison sprays or chemical fertilizers.

L. L. Olds Seed Company, P. O. Box 1069, Madison, Wisconsin 53701. The readable and informative catalogue offers a good selection of vegetables, including more than a dozen kinds of potatoes, among them the little-seen salad potatoes. (Note: They do not accept potato orders from outside the U.S. or from California, Alaska, or Hawaii.)

George W. Park Seed Company, P. O. Box 31, Greenwood, South Carolina 29646. This old, high-quality Southern house offers a good selection of vegetables, including some unique ones and such Southern favorites as Crowder peas. Many herbs are also listed.

R. H. Shumway Seedsman. 628 Cedar Street, Rockford, Illinois 61101. In its large-page catalogue with an old-time air, this house carries a good representative list of seeds plus fruit and nut trees.

Stark Bro's Nurseries, Louisiana, Missouri 63353. The oldest nursery in America, this progressive house is noted for its number of exclusive introductions in fruits. Dwarf apples are outstanding here. Disease-resistant varieties of several fruits are featured in dwarfs and standard sizes.

Stokes Seeds, Box 15, Buffalo, New York 14205. The hefty little pocket-sized catalogue does a good job of describing varieties and offering cultural suggestions. Many of the customers are Canadian, and emphasis here is on varieties adaptable to the Great Lakes area of Canada.

Southmeadow Fruit Gardens, 2363 Tilbury Place, Birmingham, Michigan 48009. For choicely good varieties of famous old fruits you won't find listed anywhere else—especially apples—this is the nursery to see. The address above is that of Mr. Robert A. Nitschke, a serious hobbyist fruit grower who directs this endeavor and handles catalogue requests. Orders are filled at Lakeside, Michigan, by Grootendorst Nurseries.

Otis S. Twilley, P. O. Box 1817, Salisbury, Maryland 21801. A good spread of varieties is listed, with here and there a Southern accent. The house is especially strong in melons, cucumbers, and tomatoes.

Vita Green Farms, P. O. Box 878, Vista, California 92083. This house specializes in organically grown vegetable, herb, and farm seeds.

Herbs

The following list a good variety of herbs—seeds, plants, or both—including many of those relied on by some gardeners for pest control.

Casa Yerba, P. O. Box 176, Tustin, California 92680.

Cedarbrook Herb Farm, Route 1, Box 1047, Sequim, Washington 98382.

Greene Herb Gardens, Greene, Rhode Island 02872.

Hemlock Hill Herb Farm, Litchfield, Connecticut 06559.

Le Jardin du Gourmet, P. O. Box 119, Ramsey, New Jersey 07446.

Meadowbrook Herb Garden, Wyoming, Rhode Island 02898.

Nichols Garden Nursery, 1190 North Pacific Highway, Albany, Oregon 97321.

George W. Park Seed Company, P. O. Box 31, Greenwood, South Carolina 29646.

Pine Hills Herb Farms, P. O. Box 144, Roswell, Georgia 30075.

Snow-Line Farm, Route 1, Box 270, Yucaipa, California 92399.

Soil Tests

An organic-concept laboratory that does soil testing is:
Bio-chemical Research Laboratory, Threefold Farms, Spring Valley, New York 10977.

Where to Ask

Here are some excellent public sources where you can get a variety of gardening information, sometimes including answers to specific questions.

The United States Department of Agriculture,
Office of Information,
Washington, D.C. 20250.
There are a great many publications available here, some of
them free. State your needs in a letter, and they will send you
a list of pertinent publications. Answers are sometimes slow.

The agricultural agent of your county.
You will find the agent at your county seat, and your tele-
phone directory may list his office under your county name.
He carries a stock of both state and federal bulletins and will
be familiar with your local growing conditions. Usually
called the county agent, or the farm adviser, he is almost
sure to be overworked, so keep this in mind when asking for
services.

Your state department of agriculture.
This will be in your state capital. It is also a source of bulletins and other publications, and the people there are conversant
with regional gardening problems.

Your state agricultural experiment station.
Address "The Director." You'll tap a source of technical
know-how here something like the county agent on a wider
scale. Here are the locations of all the stations in the United
States:

Alabama	Auburn 36830
Alaska	College 99730
Arizona	Tucson 85721
Arkansas	Fayetteville 72701
California	Berkeley 94720
Colorado	Fort Collins 80521
Connecticut, Agricultural	
College and Storrs Station	Storrs 06268
Connecticut, State Station	New Haven 06504

Delaware	Newark 19711
Florida	Gainesville 32603
Georgia, Coastal Plains Station	Tifton 31794
Georgia, Main Station	Experiment 30212
Hawaii	Honolulu 96822
Idaho	Moscow 83843
Illinois	Urbana 61801
Indiana	Lafayette 47907
Iowa	Ames 50010
Kansas	Manhattan 66504
Kentucky	Lexington 40506
Louisiana	Baton Rouge 70803
Maine	Orono 04473
Maryland	College Park 20740
Massachusetts	Amherst 01003
Michigan	East Lansing 48823
Minnesota	St. Paul 55101
Mississippi	State College 39762
Missouri, Fruit Station	Mountain Grove 65711
Missouri, Main Station	Columbia 65202
Montana	Bozeman 59715
Nebraska	Lincoln 68503
Nevada	Reno 89507
New Hampshire	Durham 03824
New Jersey	New Brunswick 08900
New Mexico	University Park 88070
New York, Cornell Station	Ithaca 14850
New York, State Station	Geneva 14456
North Carolina	Raleigh 27607
North Dakota	Fargo 58103
Ohio	Wooster 44691
Oklahoma	Stillwater 74075
Oregon	Corvallis 97331
Pennsylvania	University Park 16802

Rhode Island	Kingston 02881
South Carolina	Clemson 29631
South Dakota	Brookings 57007
Tennessee	Knoxville 37901
Texas	College Station 77843
Utah	Logan 84321
Vermont	Burlington 05401
Virginia, Main Station	Blacksburg 24061
Virginia, Truck Station	Norfolk 23501
Washington	Pullman 99163
West Virginia	Morgantown 26506
Wisconsin	Madison 53706
Wyoming	Laramie 82701

Glossary

Acid Soil. A soil with a pH value lower than 7.0 in the root zone area.

Actinomycetes. One group of micro-organisms that decompose organic matter, as in composting.

Aerobic. Requiring oxygen in order to function; aerobic bacteria are most important for efficient composting.

Alkaline Soil. Strictly speaking, a soil with a pH value above 7.0 in the root zone area; in practical gardening terms, soil with a pH value of about 7.5 or a little more.

Anaerobic. Living or functioning in the absence of oxygen; anaerobic bacteria are the cause of bad odors in too wet or too compact compost piles.

Annual. A plant that progresses from seeding to harvest in one season and then dies. Some non-annuals such as beets produce the wanted crop their first season and so are treated as annuals.

Asexual. Reproduction of a plant without sexual means, such as by grafting or from cuttings.

Ash. The residue from complete burning of organic matter, commonly made up of compounds of oxygen and some other element (oxides): aluminum, calcium, iron, magnesium, potassium, etc.

AVAILABLE NUTRIENTS. In soil, the elements that plants need and can get.

BIENNIAL. A plant that needs two growing seasons from seeding to harvest before dying. For practical uses, some biennials are treated as annuals. See Annual.

BUD. A plant part that encloses an undeveloped flower or shoot.

BORON. A trace element needed by plants for normal growth.

CALCIUM. A major plant nutrient, usually supplied by adding lime if needed. Also a corrective for too acid soil.

CARBOHYDRATE. Any of several organic compounds manufactured by plants and forming their supporting tissues. Carbohydrates are the basic source of most of the world's energy. Sugar, starch, and wood are all carbohydrates.

CARBON. A plant nutrient, and one of the commonest chemical elements. Diamonds and graphite are pure carbon, and compounds of carbon are the main part of all living tissue, from muscles to leaves.

CELL. The basic structural unit of a plant.

CELLULOSE. A compound of carbon, hydrogen, and oxygen making up most of the substance in cell walls of plants; an essential part of wood; cotton is nearly pure cellulose, as are paper and cellophane.

CHARACTER. In genetics, an identifiable inherited detail—color, pattern, structure, a strength or weakness, etc.

CHLORINE. A trace element required by plants.

CHLOROPHYLL. The green coloring matter in leaves, necessary for photosynthesis.

CHLOROSIS. A deficiency problem in plants, showing up as yellowing, caused by failure to develop chlorophyll, usually due to lack of iron.

CHROMOSOMES. The carriers of genes, which control heredity.

CLAY. Specifically, mineral soil of hydrated silicates of aluminum, made up of very small particles (more than 500 per millimeter). "Clay soil" means a soil having at least 40 percent clay content.

CLONE. A plant produced vegetatively, usually by rooting a cutting.

C/N. The symbol referring to the percentages of carbon and nitrogen in organic matter; usually called the C/N ratio and expressed as so many parts of carbon to one part of nitrogen.

COMPOST. A body of organic matter in the process of planned decomposition, for the production of fertilizer, often called artificial manure.

COPPER. A trace element needed by plants for proper respiration, and in enzyme activity.

COTYLEDONS. The first leaves that sprouting seeds produce.

COVER CROP. A crop grown to protect soil from erosion, and often turned under later as a green-manure crop.

CROSS. Short for "cross-pollinate." When used as a noun it means a hybrid plant produced in this way, by pollinating the stigma of one plant's flower with pollen from the flower of a different variety of that plant, and occasionally a different species. Crossing may be done by man, insects, wind, etc.

CUTTING. A half-tender piece of plant stem (sometimes root or leaf) to reproduce the plant vegetatively. Also called a clone or slip.

DAMPING-OFF. A fungus disease that kills seedlings.

DAY-LENGTH. The number of daylight hours in each twenty-four-hour day.

DUST MULCH. A shallow, fine cultivation of surface soil, intended to halt evaporation of moisture from below.

ECOLOGY. The science dealing with relations between organisms and environments.

ENZYMES. Complex substances, such as pepsin, produced by living cells; enzymes act as agents in producing or speeding chemical changes.

FAMILY. A broad classification of plants all belonging to the same order. The Leguminosae family, for example, belongs to the Rosales order.

FLAT. A box about 3″ high, for holding a planting mixture to sow seed in or to transplant seedlings to.

FOLIAR FEEDING. Fertilizing plants by putting appropriate nutrients on the leaves, to be absorbed.

F_1. First generation; usually applied to a hybrid plant resulting from a mating of parents selected for distinct differences that will combine beneficially in the offspring.

FUNGI. (Singular: fungus). A group of plants including mushrooms, mildews, and rusts. They lack chlorophyll for making their own food and so must live on organic matter.

GENES. Particles in cells, that control inherited characters.

GENUS. A classification of plants belonging to the same family. (Plural: genera). The *Phaseolus* genus, for example, belongs to the Leguminosae family.

GERMINATE. To sprout, as a seed.

GREEN MANURE. A crop grown for the purpose of plowing or spading it under to improve soil.

GREENSAND. An organic fertilizer rich in potassium. It consists mainly of a mineral, glauconite, a sedimentary deposit, dark green in color.

HARDEN-OFF. To condition previously protected plants to outdoors by repeated exposures.

HARDPAN. A cement-like layer of soil underlying more friable soil.

HEAVING. Disturbance of earth, and plants in it, by alternate freezing and thawing.

HEEL-IN. To store a plant temporarily by covering its roots, and sometimes the entire plant, with moist soil.

HERBACEOUS. Non-woody.

HORMONES. Natural materials in plants that regulate growth.

HOTKAP. A commercial brand name for a protective plant covering made of paper; often used for protecting tender seedlings from spring frosts.

HUMUS. Relatively stable organic matter in soil; dark brown or black; important for moisture holding and fertility.

HYBRID. See F_1.

HYBRID VIGOR. Characteristic increase in energy shown by first-generation hybrid offspring over parents. Hybrid vigor decreases with inbreeding by about 50 percent in each descending generation.

INBREEDING. Continued self-pollinating of a breeding stock over several generations. The usual purpose is to purify certain characters so they will breed true.

INORGANIC. Lacking the make-up of living matter; refers in general to minerals.

IRON. A trace element needed by plants in the formation of chlorophyll.

LEACHING. The loss of nutrients in the soil, or in such materials as manure and compost, due to the passage of water through them.

LEGUME. A member of the huge pea family, Leguminosae, represented in the garden by peas and beans, and in the field by clover and alfalfa. Legumes have the valuable ability to obtain nitrogen from the air, storing it in nodules on the roots.

LIME. A material derived from limestone and used to reduce acid content of soils. Among its many forms are ground limestone (calcium carbonate), hydrated lime (calcium hydroxide), and basic slag, a waste product in metal manufacture.

LOAM. Strictly speaking, a soil having a texture between a sandy soil and a clay soil, but containing both sand and clay, plus silt. Formerly, "loam" meant a mellow soil rich in organic matter.

MAGNESIUM. A major element needed by green plants in photosynthesis.

MANGANESE. A trace element needed by plants in enzyme activity.

MARL. A deposit of clay and calcium carbonate found around lakes and used for liming soil.

MELLOW SOIL. Crumbly, porous soil, easily worked.

MICROBE. A micro-organism.

MICROCLIMATE. The climate near ground level.

MICRONUTRIENTS. Another term for trace elements.

MICRO-ORGANISMS. A blanket term for microscopic forms of life, and including bacteria and some fungi.

MINERALIZATION. Process of changing a substance into minerals, often applied to the results of actions by micro-organisms in releasing minerals from organic matter.

MINERAL SOIL. One composed mostly of mineral matter rather than of organic matter.

MOLYBDENUM. A trace element essential to plants' enzyme activity.

MUCK. Highly decomposed peat, forming a rich organic soil, sometimes quite acid.

MULCH. Any of many materials spread around plants to retain moisture in the soil, encourage beneficial microbial activity, protect roots, etc.

NITROGEN. An element vital to plant life in the manufacture of proteins and protoplasm.

NUTRIENT. Any substance needed by a plant to sustain life and provide growth and energy.

ORGANIC. Strictly speaking, pertaining to or derived from living matter. Thus, "organic gardening" means gardening with what nature provides ("*natur*al gardening"), and nothing else. This is usually understood to mean the exclusion of so-called chemical fertilizers and poisons.

ORGANIC MATTER. For garden purposes, plant and animal materials in the process of decomposition, which changes them to carbon dioxide, water, and minerals.

PATHOGEN. An organism able to cause disease in a host.

PEAT. Plant remains found in bogs, relatively undecomposed, and accumulated during hundreds of years. Widely used as a soil conditioner and mulch. There are three types of peat:

Sphagnum peat, or peat moss, is the remains of sphagnum plants, which are mosses. It is quite acid, with pH values from 3.0 to 4.5. It has some slight nutrient use, can hold up to 15 times its weight in water, and resists rotting.

Lowmoor peat is the remains of sedges, reeds, and mosses. It ranges from quite acid to neutral, with pH values from 3.5 to 7.0. It is higher in nutrients than sphagnum peat, but can hold only about half as much water—up to 8 times its weight. It also resists rotting.

Forest peat, also called peat mold and leaf mold, is the remains of wood and leaves from trees. It lies in between the other two peats in composition, with pH values similar to lowmoor peat.

PERENNIAL. A plant that normally survives for several years.

pH. When followed by a number, this is a measure of the degree of acidity in a soil. For example, pH 4 is quite acid, pH 7 is neutral, and pH 8 is quite alkaline.

PHOSPHORUS. A major plant nutrient, necessary to growth and to fruiting.

PHOTOSYNTHESIS. Formation of carbohydrates by green plants from water and carbon dioxide, in the presence of light.

POLLINATE. To start sexual reproduction in a plant by bringing pollen, the male element, in contact with the ovule, the female element. The ultimate object is the production of seed.

POTASSIUM. A major plant nutrient, necessary to growth, strong stems, and proper development of root crops.

p.p.m. Abbreviation for "parts per million," often used to indicate the strength of a solution.

PROFILE. As applied to soil, a cross-section extending from the surface on down to bedrock.

PROTEIN. Any of several nitrogenous organic compounds formed by plants and essential to living matter.

PROTOPLASM. The living jellylike matter of all plant and animal cells. As the basic substance of life, it contains the power to reproduce and to carry on other life processes.

RESISTANT. Said of a plant able to produce a crop despite the attack of some disease. Complete resistance is called *immunity*, resistance that permits successful growth in spite of disease is called *tolerance*, and lack of enough resistance to permit successful growth is called *susceptibility*.

RESPIRATION. A plant's growth process, in which it uses oxygen from the air to burn carbohydrates, releasing carbon dioxide. All plant tissues, including seeds and harvested things, go on respiring as long as they are alive.

ROOT HAIRS. Fine, hairlike roots, the main absorbing part of a plant's root system.

ROOT ZONE. The layers of soil penetrated by a plant's roots.

SALTS. Substances resulting from chemical reaction of an acid with a base. In moist soil, salts dissolve into such substances as calcium, chloride, sodium, and sulfate.

SANDY SOIL. A soil with more than 70 percent sand and less than 15 percent clay.

SILT. Mineral particles of soil ranging from the size of fine sand, $\frac{5}{100}$ of a millimeter, to $\frac{2}{1000}$ of a millimeter. Soil having 80 percent or more silt and less than 12 percent clay is given the textural name "silt."

SLUDGE. The solids that remain after sewage is treated in disposal plants. There are two kinds of sludge:

Activated sludge, which has been worked on by air-using (aerobic) microbes, and which has no odor; it is a good soil conditioner and plant food, having 5–6 percent nitrogen, 2–4 percent phosphorus, and about .5 percent potash.

Digested sludge, which has been worked on by anaerobic microbes; it is not always safe to use on actively growing food plants, and is low in nutrients, having 1–3 percent nitrogen and .5–1.5 percent phosphorus.

SPECIES. A group of closely related plants belonging to the

same genus. The *limensis* species, for example (lima beans), belongs to the *Phaseolus* genus, as do several other beans.

SPHAGNUM MOSS. See Peat.

STUBBLE MULCH. The cut-off stumps of plants, and other trashy residue, allowed to remain on the soil to protect it from erosion. This is more a farming than a gardening practice.

SUBSOIL. The layer of soil occurring immediately under the topsoil.

SULFUR. A major plant nutrient, essential to protoplasm formation.

SYMBIOSIS. A living together by two species of organisms for the benefit of one or both. The best-known example in gardening is the existence of rhizobia bacteria on the roots of legumes. The bacteria take nitrogen from the air in the soil and turn it into forms that nourish the legumes.

SYNTHESIS. The combining of simpler parts into a complex substance, as in carbohydrate formation by photosynthesis from water and carbon dioxide.

TERRACE. An earth shelf built across a slope at the same level throughout its length. The object is to slow down the run-off of water, to control erosion.

TEXTURE. Referring to soil, the sizes and proportions of sand, silt, and clay particles in a soil mass.

TILTH. The physical condition of soil for plant growth.

TOPSOIL. The top horizon in a soil profile, usually darker than lower layers, more fertile, and ranging from less than an inch to several feet deep.

TRACE ELEMENTS. A group of elements, or nutrients, used by plants in much smaller amounts than the major elements, but thought to be vital to their well-being.

TRAIT. An aspect of inherited character involving performance and not usually concerned with form.

TRANSPIRATION. The passage of moisture from the surface of leaves and stems into the air.

VARIETY. A classification of plants, all members belonging to the same species. One variety of lima beans is called Fordhook bush lima, for example, and belongs to the *limensis* species along with all other varieties of lima beans.

VIABLE. Usually applied to seed, and meaning capable of germinating.

VIRGIN SOIL. Soil that has never been used to produce a cultivated crop.

VOLUNTEER. A plant growing from seed not deliberately planted by human means.

WEED. Any plant growing where it is not wanted, but usually applied to wild, persistent, nuisance plants.

ZINC. A trace element needed by plants in enzyme systems.

Index

Page numbers in italics refer to text illustrations.